WILDFLOWERS
OF OREGON

WILDFLOWERS
OF OREGON

A Field Guide to Over 400 Wildflowers, Trees, and Shrubs
of the Coast, Cascades, and High Desert

DAMIAN FAGAN

GUILFORD, CONNECTICUT

FALCONGUIDES®

An imprint of The Rowman & Littlefield Publishing Group, Inc.
4501 Forbes Blvd., Ste. 200
Lanham, MD 20706
www.rowman.com

Falcon and FalconGuides are registered trademarks and Make Adventure Your Story is a trademark of The Rowman & Littlefield Publishing Group, Inc.

Distributed by NATIONAL BOOK NETWORK

Map by The Rowman & Littlefield Publishing Group, Inc.
All interior photographs by Damian Fagan unless otherwise noted.

British Library Cataloguing-in-Publication Information Available

Library of Congress Cataloging in Publication Data
Names: Fagan, Damian, author.
Title: Wildflowers of Oregon : a field guide to over 400 wildflowers, trees, and shrubs of the coast, cascades, and high desert / Damian Fagan.
Description: Guilford, Connecticut : FalconGuides, [2019] | Includes index. |
   Identifiers: LCCN 2018053818 (print) | LCCN 2018055853 (ebook) | ISBN
   | ISBN 9781493036325 (paperback) | ISBN
   9781493036332 (ebook)
Subjects: LCSH: Wild flowers--Oregon--Identification.
Classification: LCC SB439.24.O7 (ebook) | LCC SB439.24.O7 F34 2019 (print) |
   DDC 635.9/67609795--dc23
LC record available at https://lccn.loc.gov/2018053818

∞™ The paper used in this publication meets the minimum requirements of American National Standard for Information Sciences—Permanence of Paper for Printed Library Materials, ANSI/NISO Z39.48-1992.

Printed in the United States of America

THIS BOOK IS DEDICATED TO THE MEMORY OF DR. MELINDA DENTON AND DR. ARTHUR KRUCKENBERG FOR INSPIRING GENERATIONS OF STUDENTS IN THE STUDY OF BOTANY.

CONTENTS

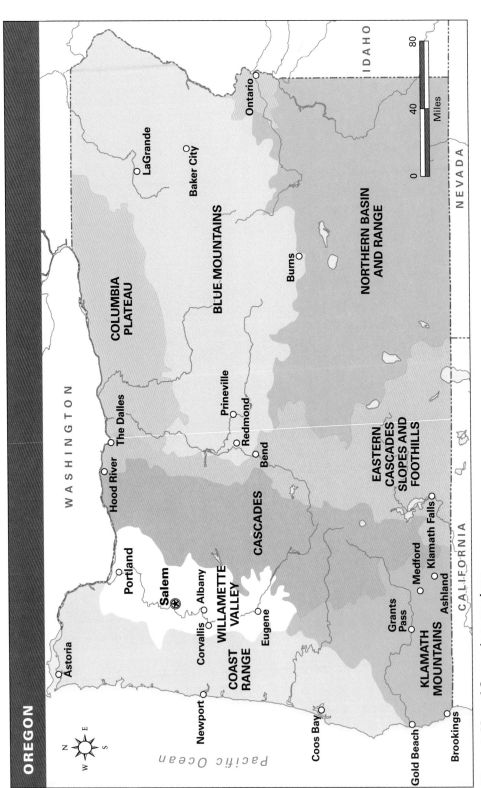

Figure 1. Map of Oregon's ecoregions.

PREFACE

What is it that draws us to wildflowers? Is it the spectacular display of color that engages our interest? Perhaps it is flower structure, refined through evolution and field-tested by millions of pollinators? Maybe it's the stories of early naturalists or Native Americans associated with the discovery and utilization of these plants? Perhaps it is just the pure joy of exploring some aspect of nature that doesn't fly or run away as we approach, offering an easy moment to connect, to explore, and to engage.

For me, it is all these things and more.

As a young student in the field of botany, I would backpack with my hardbound copy of *Flora of the Pacific Northwest* by Charles Leo Hitchcock and Arthur Cronquist. I'd stop walking and work the botanical keys trying to discover the identity of some lovely wildflower in bloom along the trail. While reading the choices in the key, I'd keep one finger wedged into the glossary, to rummage around back there learning the definitions for the technical terms. Oh, yes, there was some trial and error, moments of discovery clouded over with doubt. Were the leaf margins serrate or crenate? Did the anthers dehisce laterally or were they more vertical in orientation? Are the petals lobed or deeply lobed? So many options to wade through but well worth the effort!

After forty years of kneeling down in sagebrush flats or mountain meadows studying a flower through my hand lens, I'm still learning.

ACKNOWLEDGMENTS

A work such as this is never the product of one person. I'm reminded often of the effort expended by early plant collectors as they observed collections of plants new to science. Some gathered information from indigenous tribes as to medicinal or edible qualities during their forays. Others braved harsh conditions and explored unknown lands to broaden the scope of plant knowledge that existed at the time. Specimens sent by these collectors ended up at academic institutions, museums, Royal Societies, or in the hands of private benefactors who then proceeded to determine what they had been. For these early efforts and the continued efforts of modern-day taxonomists and collectors, I am forever indebted.

Also to thank are the wildflower enthusiasts who post wildflower reports, online images, and trip results on the various social media channels and websites. It is great to see this sharing of information, and I have poached information from these sites to locate flowers for photography more than once. I hope that we meet someday on a mountain trail that is exploding with flowers.

Thanks to my wife, Raven Tennyson, for her support during this project. Also thanks to David Legere, acquisitions editor, Kristen Mellitt, production editor, and the rest of the team at Globe Pequot/Falcon Guides for providing me the opportunity to work on this project and for their expertise in creating the final product, respectively.

INTRODUCTION

Oregon is a land of contrasts. From dry deserts to moist rainforests and coastal beaches to glaciated peaks, diversity is the rule, not the exception. Influenced by elevation, climate, and soil type, a vast array of plant life forms a mosaic of color and texture blanketing the region. Ask a resident what defines this region, and they may reply, "the Cascades," "rugged coastline," "big trees," "dense, dark forests," "clear rivers," "wild, open spaces," or "incredibly diverse."

The region's volcanic past often dominates the soils of certain regions with volcanic ash and pumice. Both metamorphic and sedimentary rocks layers also exist with these igneous types, and their weathering and erosion create variable soil conditions for plants. Some of these soil types are widespread while others are restricted to particular areas due to the rarity of the parent rock material. On these soil types occur endemics—plant species that have a very narrow distribution but may also occur where different provinces overlap to form unique situations of soils, climate, and topography.

In Oregon, elevations range from sea level to 11,249 feet at the summit of Mount Hood. Within the state, one can define broad-scale physiographic provinces, known as ecoregions. Based upon similarities of natural communities and environmental conditions that are geographically distinct, ecologists have divided Oregon into large-scale, ecologically similar divisions called ecoregions, which other states have done as well. There are 9 ecoregions represented in Oregon, and within each of these, there are finer scales defined by plant communities and environmental conditions present.

An example is the Coast Range Ecoregion that stretches along much of the Oregon Coast. The low-mountain landscape is influenced by a maritime climate and is covered in evergreen forests. Within the ecoregion, there are finer divisions, such as the Coastal Lowlands and Southern Oregon Coastal Mountains. The first is the lowlands region with beaches, dunes, and marine terraces below 400' in elevation, while the second region is a geologically and botanically unique area, representing a blend of northern and southern plant species, which represents a transition zone between the Coast Range and the Siskiyou Mountains.

Delineating the ecoregions was a collaborative effort between the Environmental Protection Agency, United States Geological Survey, United States Forest Service, other state and federal agencies, and academic institutions.

In this guide, I've tried to narrow down the type(s) of habitat(s) a plant occurs in on a finer scale than these ecoregional definitions, as well as including the geographical range it occupies across the state by area rather than by ecoregion. Ecoregional understanding is key to finding certain plants within a given portion of the state, but I've chosen to direct the user of this book to find wildflowers through the use of geographical names more so than by ecoregions.

Brief History of Plant Taxonomy

There are thousands of vascular plants, trees, shrubs, and wildflowers that occur in Oregon. This book includes descriptions and photographs of more than 400 of those flowering plants from representative habitats and elevations across the state. Representative plants from the desert, coastal, and montane areas from all ecoregions within the state were selected to provide a general exposure of this vast Northwest flora. The majority of the plants herein are native, with a few rare and endemic species included. Some of the plants are not native but have naturalized to the point they seem native just by their sheer presence. Moreover, as a gentle reminder, please observe, photograph, draw, or record these spectacular wildflowers in your own way, but please don't pick their blossoms or disturb the plants, leaving them for others to enjoy.

To facilitate looking up a species, the plants in this book were separated by floral color first, then arranged alphabetically by family, and finally by genus and species. This arrangement is to facilitate searching for a particular flower by color first and, hopefully, to make searching easier for those unfamiliar with taxonomic keys.

For each entry, there is a common name and scientific name. Swedish naturalist Carl Linnaeus (1707–1778) developed the modern system of binomial nomenclature—this structure of genus and species. Linnaeus created a descriptive system that standardized the terminology and naming of plants and animals, as well as organized the information systematically. The system, which continues to be used today, provided a common language for all to use. For instance, the binomial name *Lilium columbianum* (tiger lily) consists of the Latin or Greek rooted generic (referring to the genus) name (*Lilium*) followed by a specific epithet (*columbianum*) referring to the species. Linnaeus based his work upon that done by various individuals dating all the way back to Aristotle.

For plants, he based his system, known as the sexual system, upon the number, union, or length of stamens and the structure of the ovary. Since such features do not necessarily show evolutionary relatedness, this has been called an artificial system. Linnaeus greatly clarified and simplified the identification and description of known and newly discovered taxa, providing one system that could cross any political or language barrier.

With Linnaeus's nomenclatural hierarch, plants with similar sexual features were lumped together into families and then sorted out into finer divisions called genera. The genera were then split into finer divisions of species or even subspecies. Today, taxonomists continue to refine these associations, moving species and genera around into new families or genera based upon genetic relationships, as well as physical forms.

Experienced wildflower enthusiasts will note that some familiar scientific plant names, and the families they were placed in, have changed since the 1980s and 1990s. This is due to a better understanding of the evolutionary relationships between plants on a molecular level. The use of DNA sequencing has reshuffled the order and hierarchy of some plants; hence, bear grass (*Xerophyllum tenax*) used to be placed in the Lily Family (Liliaceae), and now it resides in the Trillium/Death-camas Family (Melanthiaceae). Though a tremendous amount of work has been on the systematics of plants, more changes are likely in the future as scientists gain a better understanding of these relationships. This guide includes updated and accepted scientific names of plants using the Oregon Floral Project at Oregon State University as the primary reference, along with revisions in the forthcoming *Flora of the Pacific Northwest* (2018) through the University of Washington Herbarium at the Burke Museum in Seattle. First published in 1973 by Charles Leo Hitchcock and Arthur Cronquist, the updated version will include nomenclatural changes to plant taxa in the Northwest.

HOW TO USE THIS GUIDE

Though there are standards for acceptance of scientific names, such a system does not occur for common names as it does for the common names of birds. Thus, one person's Tiger Lilly may be another's Oregon Lily or someone else's Columbia Lily. Common names may be regional, and they aren't standardized similar to scientific names.

Under each species is an entry for Description, Bloom Season, Habitat/Range, and Comments. The Description includes information about plant height, leaf shape and size, and flower color and structure to help identify the species. Bloom Season represents the general flowering period in the year. The Habitat/Range section is a generalized description of where the plant occurs in the region, in what type of habitat, and at what elevation. These characters may help to distinguish some species from others not shown in this guide.

The Comments section contains information about the ethnology or derivation of the scientific names. Oftentimes these names provide information about the plant's physical attributes or about the collector of the species. Along with the ethnology is random information about the ethnobotany, pollination, toxicity, or historical figures in the world of botany and exploration that have some relevance to the plant.

A word of caution: The diversity of plants within the region is both exciting and frustrating, especially for the production of a statewide field guide. It is exciting in that this guide covers a diversity of plants and frustrating in that there are too many species to include and that sometimes the best level of identification will be a broad one—"that plant looks like a lupine" or "maybe this plant is in the Lily Family." Nature itself ignores classification; it is we who affix a label on things. That aside, hopefully this guide will be used in association with other books on your shelf that will enable you to understand these wonderful wildflowers of Oregon better.

A word of encouragement. There is great wisdom in the quote "Stop and smell the roses." Our lives are often defined by time, and there certainly isn't enough to satisfy most of our appetites. At times our preference is just to hear the name of a plant but not to take a really good look at it—let alone to take a sniff of the flower or to feel the rough texture of the leaves. To observe the activities of pollinators, one should take a front-row seat, relax, and enjoy the action. More times than not, taking that extra moment will provide a greater understanding and appreciation of these wildflowers.

Please remember to enjoy the sights and fragrances of these flowers responsibly and to leave them for others, both winged and two-legged, to enjoy. If you are uncertain of the identification, create a sketch or take a photograph with a cell phone and write down some notes about the plant's feature. Resist the temptation to collect specimens and stick them inside this guide. The flowers may fade or get mashed flat, making any further identification impossible. Plus, certain plants are legally protected due to their rarity, and it would be a shame to contribute to their decline.

The Functioning Plant

A basic understanding of plant parts and their functions adds much to the appreciation of them in their native settings and to identifying them, as well. Roots absorb water and minerals from the soil and transport these to the higher parts of the plant. They also function to hold the plant in place, embedded in the earth. The stem has conduits for transporting

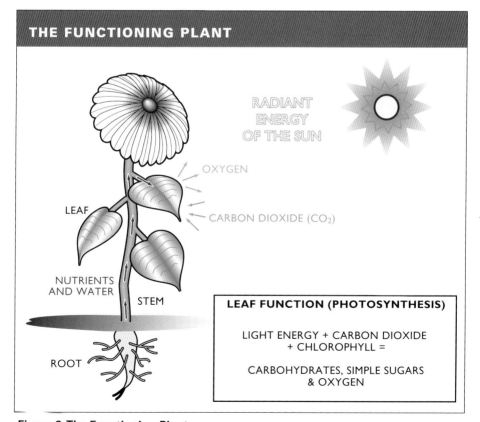

Figure 2: The Functioning Plant

water and minerals to the leaves and for taking products made by the leaves—carbohy-drates, proteins, lipids, and more—to other parts of the plant. Leaves contain chlorophyll and other pigments necessary for photosynthesis. The sugars and other products of photo-synthesis and the raw materials taken from the soil are either used immediately or stored by the plant. Beyond these basic structures are the amazing adaptations that plants have made for reproduction.

Pollination is the transfer of male spores, or pollen, from the anther at the end of the stamen to the stigmas, which is the tip of the female's part of the flower, the pistil. When pollen grains reach the stigma, they germinate much like a seed, and a pollen tube grows downward into the style, the stalk of the pistil. In these tubes, the male sex cells, or gametes, form. The pollen tube then grows through the tissues of the pistil. The pistil nourishes the tube as it grows, and when the pollen tube is near the female gamete in the ovule, the male gametes release and fertilization takes place. The transfer of pollen to the stigmas of a flower is one of the greatest technical achievements of the plant kingdom; the logistics of this have helped create the fascinating variety of flowers we see today.

The fossil record is a stone testament to the innovation of the plant kingdom over millions of years. It reveals spore-producing ferns, primitive fernlike trees that bore seeds, the cone-bearing plants (the conifers), and the more modern orchids with their specialized methods of pollination. Throughout this history, there was a noted change from wind pollination to animal pollination, a conclusion based upon the structure of fossilized flowers, which occurred at about the same time pollinating insects became numerous.

Generally, there are three main ways ovules become fertilized: by wind, animal, or self-pollination. Wind pollination is considered the more "primitive" form of pollina-tion. Wind pollination is a chancy method and used primarily by plants that grow in close proximity to one another or where there are few insects to do the job. Grasses and many trees are wind pollinated. To increase the odds of pollination, many wind-pollinated plants release tremendous amounts of pollen into the air from their usually smaller and less showy flowers. Some have separate male and female flowers, often arranged in dense clusters, to further this strategy. Some species release their huge amounts of pollen before their leaves develop in order to increase the odds of contact even more.

The evolution of animal pollination, which benefits both pollinator and plant, created a tremendous amount of variation in flower structure since no single floral type can perfectly suit all types of potential pollinators. About 85 percent of all flowering plants are insect pollinated. Differences in flower size, shape, colorations, and arrangement are shown in the simplified chart of Table 1. This does not cover all the groups of insects, and one may observe many different types of insects on one flower.

Most insects move pollen from flower to flower more reliably than the wind. Some insects are generalists and visit different types of plants, not selecting just one type of flower during their foraging. Bees, on the other hand, are more "faithful" as pollinators—they select one or a few species of plants and regularly visit only those flowers, which count on the bees for pollination and reward them with nectar and pollen.

Plants tend to attract certain insect pollinators consistently, and those pollinators evolved to select the flowers that fulfill their needs as well. Nectar, a sugary bribe or reward, attracts the pollinators. Certain plants may time their nectar release to coincide with the times of peak foraging activity of certain insects or birds and thus do not spend precious energy providing nectar to nonpollinating species.

Visual acuity for insects is less than that for humans, and the ability for insects to distinguish shape and form from a distance is relatively poor. Many flowers have developed special patterns of color, called nectar guides, that function as landing lights, attracting and guiding these pollinators and orienting them to the nectar. Most yellow and white flowers are highly reflective of light and are thus visited by a large variety of insects, but bees frequent blue flowers more than any other insect group.

Table 1: Simplified chart showing some relationships between flowers and pollinator groups. (Adapted from How and Westley, 1988).

Pollinator	Flower Color	Flower Depth	Odor
Beetles	Usually dull	Flat, bow-shaped	Strong
Flies	Variable	Moderately deep	Variable
Bees	Blue, white, pink, but not pure red	Flat or broad tube	Usually sweet
Wasps	Dull or brown	Flat or broad tube	Usually sweet
Hawk moths	Variable	Deep or narrow tube	Strong, sweet
Small moths	White or green (nocturnal moths) Red, purple, pink (diurnal moths)	Moderately deep	Moderately sweet
Butterflies	Bright red, yellow, blue	Deep, narrow, tubular	Moderately strong, sweet
Hummingbirds	Bright red (usually)	Deep, with wide spur or tubular	None

The process of pollination is a fascinating and complex subject. While observing wild-flowers, keep an eye out for pollinators on flowers or predators, such as crab spiders, that prey on insects visiting flowers.

Plant Characteristics

This section will help to define some of the terms and physical characteristics of the plants in this book. Technical terms are kept to a minimum; for their definitions, see the Glossary.

Many plants are perennials, plants with more or less woody stems and deep or long roots that last at least three years. Two types of perennials exist: woody shrubs and trees or herbaceous perennials that die back to underground roots or stems each winter. Biennials have a two-year life cycle. The plant becomes established during the first season, often producing a basal rosette of leaves. During the second season, the plant flowers, produces seeds, and then dies. Annuals complete their life cycle in one growing season, their future housed in seeds that may lay dormant for years before germinating. Annuals require specific amounts of winter and spring moisture before the seed germinates; chemical inhibitors within the seed prevent premature germination. During drought conditions, the seeds do not germinate and remain dormant, possibly for many years.

Sometimes it is difficult to distinguish perennials from annuals. To identify perennials, look for woody stems, an underground structure for food storage such as tubers, bulbs, and corms, or dried flowering stems and leaves from previous years.

Leaf Structure

Important features to note about the leaves and stems are:
- Arrangement of the leaves along the stem. Are they opposite, alternate, or whorled?
- Simple versus compound leaves. If compound, how many leaflets?
- Leaf margin. Entire, toothed, wavy, or lobed?
- Are the leaves only basal, or are they also found along the stem?
- Does the leaf have a stalk (petiole)?
- Are there hairs or other projections along the stem or on the leaf surface?

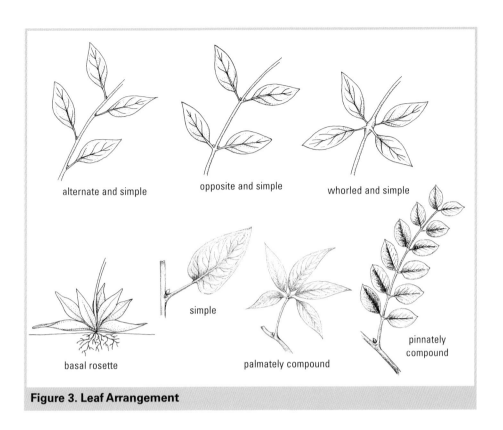

Figure 3. Leaf Arrangement

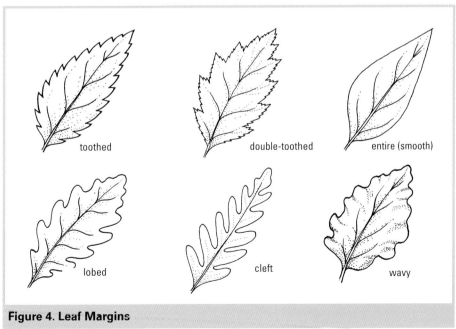

Figure 4. Leaf Margins

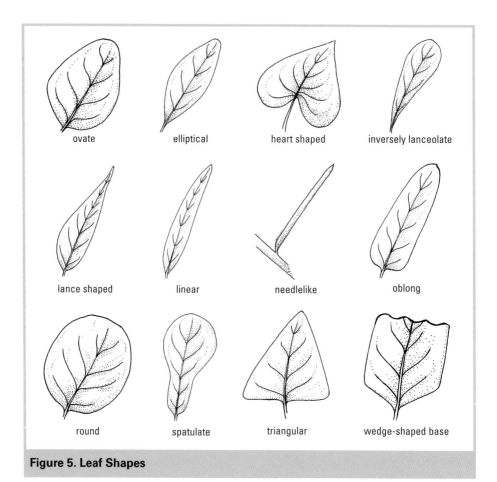

ovate · elliptical · heart shaped · inversely lanceolate

lance shaped · linear · needlelike · oblong

round · spatulate · triangular · wedge-shaped base

Figure 5. Leaf Shapes

Flower Structure

The diagrams in Figure 6 show a generalized flower in cross section. The variation and number of lower parts are key characters for identification. The sepals, or outer series of parts, surround the base of the flower. Sepals are often green and inconspicuous, but they may be colorful and showy as in the paintbrushes (*Castilleja*). Together they are called the calyx, which may be composed of separate or fused sepals.

Inside the calyx of most flowers are the petals, an inner series of generally colorful parts. Petals also vary in size and shape and may be separated or fused.

The petals are collectively called the corolla; some plants, however, may lack a corolla, or the sepals and petals may be identical. Together, the calyx and corolla function to attract pollinators and protect the sex organs at the center of the flower.

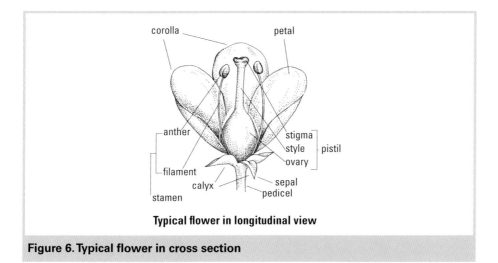

Typical flower in longitudinal view

Figure 6. Typical flower in cross section

Inside the flower are the stamens, the pollen-producing structures. Typically long and thin, the stamens have a club-like or elongate appendage at the tip—the anther—from which pollen is released. Stamens may number from zero to more than 100 per flower.

The pistil, or seed-producing structure, has three main parts: stigma, style, and ovary. Pollen reaches the stigma, or pollen receptor, which sits atop the stalk-like style. The style connects the ovary and the stigma and is the tubelike structure that the pollen tube grows through to reach the ovary. Within the ovary are the ovules, the structures that become the seeds after fertilization.

Here again, variation is the theme song. For example, some flowers lack a style; ovules may vary in arrangement and number, which determines the type of seed or fruit that develops. Many flowers have both male (staminate) and female (pistillate) parts within one flower, but some plants have separate male and female flowers on the same plant or even on separated plants. The term monoecious ("one home") is used to describe a species where male and female flowers are on one plant; dioecious ("two homes") refers to uni-sexual flowers being found on separate individual plants.

Two families with unique flower types are shown in Figures 7 and 8. These flowers are in the Pea (Fabaceae) and Aster (Asteraceae) families.

Members of the Pea Family (Fabaceae) have a calyx that surrounds five modified pet-als. The upper petal, or standard, is erect, spreading, and usually the longest of the five. The two side petals, or wings, closely surround the keel, which are the two fused lower petals. See Figure 7 for a typical flower of the Fabaceae.

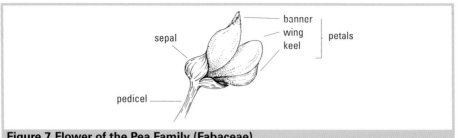

Figure 7. Flower of the Pea Family (Fabaceae)

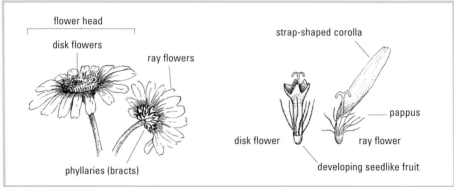

Figure 8. Flowers in the Aster Family (Asteraceae)

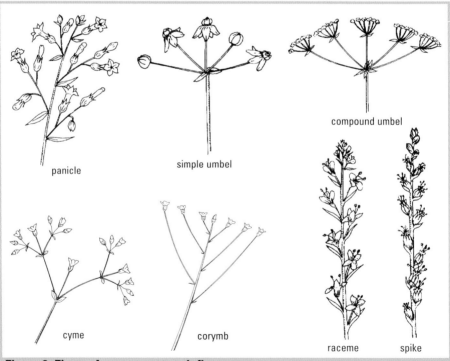

Figure 9. Flower Arrangement, or Inflorescence

Members of the Aster Family (Asteraceae) have an elaborate flower arrangement. A flower head, which looks like one flower, is actually a dense cluster of a few to several hundred tiny flowers. The flower head has a series of bracts, more or less modified leaves that surround the base of the flower head. The calyx of each of the tiny flowers is absent or reduced to bristles, scales, or hairs—the pappus—that form a crown of various characters at the top of the seed, and this is often a key in identifying the species. Members of the Asteraceae have either ray or disk flowers, or both, within a flower head. See Figure 8 for generalized flowers of this family. A strap-like limb forms the corolla or the ray flower and is usually brightly colored. The disk flower has a small, tubular corolla, usually with five lobes, but with no rays.

WHITE FLOWERS

This section includes flowers that range from creamy to bright white. Some plants produce flowers that tend toward pale yellow or pale green flowers, so if you don't find your flower here, check those sections. Flower color may fade with age or post-pollination, also creating some confusion regarding which section to search.

BLUE ELDERBERRY
Sambucus nigra
Moschatel Family (Adoxaceae)

Description: Deciduous shrub or small tree, with multiple stems, up to 20' tall. Smooth, light gray bark becomes furrowed and darker with age. Opposite leaves are 5"–15" long and divided into 3–9 leaflets. The leaflets are 2"–8" long and toothed along the margin. Tiny, 5-petaled white flowers are borne in a flat-topped cluster that is 5"–13" wide. Fruit is a blue-black berry.

Bloom Season: Late spring to midsummer

Habitat/Range: Found at mid to high elevations in rocky canyons, open slopes, and mixed coniferous forests on both sides of the Cascades and through-out the western and eastern United States.

Comments: *Sambucus* is the Greek name for a musical instrument made from elderberry wood. *Nigra* ("black") refers to the color of the edible berries, which are harvested to make jam or wine. Medicinally, the leaves, bark, flowers, and fruits may be harvested to treat respiratory infections or fevers.

RED ELDERBERRY
Sambucus racemosa
Moschatel Family (Adoxaceae)

Description: Shrub or small tree, often with multiple stems, that is 6'–18' tall. Bark is reddish-brown in color and smooth. Deciduous compound leaves have 5–7 lance-shaped leaflets that are 2"–6" long and pointed at the tip. The leaflets are smooth along the margin, darker green above, and lighter and hairy on the undersides. Tiny cream-colored, 5-petaled flowers are borne in a dense, pyramid-shaped cluster. Fruit is a reddish berry.

Bloom Season: Early to midsummer

Habitat/Range: Mostly west of the Cascades but found in mountain ranges in eastern Oregon as well.

Comments: *Sambucus* is the Greek name for a musical instrument made from elderberry wood. *Racemosa* ("raceme") refers to the unbranched, elongated flower cluster with the oldest flowers at the base. Wildlife and humans consume the edible red berries.

TOLMIE'S ONION
Allium tolmiei
Amaryllis Family (Amaryllidaceae)

Description: Perennial, from a ¾"–long bulb. Sickle-shaped leaves are flat, thick, and up to twice as long as the flowering stalk. The upright flowering stems bear clusters of white or pinkish bell-shaped flowers made up of 6 tepals with reddish midribs. The flower clusters are about ½" wide, and the anthers are purplish or yellow. Fruit is a capsule.

Bloom Season: Late spring to midsummer

Habitat/Range: Grows in open areas and mountain meadows from low to high elevations on the east side of the Cascades from Washington to northern California and east to Nevada.

Comments: *Allium* is the Greek name for garlic. *Tolmiei* honors William Fraser Tolmie (1812–1886), a Scottish physician for the Hudson Bay Company stationed at Fort Vancouver in the early 1830s who collected plants in the Northwest.

LYALL'S ANGELICA
Angelica arguta
Carrot Family (Apiaceae)

Description: Perennial that may grow up to 7' tall. The stems are hollow between the leaf joints and may be ribbed. Compound leaves, 2"–6" long, are divided into 3 or more egg- to lance-shaped leaflets that are sharply toothed along the margins. The underside of the leaflets may have hairy veins. Flat-topped clusters of 20–60 tiny white flowers arise on short stalks. The entire flower heads may be 1"–4" wide. The ¼"-long seed has 2 broad wings and several ridges.

Bloom Season: Summer

Habitat/Range: Widespread across much of western North America, Lyall's Angelica grows in moist mountain meadows, riparian areas, and bogs or wetlands from low to subalpine elevations.

Comments: *Angelica* ("angel") refers to the medicinal and angelic protection against evil properties as revealed to humans by an archangel. *Lyallii* honors David Lyall (1817–1895), a Scottish botanist who collected plants during a boundary survey between British Columbia and the United States and who first defined vegetative zones in British Columbia based upon his collections. The leaves have a parsley-like aroma when crushed. The roots were used medicinally to treat colds, sore throats, or intestinal cramps. Beetles frequent the flowers as pollinators.

SEACOAST ANGELICA
Angelica lucida
Carrot Family (Apiaceae)

Description: Perennial with stout, hollow stems 4' tall. Compound leaves are highly divided. The divisions have broad, toothed margins and sometimes partly cleft segments. Leaves are dark green above and smooth below. Tiny white flowers are arranged in rounded, umbrellalike clusters. Fruit is a seed with side wings.

Bloom Season: Summer

Habitat/Range: Coastal on bluffs, beaches, and wet meadows at low to mid elevations from Alaska to California and along the Atlantic and Siberia coasts as well.

Comments: *Angelica* ("angel") refers to the medicinal and angelic protection against evil properties as revealed to humans by an archangel. *Ludica* ("shining") refers to the glossy leaves. Seeds of a European species were made into gin and absinthe. Also called Sea-Watch.

DOUGLAS' WATER HEMLOCK
Cicuta douglasii
Carrot Family (Apiaceae)

Description: Perennial from a stout, tuberous root. Smooth stems grow upright 20"–36". The leaves are highly dissected with egg- to lance-shaped leaflets that are toothed along the margin and have a sharp tip. The umbrellalike flower cluster is borne on a long stalk and lacks bracts beneath the cluster. The tiny white, greenish, or light purplish flowers have 5 petals and stamens. Fruit is a rounded seed with corky ribs.

Bloom Season: Summer

Habitat/Range: Moist areas, ditches, swamps, meadows, and stream edges from low to high elevations across the Pacific Northwest.

Comments: *Cicuta* is a Latin name used by Pliny for this or another toxic plant. *Douglasii* is for David Douglas (1799–1834), a Scottish botanist who collected plants in the Northwest for the Horticultural Society of London. The plant contains conine, an oily alkaloid that is very toxic to people and livestock who consume their roots, young shoots, or leaves.

POISON HEMLOCK
Conium maculatum
Carrot Family (Apiaceae)

Description: Perennials with a purple-spotted stem that is 1'–8' tall. The leaves are 2–3 times dissected and fernlike. The large leaves, up to 15" long, are borne on stalks that have enlarged and sheathed bases. Small, white flowers are borne in flat-topped clusters. Fruits are egg-shaped seeds with raised, wavy ribs.

Bloom Season: Summer

Habitat/Range: Disturbed sites that are moist from low elevations throughout the Pacific Northwest.

Comments: *Conium* ("conine") refers to the toxic alkaloid that this plant produces. *Maculatum* ("spotted") refers to the splotches on the stem. This plant is extremely poisonous and was administered to Athenians condemned to die for crimes against the Roman state. This European native is now established in the United States.

AMERICAN SILVERTOP
Glehnia littoralis
Carrot Family (Apiaceae)

Description: Perennial, low-growing with stems sprawling across the sand. The compound leaves are leathery to the touch and have waxy margins. The leaflets may be toothed or lobed, egg-shaped, and very hairy on the underside. The small, round flower heads bear clusters of tiny white flowers, borne on hairy stalks. Fruit is a cluster of seeds with broad, corky wings.

Bloom Season: Summer

Habitat/Range: Sand dunes along the coast from Alaska to northern California.

Comments: *Glehnia* honors the Russian botanist and curator of the Botanic Garden at St. Petersburg, Peter von Glehn (1835–1876). *Littoralis* ("beach") refers to the plant's habitat preference. Adaptations to the sandy sites include a stout taproot that stores water, extensive horizontal root systems to combat shifting dunes, leaf stipules that act as sand anchors, and leathery leaves to reduce water loss and protect the leaf from the salty conditions. At first glance, the leaves resemble those of Coastal Strawberry, *Fragaria chiloensis*. Plants bloom in summer, and the wind acts as a dispersal agent blowing the seeds over the dunes.

GRAY'S LICORICE-ROOT
Ligusticum grayi
Carrot Family (Apiaceae)

Description: Perennial, plants to 30" tall. Stems are smooth and bear leaf sheaths at their bases. Leaves are mostly basal, 4"–12" long, and highly divided into small leaflets, of which the terminal ones are lance-shaped. There are often 1–2 smaller upper stem leaves. Small, white flowers, 7–14, are arranged in compound umbrellalike clusters. The fruit is a ½" seed with long, flat projections along the ribs.

Bloom Season: Summer and early autumn

Habitat/Range: Moist or dry open slopes and meadows at mid to subalpine elevations from Washington to California in the Cascades and east to central Idaho.

Comments: *Ligusticum* ("of Liguria") refers to an area in Italy where a relative of Gray's Lovage was first located. Grayi honors Asa Gray (1810–1888), an American botanist who wrote *Gray's Manual of Botany* (1848, 8th ed., 1950) and was a Harvard professor. Wild Carrot or Queen Anne's Lace (*Daucus carota*) also has carrot-like leaves and is a very common Eurasian weed that blooms in late summer across the region. The aromatic roots give the plant its common name. May be confused with Poison Hemlock (*Conium maculatum*) when harvesting the plants for medicinal use.

PACIFIC WATER-DOGWORT
Oenathe sarmetosa
Carrot Family (Apiaceae)

Description: Perennial, stems mostly trail along the ground and are 3'–4' long. Compound parsley-like leaves are divided 2–3 times; the leaflets are cleft and toothed, and end in a fine point. The leaflets' lateral veins reach the tip. Tiny, white flowers, 5–20, are loosely arranged in flat-topped clusters that are 1"–2" wide. A cluster may or may not have several narrow bracts below the flowering head. Fruit is a barrel-shaped seed with ribs.

Bloom Season: Summer

Habitat/Range: Wet sites along streams and rivers, marshes, wetlands, and forest edges at low to mid elevations throughout the Pacific Northwest.

Comments: *Oenanthe* is from the Greek *oinis* ("wine") and *anthos* ("flower") and refers to the flowers being wine scented. *Sarmentosa* ("bearing runners") describes the long runners that arise from nodes where the plant contacts the ground. Although the plant may contain toxins similar to Water Hemlock, some Northwest tribes used the plant as an emetic for stomach ailments or to shorten labor during childbirth.

SPREADING DOGBANE
Apocynum androsaemifolium
Dogbane Family (Apocynaceae)

Description: Perennial up to 2' tall or sprawling along the ground. Cut stems exude a white sap. Leaves are opposite and lance to egg-shaped and droop from the stem. Small urn-shaped flowers are borne in clusters at the end or along the stem. The white to pinkish corolla is greater than twice the length of the calyx. Fruit is a slender pod up to 3" long that hang downward.

Bloom Season: Summer

Habitat/Range: Widespread in dry soils from low to mid elevations throughout the United States.

Comments: *Apocynum* is from the Greek words *apo* ("away from") and *kyon* ("dog"); although the derivation is confusing, the plant may have been used to poison wild dogs. *Androsaemifolium* ("*Androsaemum*-leaved") refers to leaf similarity with another plant. Native peoples used the fine fibers of the stem as thread or plaited them into cordage. The plant was also used medicinally to treat venereal disease. Sometimes called Fly-Trap Dogbane because of the 5 peg-like nectaries at the base of the pistil. The V-shaped openings trap smaller flies and moths not strong enough to pull their mouthparts out of the narrow openings. Larger butterflies or bumblebees have no trouble with these openings.

INDIAN HEMP
Apocynum cannabinum
Dogbane Family (Apocynaceae)

Description: Perennial, grows 1'-3' tall with stout, upright stems. A milky sap exudes when the stem or leaves are cut. The upright leaves are elliptical to egg-shaped, 2"–3" long, arranged oppositely along the stem, and have pointed tips. Small white or green bell-shaped flowers, ⅛"–¼" wide, arise on short stalks in clusters along the stem. Fruit is a long, thin pod.

Bloom Season: Summer

Habitat/Range: Disturbed moist sites in meadows, forest openings, coastal areas, and sagebrush steppe on both sides of the Cascades in Oregon, and it is widely distributed throughout the United States.

Comments: *Apocynum* is from the Greek words *apo* ("away from") and *kyon* ("dog"); although the derivation is confusing, the plant may have been used to poison wild dogs. *Cannabinum* is from a Greek word meaning "hemp," hence the common name, as well. Native Northwest tribes used the strong fibers of Indian Hemp to make cordage for fishing nets, snares, sewing, and as a string.

ELK CLOVER
Aralia californica
Ivy/Pennywort/Devil's Club Family (Araliaceae)

Description: Herbaceous perennial that grows up to 6'–9' tall on thick, nonwoody stems. Leaves pinnately or tripinnately compounded and 3"–6" long. Leaflets oppositely arranged, 6"–12" long, toothed along the margins, and with a single, terminal leaflet. Small greenish-white flowers are borne in an umbrellalike arrangement with each cluster appearing round or starlike. Individual flowers are ⅛" wide. Fruit is a purple to black berry, ¼" long, containing 3–5 seeds.

Bloom Season: Midsummer to early fall

Habitat/Range: Moist forests, riparian areas, seeps, and chaparral at low elevations from southwest Oregon to central California.

Comments: Aralia is from the French Canadian *aralie*, the name under which the plant was first collected. *Californica* ("of California") refers to its distribution. Medicinally harvested for use as a cough suppressant, arthritis treatment, and as an anti-inflammatory. Deer resistant, but birds consume the berries. Also called California Spikenard.

DEVIL'S CLUB
Oplopanax horridus
Ivy/Pennywort/Devil's Club Family (Araliaceae)

Description: Perennial, with thick stems 3'–10' tall. The stems have a sweet aroma and numerous ¼"–½"-long yellow spines. The large, maple-shaped leaves are up to 18" wide and have 7–9 shallow-pointed lobes. The lobes are toothed, and there are numerous spines on the leaf's underside, as well as the petioles. The tiny, white flowers are borne along an elongated stalk. The ¼"-wide flowers are arranged in rounded clusters along the stalk. Fruit is a red berry.

Bloom Season: Early summer

Habitat/Range: Moist woods, particularly near streams, at low to mid elevations from Alaska to Oregon and east to Idaho and Montana.

Comments: *Oplopanax* is from the Greek *oplo* ("tool" or "weapon") and *Panax*, which is another genus. *Horridus* ("very prickly") describes the stems and leaf undersides. Native coastal tribes used the roots and inner bark to treat various ailments, the stem wood was carved into fishing lures, and the berries were mashed and used to cleanse the hair of dirt or lice. Charcoal from the wood was added to bear grease for face painting. A tea is made from the leaves to treat diabetes.

SAND LILY
Leucocrinum montanum
Asparagus Family (Asparagaceae)

Description: Perennial, from deeply buried roots. The numerous strap-like leaves arise from the top of the root as these plants lack stems. The tufted leaves are up to 10" long and have a whitish margin. The fragrant flowers are borne on stalks, 2"–5" long, that may barely rise above the ground. The showy, white flowers are often borne in clusters; individual flowers are 1"–2" across. Fruit is an egg-shaped capsule.

Bloom Season: Spring

Habitat/Range: Sandy or rocky soils in sagebrush steppe and open woodlands from low to mid elevations from Oregon to California and east to South Dakota.

Comments: *Leucocrinum* is from the Greek *leukos* ("white") and *crinon* ("lily"), while *montanum* ("of the mountains") refers to the plant's distribution. Plants may lie dormant during dry years, and then sprout the following spring when soil moisture is sufficient.

FALSE LILY-OF-THE-VALLEY
Maianthemum dilatatum
Asparagus Family (Asparagaceae)

Description: Perennial, often found in dense clusters as the plants sprout from underground lateral roots. Each plant bears 1–3 heart-shaped, glossy leaves that may be 5" long. Floral stalks rise above the leaves and bear a cluster of small, white flowers; floral parts are in 4s (instead of the usual 3 for members of this family). Fruit is a light green to mottled brown berry that turns red with age.

Bloom Season: Spring

Habitat/Range: From low to mid elevations in moist, shady forests, along stream banks, and under Sitka Spruce forests near the coast.

Comments: *Maianthemum* is from the Greek *maios* ("May") and *anthemon* ("flower"), which reflects the plant's springtime blooming. *Dilatatum* ("expanding") refers to the sprouting from the roots. Native coastal tribes used the plant medicinally to treat wounds, eyestrain, and internal injuries.

PLUMED SOLOMON'S SEAL
Maianthemum racemosa
Asparagus Family (Asparagaceae)

Description: Perennial, often in clumps, with upright or arched stems, 1'–3' long. Broad egg-shaped leaves are 3"–10" long. Numerous, tiny white flowers are borne in a terminal cluster. Individual flowers of 6 distinct tepals. Fruits are fleshy red berries that may have purple spots.

Bloom Season: Spring to early summer

Habitat/Range: Grows in moist woods, meadows, and along stream banks from low to mid elevations throughout the Pacific Northwest.

Comments: *Maianthemum* is from the Greek *maios* ("May") and *anthemon* ("flower"), which reflects the plant's springtime blooming. *Racemosa* ("flowers in a raceme") describes the floral arrangement. Native Northwest tribes used the boiled roots as either a tea for rheumatism, back injuries, or kidney problems or as a poultice for wounds. Although the berries are nontoxic and eaten by wildlife, they are poor tasting.

STARRY SOLOMON'S SEAL
Maianthemum stellatum
Asparagus Family (Asparagaceae)

Description: Perennial with upright or arched stems 10"–30" tall. Broad, lance-shaped leaves are 2½"–8" long. Five to 10 white, star-like flowers are born in an unbranched terminal cluster. The fruit is a greenish-yellow berry with 3 or 6 bluish-purple stripes that darken with age.

Bloom Season: Spring to midsummer

Habitat/Range: Moist woodlands and stream banks or drier meadows and clearings throughout the Pacific Northwest.

Comments: *Maianthemum* is from the Greek *maios* ("May") and *anthemon* ("flower"), which reflects the plant's springtime blooming. *Stellatum* ("star-like") refers to the flowers. The berries are edible but of poor quality. This species and *M. racemosa* resemble Solomon's Seal (*Polygonatum multiflorum*), hence the "false" name in the title.

WHITE TRITELEIA
Triteleia hyacinthia
Asparagus Family (Asparagaceae)

Description: Perennial, plants 1'–2' tall. The grasslike leaves are longer than the flowering stem but wither at flowering. Dense clusters of white flowers are borne in an umbrellalike pattern. The tepals form a short tube with flaring lobes; the lobes have a green midline. Flowers are ½"–¾" long. Fruit is a capsule.

Bloom Season: Mid spring to early summer

Habitat/Range: Meadows, grasslands, and sagebrush steppe at low elevations throughout the region.

Comments: *Triteleia* is from the Greek *tri* ("three") and *teleios* ("perfect"), in reference to the floral parts in 3's. *Hyacinthia* ("resembling a hyacinth") refers to the resemblance of the flowers to those of hyacinths. Also called Fool's Onion or WhiteBro-diaea; the edible bulbs lack an onion odor.

YARROW
Achillea millefolium
Aster Family (Asteraceae)

Description: Aromatic perennial from 5" to several feet tall. The fernlike leaves are pinnately dissected, meaning the individual divisions on a leaf are again divided into smaller segments. Lower leaves have stalks while the upper leaves are smaller and stalkless. White flowers are borne in large, flat, or rounded clusters, and contain mostly disk flowers (10–30) with a few ray flowers (3–5). The tiny, flat seeds lack a pappus.

Bloom Season: Spring to fall

Habitat/Range: Widespread from lowlands to high elevations throughout the northern hemisphere.

Comments: *Achillea* is after the Greek mythological hero Achilles, who also benefited from the plant's medicinal properties. *Millefolium* ("1,000-leaved") refers to the finely divided leaf segments. Native coastal tribes used Yarrow for poultices, cold and bronchitis treatments, blood purifiers, eyewashes, and other treatments. Yarrow was a parish on the Yarrow River in Scotland's Southern Uplands.

TRAILFINDER
Adenocaulon bicolor
Aster Family (Asteraceae)

Description: Slender-stemmed annual or perennial that grows 1'–3' tall. Stems have dense, white hairs below and stalked glands above. Large leaves, 3"–6" long, are triangular or heart-shaped in outline and may have toothed margins. Undersides of leaves have dense, white hairs. The small, white flower heads bear only disk flowers, and the floral bracts curve downward and drop off when the flowers mature. Fruits are club-shaped seeds with tiny, hooked hairs.

Bloom Season: Midsummer

Habitat/Range: Moist, shady forests from sea level to mid elevations from British Columbia to California and east to Montana.

Comments: *Adenocaulon* is from the Greek *aden* ("gland") and *kaulos* ("stem"), which refers to the stalked glands on the upper stem. *Bicolor* ("two colors") refers to the green uppersides and silver undersides of the leaves. Also named Pathfinder because the silvery undersides of the overturned leaves create trail blazes. The flowers produce a slightly offensive aroma to attract small flies. When mature, the seeds attach to passing animals and "hitchhike" a ride for dispersal.

LOW PUSSYTOES
Antennaria dimorpha
Aster Family (Asteraceae)

Description: Perennial, mat-like growth 1"–4" high. Leaves are lance- to inversely lance-shaped and covered with dense, white hairs. Flowering heads are borne solitary on short stalks; the disk flowers are white to brownish in color. Fruit is a seed with white hairs.

Bloom Season: Early spring to early summer

Habitat/Range: Dry grasslands, prairies, and open areas in forests from low to mid elevations throughout the western United States.

Comments: *Antennaria* is from the Latin *antenna* ("antennae"), after the resemblance of the flower's pappus (modified calyx) to insect antennae. *Dimorpha* ("2 forms") refers to the plant's different leaf shapes. Attracts flies, beetles, and butterflies as pollinators.

PEARLY EVERLASTING
Anaphalis margaritacea
Aster Family (Asteraceae)

Description: Underground stems (rhizomes) bear numerous upright, unbranched stems covered with white hairs. These woolly stems may grow 1'–4' tall. Numerous lance-shaped or linear leaves bear a prominent midvein and are white-woolly below and green above. Small, yellow disk flowers are borne in dense clusters; the white involucre bracts have a dark basal spot. Fruit is a tiny seed that may bear some white pappus hairs.

Bloom Season: Summer through fall

Habitat/Range: Widespread from lowland to subalpine regions in open forests, meadows, rocky slopes, and pastures. Sometimes considered a weedy native plant.

Comments: *Anaphalis* is a near anagram of *Gnaphalium*, a similar looking genus. *Margaritacea* ("pearl-like") identifies the shape and color of the flower heads. The dry, white involucre bracts retain this pearly coloration when dried, hence the common name.

ROUGH EYELASHES

Blepharipappus scaber
Aster Family (Asteraceae)

Description: Annual with slender upright stems, 5"–15" tall, covered with hairs. Alternate leaves are stemless, 1"–2" long, and linear with rolled-in margins. Flowerheads bear a narrow center of disk flowers with purplish extended pistils surrounded by 3–5 ½"-long white ray flowers that are purple below and 3-cleft. Fruit is a seed with stiff bristles.

Bloom Season: Spring

Habitat/Range: Grows in dry sites in grasslands, shrublands, and open woodlands at low to subalpine elevations mostly east of the Cascades from Washington to California and east to Nevada.

Comments: *Blepharipappus* is from the Greek words *blepharis* ("eyelash") and *pappus* ("seed down"), which refers to the fringed scales on the seeds hairs that resemble an eyelash. *Scaber* ("rough") refers to the texture of the stems and leaves.

DOUGLAS' DUSTYMAIDEN

Chaenactis douglasii
Aster Family (Asteraceae)

Description: Biennial, with 1 to several erect stems that are 4"–20" tall. Basal cluster of leaves is highly dissected and may have glandular or dense hairs. The ¾"–1" flower heads bear only disk flowers that are white or pinkish. The bracts that subtend the flower head are blunt and have glandular hairs. Seeds are club- to cigar-shaped, somewhat flattened, and topped with rough scales.

Bloom Season: Late spring to summer

Habitat/Range: Dry sandy or gravelly sites from low to mid elevations from British Columbia to Montana and south to California and Arizona.

Comments: *Chaenactis* is from *chaino* ("gape") and *actis* ("ray"). This name refers to the opening mouth of the tiny disk flowers. *Douglasii* honors the Scottish plant collector David Douglas (1799–1834), who collected plants throughout the Northwest. Douglas died in Hawaii after he fell into a feral pig trap and was gored to death. Native Americans used crushed leaves as a poultice to reduce swelling. Also called Hairy Chaenactis.

GRAY THISTLE
Cirsium undulatum
Aster Family (Asteraceae)

Description: Perennial, 2'–5' tall. Stems covered with white hairs. The basal leaves are 2"–10" long, deeply divided or lobed, and the lobes are toothed or divided with spines along the margins. Stem leaves are smaller. Flower heads are borne at the top of the stems. The round heads are 1"–3" wide and have white, pale lavender to pinkish-purple disk flowers. The bracts below the heads are brown and lance-shaped with spiny tips. Fruit is a seed with fine hairs.

Bloom Season: Summer

Habitat/Range: Dry, open sites at low elevations throughout the dry portions of the Pacific Northwest.

Comments: *Cirsium* is from the Greek *kirsion* ("swollen vein") after one species of thistle was used to treat swollen veins. *Undulatum* ("wavy") refers to the leaf edges. Though many thistles are introduced, Gray Thistle is native. The flowers attract numerous types of insects as pollinators, especially bees.

ALICE EASTWOOD'S FLEABANE
Erigeron aliceae
Aster Family (Asteraceae)

Description: Perennial, with upright stems 8"–28" tall. Hairy basal leaves are large, up to 8" long, oblong, and have either smooth or toothed margins. Upper leaves are smaller and lance-shaped. The stems bear 1–7 flower heads at their tip; each head is ½"–¾" wide and made up of 15–80 narrow, pink, white, or lavender ray flowers surrounding a center of yellow disk flowers. Fruit is a seed.

Bloom Season: Summer

Habitat/Range: From mid to high elevations growing in meadows and open forests mostly on the west side of the Cascades from Washington to northwestern California.

Comments: *Erigeron* is from the Greek *eri* ("early") and *geron* ("old man"), which refers to the white hairs on the seeds. *Aliceae* is for Alice Eastwood (1859–1953), an American botanist and curator at the California Academy of Sciences. Thomas Howell (1842–1912) and his brother, Joseph Howell (1830–1912), collected this plant for science in 1900 in the Siskiyou Mountains.

CUTLEAF DAISY
Erigeron compositus
Aster Family (Asteraceae)

Description: Perennial, grows up to 10" tall from a small tuft. Basal leaves are spoon-shaped in outline, sometimes divided, but lobed and covered with dense hairs. The floral stem bears one 1"–1½"-wide flower head made up of 20–60 white (tinged with purple), pinkish, or lavender ray flowers that surround a center of yellow disk flowers. At higher elevations, the plants may lack ray flowers and be very low growing. Fruit is a seed.

Bloom Season: Late spring through early fall

Habitat/Range: Widely distributed in forests, shrub steppe, or subalpine to alpine habitats from Alaska across Canada and in the United States from the Pacific Northwest to New Mexico.

Comments: *Erigeron* is from the Greek *eri* ("early") and *geron* ("old man"), which refers to the white hairs on the seeds. *Compositus* ("compound") refers to the leaves.

SPREADING FLEABANE
Erigeron divergens
Aster Family (Asteraceae)

Description: Annual, biennial, or short-lived perennial, 2"–20" tall. Stems have soft, spreading hairs. Basal leaves are inversely lance- or spatula-shaped, ⅜"–2½" long, narrow, and covered with hairs. Leaves along the stem are similar but smaller. Flower heads may be numerous per plant, with 75–150 blue, pink, or white ray flowers, surrounding yellow disk flowers. Fruit is a seed.

Bloom Season: Mid spring to midsummer

Habitat/Range: Wide range of habitats and elevations from riparian to aspen communities at low to high elevations across the West.

Comments: *Erigeron* is from the Greek *eri* ("early") and *geron* ("old man"), which refers to the white hairs on the seeds. *Divergens* ("spreading") refers to the plant's growth habit.

ROUGHLEAF ASTER
Eurybia radulina
Aster Family (Asteraceae)

Description: Perennial, 4"–40" tall with slightly zigzagged stems between the leaf nodes. Lance-shaped to oval leaves have toothed margins and stiff hairs. Flowering heads, subtended by bracts with purple margins, bear 10–15 white to lavender or purple ray flowers surrounding a center of yellow disk flowers. Fruit is a seed with hairs.

Bloom Season: Midsummer to fall

Habitat/Range: Open areas, dry meadows, and brushy hillsides in mountain woods from low to mid elevations throughout the Pacific Northwest.

Comments: *Eurybia* is from two Greek words meaning "wide" and "few," which may be in relation to the few but wide ray flowers. *Radulina* ("rough") refers to the texture of the leaves.

TIDYTIPS
Layia glandulosa
Aster Family (Asteraceae)

Description: Annual, 4"–12" tall. Basal narrow leaves are lobed or toothed, ½"–3" long, and covered with stiff, glandular hairs; upper leaves are not lobed. Flowering heads have a center of yellow disk flowers surrounded by several white, 3-lobed (toothed) ray flowers. Fruit is a seed with about 10 flat, white hairs.

Bloom Season: Spring

Habitat/Range: Open areas and sandy sites at low elevations on the east side of the Cascade Mountains from Washington to northern California.

Comments: *Layia* honors George Tradescant Lay (died 1845), an English naturalist on the Beechey Voyage (1825–1828) who collected plants in Asia, Hawaii, Alaska, California, and South America. *Glandulosa* ("glandular") refers to the sticky hairs that cover the plant. Tidytips refers to the "tidiness" of the ray flowers.

ARCTIC SWEET COLTSFOOT
Petasites frigidus
Aster Family (Asteraceae)

Description: From slender rhizomes arise numerous flowering stems, 5"–25" tall before the leaves appear. Stem leaves are small, but the deeply divided basal leaves may be 1' wide. These leaves are heart- or kidney-shaped and have 5–7 lobes that are toothed along the margin. The uppersides of leaves are green and hairless; undersides are woolly. Flower heads are arranged in flat-topped clusters. Creamy white ray flowers surround a cluster of whitish or pinkish disk flowers. The lance-shaped bracts that are below the individual flower heads have hairy bases. The ribbed seeds bear a crown of numerous white hairs.

Bloom Season: Spring

Habitat/Range: Low to mid elevations in moist forests, swamps and meadows, and along lakes on the west side of the Cascade Mountains throughout the region.

Comments: *Petasites* is from the Greek *petasos* ("a broad-brimmed hat") and refers to the large basal leaves. *Frigidus* ("growing in cold regions") refers to the habitat preference. The common name comes from a European relative with leaves that resemble the shape of a young horse's hoof. The light, winged seeds are easily dispersed by the wind, enabling this plant to colonize newly disturbed areas.

WHITE MULE'S EARS
Wyethia helianthoides
Aster Family (Asteraceae)

Description: Perennial, 1'–2' tall, often covering large areas. Basal leaves are egg-shaped, up to 1' long, and have smooth margins; stem leaves are smaller. Solitary, large white flower heads have numerous 1"–2"-long ray flowers that surround a center of yellow disk flowers. Flowers may turn pale yellow with age. Fruit is a seed.

Bloom Season: Late spring and early summer

Habitat/Range: Often abundant in moist meadows, stream banks, and open areas at mid- to subalpine montane elevations from central Oregon to southern Montana.

Comments: *Wyethia* is for Nathaniel Wyeth (1802–1856), the "Cambridge Iceman" who led 2 expeditions to Oregon in 1832 and 1834. *Helianthoides* ("resembling *Helianthus*") refers to the similarity of this plant to sunflowers in the *Helianthus* genus. The showy flowers attract a myriad of pollinators, including butterflies, bumblebees, flies, and hawk moths. Also known as Whitehead Mule's Ears, referring to the large, ear-like shape of the leaves.

VANILLA-LEAF
Achlys triphylla
Berberis/Vancouveria Family (Berberidaceae)

Description: From thin, underground rhizomes arise leaf stalks that are 4"–16" tall. The broad leaf is divided into 3 fan-shaped leaflets. The asymmetrical segments are coarsely toothed along the margin; the smaller middle segment may be roughly divided into 3 lobes. The tiny, white flowers are borne on a leafless stalk and arranged in a tight, 1"–3"-long spike that rises above the leaves. Flowers lack sepals and petals but bear 8–20 white stamens. The small, crescent-shaped, reddish-purple fruits are covered with fine hairs.

Bloom Season: Late spring to midsummer

Habitat/Range: From low to mid elevations in shady forests to openings often near streams from southern British Columbia to northwest California, mainly west of the Cascades.

Comments: *Achlys* is from the Greek word *achlus* ("mist") and is perhaps a reference to the misty appearance of the white flowers. *Triphylla* ("3-leaved") refers to the one leaf divided into 3s. To some, the lobed middle leaf resembles either a goose's foot or a deer's hoof: hence, another common name for the plant is Deer-Foot. The leaves have a vanilla-like aroma when dry or crushed.

NORTHERN INSIDE-OUT FLOWER
Vancouveria hexandra
Berberis/Vancouveria Family (Berberidaceae)

Description: Perennial, up to 20" tall. Compound leaves arise on long basal stalks and are divided into 3 divisions that bear 9–15 heart- to egg-shaped leaflets. Flowering stalks bear small, white, starlike, nodding flowers. Flowers have 6 sepals and petals; the petals are shorter than the sepals and have hooded tips. Both the sepals and petals bend backward and flare open at the base (top of the flower). Fruit is a purplish pod with sticky hairs that bears black seeds.

Bloom Season: Late spring to early summer

Habitat/Range: Moist, shady coniferous forests from low to mid elevations west of the Cascade Crest from Washington to northwestern California.

Comments: *Vancouveria* is for Captain George Vancouver (1757–1798), the British explorer who sailed twice with Captain Cook and who explored and mapped the Pacific Northwest coast from 1791–1795. *Hexandra* ("six stamens") refers to the number of stamens. The flowers have 6–9 outer sepals that fall off before the flower opens. The black seeds have a fleshy appendage that almost covers the seed; this coating attracts ants and wasps that help to disperse the seeds. Redwood Ivy (*V. planipetala*) has a white or purple-tinged flower and grows in the Klamath Mountains in southern Oregon and the northern California coast range.

NORTHERN CRYPTANTUM
Cryptantha celosioides
Borage Family (Boraginaceae)

Description: Biennial or perennial, 4"–20" tall, with one or several stems covered with bristles. Basal leaves are tufted, spatula-shaped, or broadly oblong, 1"–4" long, with rounded tips and also covered in bristles. Upper leaves are similar but smaller. Numerous small, white flowers crowd along the flowering stem; the flowers are about ½" wide and have 5 white petals that flare open at the top of a short tube. Fruits are nutlets joined together.

Bloom Season: Mid spring to early summer

Habitat/Range: Grows in drier low- to mid-elevation locations such as fields, shrub steppe, grasslands, and open forests on the east side of the Cascades in Oregon and from British Columbia to Utah.

Comments: *Cryptantha* is from the Greek *krypto* ("to hide") and *anthos* ("flower"), in reference to the bracts obscuring the flowers on some species. *Celosioides* ("like *Celosia*") refers to the resemblance of this plant to those in the *Celosia* genus of the Amaranth family. Also called Buttecandle.

SEA KALE
Crambe maritima
Mustard Family (Brassicaceae)

Description: Mound-forming perennial, grows up to 30" tall and 35" wide. Large, fleshy leaves have wavy, toothed margins and broad, egg-shaped blades that are bluish-green. Cream-colored flowers are borne on short stems. The flowers have 4 petals and are about ½"–¾" long. Fruit is a long capsule.

Bloom Season: Early summer

Habitat/Range: Coastal, growing on rocky outcrops or ledges at low elevations. A European species that is naturalized in the United States. Found growing at Yaquina Head Outstanding Natural Area near Newport, Oregon.

Comments: *Crambe* is from the Greek *Krambe* ("cabbage") and *maritima* ("maritime"), which is in reference to its coastal distribution. Edible, this plant appeared in Thomas Jefferson's *Garden Book of 1809* as a garden crop.

SPRING WHITLOW-GRASS
Draba verna
Mustard Family (Brassicaceae)

Description: Annual, plants 2"–7" tall. The basal leaves are oval to spoon-shaped and about 1" long and have small hairs. The ⅛"-wide, white flowers are borne on a short, flowering stalk. The 4 petals are deeply cleft into 2 lobes. Fruit is a flat seedpod.

Bloom Season: Spring

Habitat/Range: Open areas in grasslands, shrub steppe, or lower elevation woodlands on the east side of the Cascades.

Comments: *Draba* is from the Greek *drabe*, which is the name of a related plant. *Verna* ("springtime") refers to the spring blooming. *Draba* were used to treat infections near the finger or toenails that were called "whitlows" or "felons." Also called Vernal Whitlow Grass or Common Draba.

WHITETOP
Lepidium draba
Mustard Family (Brassicaceae)

Description: Weedy perennial often growing in profusion due to spreading rhizomes. Plants 1'–2' tall with 1"–2" long leaves that clasp the stem and are lance- to egg-shaped. The basal leaves have short stalks. Flowering head is a dense cluster of tiny, white, 4-petaled flowers. Fruit is a heart-shaped seedpod.

Bloom Season: Late spring to midsummer

Habitat/Range: Disturbed areas, meadows, agricultural fields, and roadsides across much of North America. Whitetop is native to western Asia and eastern Europe, but it is considered a noxious weed in the United States.

Comments: *Lepidium* is from the Greek *lepidion* meaning "little scale" after the small seedpods. *Draba* is from the Greek word meaning "acrid," a name applied to other Mustard-like plants.

CUTLEAF THELYPODY
Thelypodium laciniatum
Mustard Family (Brassicaceae)

Description: Biennial, from stout stems, the upright branches reach to 3' or more. Stems are hairless. The basal rosette of leaves is divided into several lance-shaped leaflets or lobes. These flowers wither before flowering. Upper leaves are less divided, smaller, and pointed at the tip. A long plume of white to pale lavender flowers with linear petals is borne along a central stalk. Fruit is a narrow, cylindrical seedpod.

Bloom Season: Mid spring to early summer

Habitat/Range: Rocky cliffs, plateaus, or slopes in open sagebrush and grassland communities from low to mid elevations from British Columbia to southern California, mainly on the east side of the Cascades.

Comments: Thelypodium is from the Greek *thelys* ("female") and *podoin* ("little foot"), which refers to the short-stalked ovary of many species. *Laciniatum* ("shredded" or "torn to pieces") refers to the highly dissected leaves. Manyflower Thelypody (*T. milleflorum*) also has upright flowering stalks bearing numerous flowers.

SIMPSON'S HEDGEHOG CACTUS
Pediocactus simpsonii
Cactus Family (Cactaceae)

Description: Solitary or colonial rounded stems grow 1"–7" high and 1½"–10" wide. Stems are covered with tubercles (swollen areas) that bear brown to blackish central spines and white radial spines. Flowers are ½"–1½" wide; petallike parts range from white to greenish, yellowish, or pinkish. Fleshy fruit is green and may turn reddish with age.

Bloom Season: Late spring to midsummer

Habitat/Range: Mixed desert shrub to ponderosa pine woodlands at mid to high elevations from Washington to New Mexico.

Comments: *Pediocactus* is from the Greek *pedio* ("plains"), referring to the growing location of this cactus. *Simpsonii* honors James H. Simpson (1813–1883), a topographical engineer who first collected this cactus in Nevada.

MOUNTAIN SNOWBERRY
Symphoricarpos oreophilus
Pink Family (Caprifoliaceae)

Description: Deciduous shrub, 2'–5' tall. Opposite leaves are oval- to egg-shaped, about 1" long, and borne on short stems. Small, bell-shaped flowers are made up of 5 pinkish-white petals that are lobed at the tip and hairy inside. Fruit is a white berry.

Bloom Season: Mid spring to early summer

Habitat/Range: Widely distributed from coast to east side forests in moist locations across most of Canada and the western and northern United States.

Comments: *Symphoricarpos* ("to bear fruit together") refers to the tight cluster of berries that forms on the shrub. *Oreophilus* ("mountain loving") refers to the plant's habitat preference. The common name refers to the color of the fruit. The berries have saponins and are not considered edible.

FIELD CHICKWEED
Cerastium arvense
Pink Family (Caryophyllaceae)

Description: Perennial that grows in tufts or clumps, with stems either upright or trailing along the ground. The upper portion of the stems has sticky hairs, as do the flowers. Leaves are ½"–1½" long, mostly linear to narrowly lance-shaped, covered with fine hairs, and pointed at the tip. Whorls of finer, small leaves grow in the axils of most stem leaves. Flat-topped clusters bear 5–9½"-wide white flowers with deeply notched petals. The 5 petals are at least 1½ times longer than the sepals. Sepals and floral stalks have sticky hairs. Fruit is a 1-seed capsule that contains numerous tiny black seeds.

Bloom Season: Mid spring to summer

Habitat/Range: Widespread from sea level to alpine elevations on dry meadows and rocky outcrops, but also found in moist, open meadows from Alaska to California.

Comments: *Cerastium* is from the Greek word *keras* ("a horn"), which describes the shape of the seed capsule. *Arvense* ("growing in fields") reflects a habitat preference for cultivated or fallow fields and meadows. Field Chickweed is widely distributed across North America.

FESCUE SANDWORT
Eremogone capillaris
Pink Family (Caryophyllaceae)

Description: Perennial, matted growth. Basal linear leaves often larger than 1" long and end in a soft, pointed tip. Stem leaves in pairs, oppositely arranged, but shorter than the basal leaves. The flowering stalk rises 4"–8" and bears a loose cluster of ½"-wide flowers. White flowers are cup-shaped and have 5 petals. Fruits are tiny seeds.

Bloom Season: Summer

Habitat/Range: Sandy or gravelly sites in mid to subalpine elevations from Alaska to central Oregon and east to Montana.

Comments: *Eremogone* is from the Greek *erem* ("a lonely place") and *gon* ("seed"), although the meaning is unclear. *Capillaris* ("very slender") refers to the leaves; also called Thread-Leaved Sandwort. The common name may refer to many of the plants growing in thin, sandy soils. King's Sandwort (*E. kingii*) is similar, but the lance- to egg-shaped sepals narrow to a pointed tip.

DOUGLAS' CATCHFLY
Silene douglasii
Pink Family (Caryophyllaceae)

Description: Perennial. Grows 4"–16" tall with multiple stems arising from a basal cluster of leaves. The leaves are lance-shaped, 1"–2½" long, oppositely arranged, and may have some fine, sticky hairs. Stem leaves are smaller. The white to greenish flowers are ½"-wide and each of the 5 petals is cleft at the tip into 2 lobes. The greenish calyx is inflated, resembling a tube, with reddish-brown streaks along its flanks. Fruit is a many-seeded capsule.

Bloom Season: Summer

Habitat/Range: Dry slopes, sagebrush steppe, and rocky ledges from mid to high elevations from British Columbia to California and east into Utah and Nevada.

Comments: *Silene* is from either the Greek *sialon* ("saliva"), which refers to the stem's sticky hairs or to *selinos*, Silenus, the intoxicated foster-father of Bacchus (god of wine) who was covered with foam. *Douglasii* honors David Douglas (1799–1834), a British horticulturalist and explorer who made three plant collecting trips to North America and introduced many western US trees into British forestry. He met his fate while climbing Mauna Kea volcano in Hawaii at age 35.

MENZIES' CAMPION
Silene menziesii
Pink Family (Caryophyllaceae)

Description: Perennial, with sticky stems, 2"–15" tall, either upright or trailing. The opposite, lance-shaped leaves are 1"–3" long. The white flowers have 5 deeply notched petals and are ¾" long. Fruit is a capsule.

Bloom Season: Summer

Habitat/Range: Meadows, open forests, or stream edges from low to mid elevations widespread throughout western North America.

Comments: *Silene* is from either the Greek *sialon* ("saliva"), which refers to the stem's sticky hairs, or from *selinos*, referring to Silenus, the intoxicated foster-father of Bacchus (god of wine), who was covered with foam. *Menziesii* is for Archibald Menzies (1754–1842), a Scottish naval physician and naturalist who sailed with Captain George Vancouver on his Pacific exploration from 1791–1795. Carl Linnaeus (1707–1778) concluded that a "flower clock" existed, with various species opening at different hours of the day. The night-blooming flowers of *Silene* opened around 11:00 p.m. and attracted hawk moths as pollinators.

FRINGED GRASS-OF-PARNASSUS
Parnassia fimbriata
Bittersweet Family (Celastraceae)

Description: Perennial, with flowering stems 6"–20" high. The basal leaves are kidney-shaped, glossy, and borne on long stems. The leafless flowering stalks bear a solitary, 1"-wide flower with 5 fringed petals. The petals have green or yellow veins, and the lower portion of the petal has hairs along the fringe. The flowers produce 5 fertile stamens alternating with sterile stamens that are divided into fingerlike lobes. Fruit is a capsule.

Bloom Season: Summer

Habitat/Range: Wet meadows, bogs, stream edges, and most sites in forests at mid to alpine elevations from Alaska to California and east to the Rocky Mountains.

Comments: *Parnassia* is from a sixteenth-century name for an unrelated plant growing on Mount Parnassus in Greece but refers to its high elevation preference. *Fimbriata* ("with a small fringe") describes the petals. Flies and mosquitoes pollinate these flowers as they obtain nectar from the exposed aromatic glands.

CHAPPARAL FALSE BINDWEED
Calystegia occidentalis
Morning-Glory Family (Convolvulaceae)

Description: Perennial vine that may twist and climb up other vegetation, the stem is covered with fine hairs. Arrow- or spade-shaped leaves are about 2" long, covered with fine hairs, lobed at the base, and pointed or rounded at the tip. The basal lobes may be as long as the main lobe. Funnel-shaped white flowers, 1–4, are borne along a single stem. The 5-petaled flowers are 1"–2½" wide. Fruit is a capsule.

Bloom Season: Late spring through summer

Habitat/Range: Shrub steppe, dry chaparral, and forests on either side of the Cascades from Oregon to Baja California.

Comments: *Calystegia* is from the Greek *kalux* ("calyx") and *stege* ("a covering"), meaning "a covering cup." The name may relate to the way the petals close over the capsule. *Occidentalis* ("western") refers to the distribution of this plant.

WESTERN BUNCHBERRY
Cornus unalaschkensis
Dogwood Family (Cornaceae)

Description: Low-growing perennial. Plants have 4–7 short-stalked oval to elliptically shaped leaves arranged in a whorl or common ring. The 1"–4"–long leaves are greenish above and white below, with parallel veins. Flower color is variable from greenish-white to yellowish to purplish. Fruit resembles a red berry: the red, pulpy flesh surrounds a stony cover that houses the single seed, known as a drupe.

Bloom Season: Mid spring to midsummer

Habitat/Range: Shady forests at mid to subalpine elevations across the Pacific Northwest and south to New Mexico.

Comments: *Cornus* is from the Latin name for the Cornelian Cherry (*C. mas*). *Unalaschkenis* ("of Aleutian Islands") is a reference to the plant's first discovery. A feature of the *Cornus* genus is the thin leaf veins that will keep connected after gently separating a leaf. The ripened fruits were eaten either cooked or raw. The stamen's springy filaments are held in place by elastic petals, and when mature, the stamens snap upward and release pollen. Canadian bunchberry (*C. canadensis*) is similar but grows outside the region of Western Bunchberry.

PACIFIC DOGWOOD
Cornus nuttallii
Dogwood Family (Cornaceae)

Description: Tree; grows 10'–50' tall. Leaves are opposite, 1"–4" long, and have deeply curved parallel veins. Upper sides are dark green, and undersides are lighter and slightly hairy. White flowers have 4–7 2"–3" long petallike bracts that subtend a center cluster of tiny greenish-white flowers. Fruit is a cluster of red fleshy berries each containing one seed.

Bloom Season: Late spring to early summer

Habitat Range: Moist, shaded locations at low to mid elevations mainly west of the Cascades from Alaska to northern California.

Comments: *Cornus* is from the Latin name for the Cornelian Cherry (*C. mas*). *Nuttallii* honors Thomas Nuttall (1786–1859), an English naturalist who collected plants and birds in the United States from 1811–1834. Pacific Dogwood is British Columbia's Provincial Flower.

RED-OSIER DOGWOOD
Cornus sericea
Dogwood Family (Cornaceae)

Description: Deciduous shrub that grows from 5'–15' tall. Reddish stems branch upward from the base; the stems may turn grayish with age. Opposite leaves show strong parallel venation. The leaves are 2"–4" long, narrowly oval, and dark green above but lighter below. Tiny, white flowers are borne in dense clusters at the branch tips; the clusters are 1½"–3" wide. Fruit is a white to tan berry.

Bloom Season: Late spring to midsummer

Habitat/Range: Moist locations along streams and rivers through the Pacific Northwest, Canada, northern United States, and into California and the Midwest.

Comments: *Cornus* is from the Latin name for the Cornelian Cherry (*C. mas*). *Sericea* ("silky") refers to the texture of the leaves. Native Americans collected the bark for use as a dye or added it to other plants to create a tobacco product. Others ate the berries to cure colds or slow bleeding. Modern-day uses include horticultural varieties used in landscaping and nursery-grown native stock used in controlling stream bank erosion.

MANROOT
Marah oregana
Gourd Family (Cucurbitaceae)

Description: Climbing perennial with branched or coiled tendrils. Irregularly lobed, maplelike leaves are large (up to 10" wide) and have stiff hairs on the upper surface. The male bell-shaped flowers, ½"–1" wide and white, are borne in loose clusters. The fused petals (5–8) form a short tube that flares open at the end, often resembling a 5-pointed star. Male and female flowers are borne separately but on the same plant; the female flowers are small, green, and inconspicuous. Fruit is a rounded, fleshy melon that may or may not have weak spines.

Bloom Season: Spring to midsummer

Habitat/Range: Open, grassy fields, thickets, bottomlands, and rocky areas at low elevations from British Columbia to California, mostly west of the Cascades.

Comments: *Marah* ("bitter") is from a Hebrew word that describes the flavor of the pounded roots. *Oregana* ("of Oregon") refers to the type specimen being collected in the Oregon Territory. Native coastal tribes used the plant to treat kidney problems and skin sores. Also known as Wild Cucumber, this plant is related to cultivated plants such as gourds and cucumbers, but the fruit is considered inedible.

GREENLEAF MANZANITA
Arctostaphylos patula
Heather Family (Ericaceae)

Description: Shrub, 3'–6' tall. Reddish bark of stems contrasts with the evergreen leaves. Leaves are 1"–2" long, rounded or broader at the upper end, and often have a pointed tip. Urn-shaped flowers are pink or whitish, ¼" long, and borne in clusters. Fruit is a reddish-brown berry.

Bloom Season: Spring

Habitat/Range: Open woods, often with ponderosa pine, and basalt outcrops on the east side of the Cascades from Washington to California and east to Colorado.

Comments: *Arctostaphylos* is from the Greek *arktos* ("bear") and *staphyle* ("bunch of grapes"), referring to the abundant berries. *Patula* ("spreading") refers to the plant's sprawling nature. *Manzanita* means "little apple" in Spanish and refers to the fruits. Northwest tribes consumed the mealy berries. Manzanita often colonizes burned areas as plants sprout from the root crown. Bees, butterflies, and other insects hang on the undersides of the flowers as they probe upward for nectar.

LITTLE PRINCE'S PINE
Chimaphila menziesii
Heather Family (Ericaceae)

Description: Perennial, low-growing, 2"–6" tall. Evergreen leaves are elliptical and have a white midvein and fine teeth along the margins. One to 3 ½"-wide white to pink flowers have recurved petals and a stout center. Fruit is a capsule.

Bloom Season: Summer

Habitat/Range: Grows in moist coniferous forests from mid to subalpine elevations throughout the Pacific Northwest.

Comments: *Chimaphila* is from the Greek *cheima* ("winter weather") and *phileo* ("to love"), in reference to the plant's evergreen leaves. *Menziesii* honors Archibald Menzies (1754–1842), a Scottish naval physician and naturalist who sailed with Captain George Vancouver on his Pacific exploration from 1791–1795.

PIPSISSEWA
Chimaphila umbellata
Heather Family (Ericaceae)

Description: Perennial "semishrub" with a woody base and evergreen leaves. Plants are 4"–12" tall. Leaves are narrowly rectangular with sharp teeth along the upper margin, arranged in a whorl pattern, and 2"–4" long. Saucer-shaped flowers (3–15) hang downward and are a waxy, whitish-pink to rose color. The flowers are borne in loose clusters. Fruits are round capsules that contain tiny seeds.

Bloom Season: Summer

Habitat/Range: Grows in moist coniferous forests from mid to subalpine elevations throughout the Pacific Northwest and in Asia.

Comments: *Chimaphila* is from the Greek *cheima* ("winter weather") and *phileo* ("to love"), in reference to the plant's evergreen leaves. *Umbellata* ("with an umbel") refers to the flower stalks arising from one spot.

SALAL
Gaultheria shallon
Heather Family (Ericaceae)

Description: A low-growing or tall shrub, up to 15'. Large, evergreen leaves are egg-shaped and shiny on the upper surface and have fine, sharply toothed margins. Urn-shaped flowers are white or pinkish and ¼"–½" long. Edible berries are dark purple to reddish-blue in color.

Bloom Season: Spring to midsummer

Habitat/Range: Low to mid elevations from coastal to coniferous forests on the west side of the Cascades from Alaska to California.

Comments: *Gaultheria* honors Dr. Jean-François Gaultier (1708–1756), a French botanist and physician from Quebec. *Shallon* is from the native name Shallon or Sabal for this plant. Many Northwest tribes collected the fruits and ate them raw or dried, often mixed with other berries.

INDIAN PIPE
Monotropa uniflora
Heather Family (Ericaceae)

Description: Saprophyte. Stems often arise in clusters, 4"–10" tall and turn black at maturity. The plant lacks green leaves but has whitish, overlapping, scalelike leaves that are narrow to oval in shape. The single 1"-long flower is white and bell-shaped and either hangs downward or to the side until mature. At that point, the flower points upward. Fruit is a capsule.

Bloom Season: Midsummer

Habitat/Range: Humus-rich sites in dense, moist forests at low to mid elevations from British Columbia to California.

Comments: Both *Monotropa* ("one direction") and *uniflora* ("one flower") refer to the plant's single flower, while the common name indicates the plant's resemblance to a white, clay pipe. The plant lacks chlorophyll and derives nutrients from fungi associated with its roots.

WHITE-VEINED WINTERGREEN
Pyrola picta
Heather Family (Ericaceae)

Description: Perennial. Basal leaves are a dark, glossy green, oval- to egg-shaped, 1"–4" long, and have broad white markings or mottling along the veins. A single, reddish flower stalk arises from the leaves, 4"–8" tall, and bears 10–25 flowers that hang downward. The sepals are reddish to greenish and subtend the whitish to greenish flowers comprised of 5 petals and a curved style. Fruit is a capsule.

Bloom Season: Summer

Habitat/Range: Coniferous forests on the east and west sides of the Cascades from British Columbia to California and east to the Rocky Mountains.

Comments: *Pyrola* is from the Latin *pirus* or *pyrus* ("the pear"), in reference to the leaf shape of certain species in the genus to that of pears. *Picta* ("painted" or "decorated") refers to the patterning on the leaves.

WESTERN AZALEA
Rhododendron occidentale
Heather Family (Ericaceae)

Description: Shrub, up to 15' tall but often smaller. The deciduous leaves are elliptical to inversely lance-shaped and 1"–4" long. White to deep pink, irregularly shaped flowers, 1"–2" long, have 5 petals—the upper one has a yellow, pink, or orange stripe or large spot at the base. The funnel-shaped flower has a long tube. The 5 stamens protrude from the flower. Fruit is a capsule.

Bloom Season: Mid spring to early summer

Habitat/Range: Moist woods or stream banks at low to mid elevations from southwest Oregon to California along the coast and mountains.

Comments: *Rhododendron* ("rose tree") describes the stature of the plants and the colorful flowers. *Occidentale* ("western") describes the range of this plant. The crushed leaves have an unpleasant odor. This shrub is often planted as an ornamental. The fragrant flowers attract various flying insects as pollinators.

BASALT MILKVETCH
Astragalus filipes
Pea Family (Fabaceae)

Description: Perennial, with stems 1'–3' tall, often in a cluster. Compound leaves generally with 9–19 linear leaflets; leaflets may be larger toward the tip. Elongated flower stalks bear cream to yellow pea-shaped flowers that hang downward from short stems. The calyx is covered with fine, black hairs. Fruit is a long, flat seedpod that hangs downward.

Bloom Season: Spring

Habitat/Range: Dry areas from sagebrush flats to juniper woodlands on the east side of the Cascades in Washington and Oregon to Idaho and up into south-central British Columbia.

Comments: *Astragalus* ("anklebone") is a Greek name that refers to the shape of the pods. *Filipes* ("threadlike stalks") refers to the thin pod stems.

BALLOON-POD MILKVETCH
Astragalus whitneyi
Pea Family (Fabaceae)

Description: Low-growing perennial with sprawling stems 4"–10" long. Compound leaves bear 5–21 narrow leaflets. Small, white (occasionally pink or purple), pea-shaped flowers are ⅛"–¼" long. Flowers are borne in small clusters. Fruit is a stalked, inflated, balloon-like, red-spotted pod that is ½"–2½" long.

Bloom Season: Late spring and summer

Habitat/Range: Rocky outcrops, dry slopes, and sagebrush steppe habitat in subalpine or alpine areas from Washington to southern California and east into Idaho and Nevada.

Comments: *Astragalus* ("anklebone") is a Greek name that refers to the shape of the pods. *Whitneyi* honors Josiah Whitney (1819–1896), a geologist, explorer, Harvard professor, and chief of California's Geologic Survey from 1860–1874. California's Mount Whitney, the highest point in the lower 48 states, is named for him.

VELVET LUPINE
Lupinus leucophyllus
Pea Family (Fabaceae)

Description: Perennial, stems up to 3' tall. The compound leaves bear 7 leaflets covered with gray- or rust-colored hairs. The pea-shaped flowers are borne in a tight, upright cluster, and the ¼"-long flowers are white to pale lavender. Fruit is a hairy pod.

Bloom Season: Late spring to early summer

Habitat/Range: Dry grasslands, sagebrush steppe, or open woodlands on the east side of the Cascades from central Washington to Montana and south to Nevada.

Comments: *Lupinus* is from *lupus* ("wolf"), since the plants were thought to "wolf" nutrients from the soil. *Leucophyllus* ("white-leaved") refers to the coloration of the leaves. Bees and bumblebees are the primary pollinators of plants in the Pea Family. Silky Lupine (*L. sericeus*) is another white-flowered lupine that occurs in the Northwest.

WILD LICORICE
Glycyrrhiza lepidota
Pea Family (Fabaceae)

Description: Perennial, 1'–4' tall. Compound leaves, 3"–6½" long, have 12–19 lance-shaped leaflets. Leaflets are pointed at the tips, smooth above, and glandular dotted or slightly hairy below. Flowers are arranged along elongated axis with 20–50 flowers per axis. Bell-shaped calyx is less than ⅛" long; corolla is white- to cream-colored and ⅜"–½" long. Pods, ½"–¾" long, are covered with hooked spines.

Bloom Season: Mid spring to midsummer

Habitat/Range: Moist sites in riparian or wet sites across most of the United States at lower elevations.

Description: *Glycyrrhiza* is from the Greek *glykos* ("sweet") and *rhiza* ("root"), referring to the sweet flavor of the roasted roots, which were eaten by Native Americans and still harvested by herbalists today. *Lepidota* ("scaly") refers to the brown scales on the leaves. The hooked pods catch on animal fur, which helps to disperse the seeds. European Licorice (*G. glabra*) is commercially used in cough syrups, laxatives, and confections.

WAX CURRANT
Ribes cereum
Currant Family (Grossulariaceae)

Description: Shrub, 2'–4' tall. Branches and flowers have sticky hairs that are foul smelling. The leaves are ½"–1" wide, fan-shaped, borne on long stems, and lobed. White to pinkish tubular flowers are borne in small clusters, where the sepals are fused into a tube with a flaring tip. The petals are tiny. Fruit is an orangish-red berry.

Bloom Season: Late spring and early summer

Habitat/Range: Drier locations in sagebrush steppe and pine woodlands from British Columbia to California and east to the Rocky Mountains.

Comments: *Ribes* is from the Arabic or Persian *ribas* ("acid-tasting"), in reference to some of the fruits. *Cereum* ("waxy") refers to the coating on the leaves or edible fruits. Pollinated by bees, butterflies, flies, and other small insects.

NORTHERN BLACK CURRANT
Ribes hudsonianum
Currant Family (Grossulariaceae)

Description: Shrub, 2'–6' tall, and stems have yellow dotted glands and lack spines. Leaves and stems are strong-scented. Leaves are 1"–4" long and wide, with 3–5 lobes that may be partially lobed again (maplelike) and are toothed along the margins. Lower leaf surface has yellowish, sticky glands. Small, white flowers, 8–50, are borne along an elongated stalk. Flowers are ¼"-long, bell-shaped, and have spreading petals. Fruit is a round berry that is black at maturity.

Bloom Season: Late spring to midsummer

Habitat/Range: Moist or wet forests, riparian areas east of the Cascades from British Columbia to Nevada and east across Canada to the Mid-West.

Comments: *Ribes* is from the Arabic or Persian *ribas* ("acid-tasting"), in reference to some of the fruits. *Hudsonianum* ("of Hudson Bay") refers to the first collection of this plant for science. The fruits are edible but bitter.

STICKY CURRANT
Ribes viscosissimum
Currant Family (Grossulariaceae)

Description: Shrub, 2'–6' tall, covered with sticky glands. Stems grow upright to 40" long and lack spines. Leaves are up to 3½" long and palmately divided in 5 toothed lobes (maplelike), are thick and fragrant, and sometimes a little sticky. Bell-shaped, white to greenish-white flowers are borne in small clusters that may hang downward. The petal tips may flare open. Fruit is a blue-black berry.

Bloom Season: Summer

Habitat/Range: Damp or dry woods and along streams or other wet places from mid to high elevations on either side of the Cascades from British Columbia to California and east along the Rocky Mountains.

Comments: *Ribes* is from the Arabic or Persian *ribas* ("acid-tasting"), in reference to some of the fruits. *Viscosissimum* ("sticky") refers to the texture of the leaves and stems. The fruits are not eaten by humans.

DWARF HESPEROCHIRON
Hesperochiron pumilus
Waterleaf Family (Hydrophyllaceae)

Description: Low-growing perennial, up to 2" tall. Leaves have narrowly egg-shaped blades and arise from the top of the taproot. Saucer-shaped, white flowers have yellow centers and purplish nectar guides on the petals. Flowers are ¾"–1½" wide; fruit is a 1-celled capsule that contains numerous tiny seeds.

Bloom Season: Mid spring to early summer

Habitat/Range: Moist meadows, sagebrush flats, and dry woodlands from low to mid elevations on the east side of the Cascade Mountains.

Comments: *Hesperochiron* is from the Greek *hesperos* ("evening") and *Chiron* ("a centaur, the half-man, half-horse of Greek mythology who supposedly was skilled in medicine"), but the meaning is obscure. *Pumilus* ("dwarf") refers to the plant's stature. The Dwarf Hesperochiron attracts flies, bees, beetles, and small butterflies to its opened flowers.

BALLHEAD WATERLEAF
Hydrophyllum capitatum
Waterleaf Family (Hydrophyllaceae)

Description: Perennial, plants are 5"–20" high. The compound leaves are mostly basal and borne on long stems. The deeply divided 7–11 leaflets are also lobed or divided. The small, purplish-blue to white flowers are borne in a rounded cluster, 1"–2" wide and have stamens that protrude beyond the flowers. Fruit is a capsule.

Bloom Season: Spring

Habitat/Range: Woodlands, thickets, and meadows at low to mid elevations on the east side of the Cascades.

Comments: *Hydrophyllum* is from the Latin *hydro* ("water") and *phyllos* ("leaf") and may refer to the habitats this group occurs in, the fleshy nature of the leaves, or the spots on the leaves that resemble water stains. *Capitatus* ("growing in a dense head") describes the flowers.

FENDLER'S WATERLEAF
Hydrophyllum fendleri
Waterleaf Family (Hydrophyllaceae)

Description: Perennial, up to 40" tall. Large compound leaves, up to 12" long, have 7–15 leaflets that are toothed along the margin and may be cleft in the blade; blades are longer than they are wide. The undersides of the leaves have soft, white hairs. Bell-shaped, white flowers arise from the leaf axils in dense clusters. The flowers may have a purple tinge, and the 5 stamens protrude beyond the flowers. Fruit is a capsule that contains 1–3 seeds.

Bloom Season: Late spring and early summer

Habitat/Range: Moist thickets, avalanche chutes, and open areas from mid to subalpine elevations from Washington to California and east to Idaho.

Comments: *Hydrophyllum* is from the Latin *hydro* ("water") and *phyllos* ("leaf") and may refer to the habitats this group occurs in, the fleshy nature of the leaves, or the spots on the leaves that resemble water stains. *Fendleri* is for Augustus Fendler (1813–1883), a German immigrant who went to New Mexico for Asa Gray to collect plants in the mid-1880s.

SILVERLEAF PHACELIA
Phacelia hastata
Waterleaf Family (Hydrophyllaceae)

Description: Perennial that is variable in height but may grow 25" tall or more. Several stems arise from a woody base and may either grow upright or are semi-erect. Abundant silver hairs cover the broad, lance-shaped leaves that show deep veins. The small white to purplish bell-shaped flowers are arranged in a tight-coiled cluster. The stamens stick out above the flowers. The fruit is a capsule.

Bloom Season: Early spring to autumn

Habitat/Range: In abundance in dry, open sites, often in sand, from low to subalpine elevations throughout the Pacific Northwest.

Comments: *Phacelia* is from the Greek *phakelos* ("fascicle") and refers to the tight floral clusters. *Hastata* ("arrowhead-shaped") refers to the shape of the leaves that may have basal lobes. Varileaf Phacelia (*P. heterophylla*) is similar with a single erect stem and some leaves with lower lateral lobes.

TRACY'S MISTMAIDEN
Romanzoffia tracyi
Waterleaf Family (Hydrophyllaceae)

Description: Perennial, arises from woolly tubers. Leaves are kidney-shaped to round, with broad, scalloped lobes. Basal leaves are 1"–1½" wide and have sticky hairs. Flowers are ½" wide and have 5 white petals that are fused into a funnel-shaped flower. Flowers have a yellow center and rise barely above the leaves. Fruit is a many-seeded capsule.

Bloom Season: Summer

Habitat/Range: Grows on coastal cliffs and rocky outcrops, close to sea spray, from Vancouver Island to northern California.

Comments: *Romanzoffia* honors Nikolai Rumyantsev (1754–1826), better known as Count Romanzoff, a Russian sponsor of the Kotzebue expedition to the Pacific Northwest (1815–1818), which was an expedition to locate a navigable sea route through the Arctic around North America. *Tracyi* is for Samuel Mills Tracy (1847–1920), a botanist with the US Department of agriculture. Sitka Mistmaiden (*R. sitchensis*) is a related species that grows on wet cliffs and rocky outcrops in the Cascade Mountains and Columbia River Gorge.

YELLOWLEAF IRIS
Iris chrysophylla
Iris Family (Iridaceae)

Description: Perennial, spreads by underground roots and often forms a small cluster. Basal leaves are narrow, grasslike, and up to 16" long. Stem leaves smaller. The flowers are 1½"–3" wide, have a long (2"–4") floral tube, and have white to cream-colored petals that have dark-purple veins and yellow centers. Fruit is a capsule.

Bloom Season: Mid spring to early summer

Habitat/Range: Mostly open coniferous woods at mid elevations from western Oregon to northwest California.

Comments: *Iris* is after the Greek goddess of rainbows. *Chrysophylla* ("with golden leaves") refers to the leaves. Siskiyou Iris (*I. bracteata*) has white to pale petals that have dark veins, yellow centers, and very short floral tubes.

FIELD MINT
Mentha arvensis
Mint Family (Lamiaceae)

Description: Perennial, with square stems, 1'–3' tall. The opposite leaves are broadly lance-shaped, 1"–3" long, and toothed along the margin. The leaves extend beyond the flower clusters. The purplish to pink or white flowers are borne in small clusters in the upper leaf axils. The tiny flowers have 4 stamens that protrude above the flowers. Fruit is a tiny nutlet.

Bloom Season: Summer

Habitat/Range: Moist sites in fields, meadows, streams, marshes, and coastal flats from sea level to mid elevations throughout the region and most of North America.

Comments: *Mentha* is named after the Greek nymph Menthe who was transformed into a mint plant by a jealous Persephone. *Arvensis* ("growing near fields") refers to the type of habitat where this plant occurs. The leaves were brewed for a tea to aid digestion or for colds.

CAT'S EAR
Calochortus elegans
Lily Family (Liliaceae)

Description: Perennial, low-growing, 3"–6" tall. Each stem has 1 or 2 narrow, grasslike basal leaves, 4"–8" long. Bears 1–6 flowers per plant. Flowers are 2" wide with hairy petals that are white to pale lavender; petals have a purplish crescent at the base. Fruit is a capsule.

Bloom Season: Mid spring to early summer

Habitat/Range: Forests, woodland edges, grasslands, and mountain slopes from mid to alpine elevations from southeastern Washington to California and east to Montana. Occurs on both sides of the Cascades.

Comments: *Calochortus* ("beautiful grass") describes the leaves of this genus. *Elegans* ("elegant") refers to the flowers. The common name refers to the flower resembling the hairy insides of a cat's ear. Mariposa Lilies are "pollinator generalists," meaning the flowers attract a wide variety of bees, flies, beetles, and wasp pollinators.

SUBALPINE MARIPOSA LILY
Calochortus subalpinus
Lily Family (Liliaceae)

Description: Perennial to 15" tall. The grasslike leaves arise basely from the stem, are flattened, and are about as long as the flowering stalk. Stems bear 1–5 flowers that arise from the same point. Flowers are 1½"–2" wide, yellowish-white, and the centers are yellow and fringed with fine hairs. Petals often have a narrow, purple crescent gland low on the petal, and the sepals have a purple dot at their base. Fruit is a 3-winged capsule that hangs downward.

Bloom Season: Summer

Habitat/Range: Dry meadows, volcanic soils, and open forests from mid to subalpine elevations in the Cascade Mountains from southern Washington to central Oregon.

Comments: *Calochortus* ("beautiful grass") describes the leaves of this genus and *subalpinus* ("subalpine") defines the elevational distribution of this species. Tolmie's Mariposa Lily (*C. tolmiei*) is a spring bloomer with white or lavender flowers and hair covering the inside of the flower.

QUEEN'S CUP
Clintonia uniflora
Lily Family (Liliaceae)

Description: Perennial, several broad, elliptical to oblong leaves, generally 3"–7" long, arise from an underground stem (rhizome). The leaves have hairy margins and end in a pointed or rounded tip. A single (rarely 2), white, cup-shaped flower arises on a long stalk. The 1"-wide flower has 6 petallike tepals. Fruit is a blue, beadlike berry.

Bloom Season: Early to midsummer

Habitat/Range: Mostly in moist coniferous forests from low to subalpine elevations from Alaska to California and east to Montana.

Comments: *Clintonia* honors DeWitt Clinton (1769–1828), a former New York state senator, mayor of New York City, presidential candidate (Peace Party in 1812), and governor of New York, who also wrote natural history books. His political support of the Erie Canal led doubters to label it "Clinton's Ditch." *Uniflora* ("one flower") refers to the single flower. Also known as Blue-Bead Lily after the fruit, which grouse consume.

WHITE AVALANCHE LILY
Erythronium montanum
Lily Family (Liliaceae)

Description: Perennial, plants are 6"–8" tall. One or 2 basal leaves are broadly elliptical to lance-shaped, 4"–8" long, and ½ as wide; the tips are sharply pointed, and the margins are wavy. The leaves lack mottling. A flowering stalk bears 1–4 white flowers that are yellow to orange-yellow at the base and have 6 tepals that curve backward. Fruit is a capsule.

Bloom Season: Mid spring to early summer

Habitat/Range: Damp meadows at subalpine to alpine elevations from British Columbia to southern Oregon.

Comments: *Erythronium* is from the Greek *erythros* ("red") and refers to a red dye made from a pinkish flowering relative. *Montanum* ("of the mountains") describes where the plant grows. The flowers often bloom while there is still snow on the ground, and they may turn pink when mature.

GIANT WHITE FAWN LILY
Erythronium oregonum
Lily Family (Liliaceae)

Description: Perennial, plants are 6"–12" tall. The pair of basal leaves are broadly elliptical to lance-shaped, 5"–8" long, and they often have pale green, purple, or brown mottling. A single (sometimes 2 or more) nodding flower is borne on a long, 7"–13" flowering stalk. The similar white to cream-colored petals and sepals curve backward with age and have an orange-yellow blotch at their base. The flowers are 1"–6" wide. Fruit is a capsule.

Bloom Season: Early to mid spring

Habitat/Range: Well-drained moist sites in open or dense forests, fields, rocky slopes, and meadows at low (mostly) to mid elevations on the west side of the Cascade Mountains from British Columbia to southwest Oregon.

Comments: *Erythronium* is from the Greek *erythros* ("red") and refers to a red dye made from a pinkish flowering relative. *Oregonum* ("of Oregon") refers to the type locality. The roots were eaten either raw or cooked by native tribes, as well as by bears that may consume the whole plants. Though the flowers are very showy, there may be small pollinators such as beetles or flies crawling around inside the flowers. Also called Giant Dog-Toothed Lily or Lambs-, Deer's-, or Adder's-Tongue.

WASHINGTON LILY
Lilium washingtonianum
Lily Family (Liliaceae)

Description: Perennial, from 2'–6' tall. The 2"–4" long, lance-shaped leaves are arranged alternately on the lower stem and have wavy margins. Upper stem leaves arise in a whorled pattern and are smaller. The fragrant, 2"–4" long flowers are bell-shaped and have white to pale-pink tepals with purplish spots that fade to pink or purple when mature. Fruit is a capsule.

Bloom Season: Early summer

Habitat/Range: Open forests or clearings at mid elevations in the Cascade Mountains and foothills in Oregon and California.

Comments: *Lilium* is the Latin name for this genus, and *washingtonianum* is for Martha Washington. These plants resemble the cultivated Easter Lily; indiscriminate collecting has made this species difficult to locate.

HOOKER FAIRY-BELL
Prosartes hookeri
Lily Family (Liliaceae)

Description: Plants 1'–3' tall with few branches. Stalkless leaves are broadly lance-shaped to oval, slightly hairy, with pointed tips and wavy margins. The ¾"-long, greenish-white, bell-shaped flowers are borne mostly in pairs and hang downward. Flowers flare open at the end. Fruit is a yellowish to red, oval berry.

Bloom Season: Late spring to midsummer

Habitat/Range: Dense, moist woods or mixed forests at low elevations in the Cascade Mountains from British Columbia to western Montana and into northeast Oregon.

Comments: *Prosartes* ("attached") refers to the flowers. *Hookeri* honors Joseph Hooker (1817–1911), a widely traveled British plant hunter and explorer. The common name describes the fairylike quality of the flowers.

SMITH'S FAIRYBELLS
Prosartes smithii
Lily Family (Liliaceae)

Description: Perennial, 1'–3' tall, with numerous branches and smooth stems and leaves. Leaf bases clasp the stem. The 2"–5" long leaves are broadly lance-shaped and pointed at the tip. Bell-shaped, 1"-long flowers hang downward and are arranged in groups. The cream-colored tepals do not flare open to expose the stamens. Fruit is a yellowish to orange-red berry.

Bloom Season: Late spring to midsummer

Habitat/Range: Moist sites in woods and along stream banks in the Coast Range and west slope of the Cascade Mountains from British Columbia to California.

Comments: *Prosartes* ("attached") refers to the flowers. Common and specific name honors Sir James E. Smith (1759–1828), an English botanist who purchased the Linnaeus collection and later formed the prestigious Linnean Society of London, the oldest existing biological society in the world.

CLASPING TWISTED-STALK
Streptopus amplexifolius
Lily Family (Liliaceae)

Description: Perennial, 1'–3' tall. Branched stems are bent in zigzag patterns. Egg- to lance-shaped leaves are 2"–6" long and clasp the stem. Whitish, bell-shaped flowers are green-tinged with flaring tips and are borne on twisted stalks below a leaf. Fruit is a translucent yellow to red berry that may darken at maturity.

Bloom Season: Summer

Habitat/Range: Moist sites along stream banks, clearings, and thickets in forests in subalpine elevations from Alaska to California and east through much of Canada and the northern United States.

Comments: *Streptopus* ("twisted foot") refers to the flower stalks' twisting habit beneath the leaf. *Amplexifolius* ("stem-clasping leaf") refers to the way the leaf attaches to the stem. Rosy Twisted-Stalk (*S. roseus*) is similar in appearance but with rosy flowers with magenta spots. The edible fruits reportedly taste like cucumbers.

TWINFLOWER
Linnaea borealis
Twinflower Family (Linnaeaceae)

Description: Perennial; long, slender runners arise on leafy stems less than 5" tall. The dark-green (above) and broadly elliptical leaves have an opposite arrangement. Upper half of leaf has few shallow teeth along the margin. Pairs of pink ¼" flowers are borne at the end of a Y-shaped stalk. Fruits are small nutlets with sticky hairs.

Bloom Season: Summer

Habitat/Range: Various elevations to subalpine in forests, shrub thickets, or rocky shorelines throughout the Pacific Northwest.

Comments: *Linnaea* is after Carl Linnaeus (1707–1778), a Swedish scientist who devised the current taxonomic binomial system of genus and species. In many portraits, Linnaeus is often holding a sprig of this plant. *Borealis* ("northern") refers to the plant's distributional range. The common name describes the fragrant flowers borne in pairs.

MEADOW DEATH CAMAS
Toxicoscordion venenosum
Trillium/Death-Camas Family (Melanthiaceae)

Description: Perennial, from an onion-like bulb arise grasslike, linear leaves up to 15" long. Tiny, creamy-white flowers are borne on short stalks in a pyramid-shaped cluster. Tepals are shorter than the stamens and have a greenish, oval dot at the base. Flowers have a strong aroma. Fruit is a narrow capsule.

Bloom Season: Mid spring to midsummer

Habitat/Range: Rocky or grassy slopes, open forests, meadows (dry in summer), and forest edges from eastern Washington to southern Idaho and south to California.

Comments: *Toxicoscordion* ("toxic garlic") refers to the poisonous nature of the plant. *Venenosum* ("poisonous") refers to the bulbs, which contain toxic alkaloids. Fremont's Death Camas (*T. fremontii*) grows on open or rocky slopes in southwestern Oregon and has a spherical bulb, long leaves up to 1½" long, and star-shaped flowers.

FOOTHILL DEATH CAMAS
Toxicoscordion paniculatum
Trillium/Death-Camas Family (Melanthiaceae)

Description: Perennial, from a bulb with slender stems 20" high. Basal leaves are strap-like and up to ½" wide. The flower heads are arranged in a loose cluster with the younger flowers at the top or middle. The whitish ¼"-wide flowers are borne on small stalks alongside branches of the main flowering stalk. Flowers made up of 6 tepals, each bearing a yellowish-green, egg-shaped gland. Fruit is a capsule.

Bloom Season: Spring

Habitat/Range: Open meadows, sagebrush flats, open ponderosa, or lodgepole woodlands across much of the western United States.

Comments: *Toxicoscordion* ("toxic garlic") refers to the poisonous nature of the plant. *Paniculatum* ("flowers in a panicle") describes the arrangement of the flowers. Death Camas contains toxic alkaloids; hence the native tribes had to be careful when digging the edible Camas bulbs (*Camassia quamash*), which may grow in meadows intermixed with Death Camas. Thomas Nuttall first named this plant *Helonias paniculata* in 1834 from a collection that Nathaniel Wyeth made in 1833.

PACIFIC TRILLIUM
Trillium ovatum
Trillium/Death-Camas Family (Melanthiaceae)

Description: From a fleshy rhizome arises a single, hairless stem that bears large leaves shaped like a rounded-edge triangle in whorls of 3 (may be up to 5). Stalkless leaves (sessile) are dark green and not mottled. Normally a single, white, turning pink to purplish with age flower is borne at the end of a short stalk. The 3 flower petals may be up to 3" long. Fruits are a many-seeded, berrylike capsule.

Bloom Season: Spring

Habitat/Range: Prefers moist open forests and boggy areas from lowland to high elevations from British Columbia to central California and east to the Rocky Mountains.

Comments: *Trillium* ("in 3s") refers to the number of leaves and floral parts. *Ovatum* ("oval-like") refers to the leaf shape. Ants collect the seeds and eat the oil-rich appendage on the tip. Discarded seeds may sprout to form future plants, although it takes 6–8 years from germination to flowering. Sessile or Giant Trillium (*T. albidium*) has stalkless, mottled leaves and greenish-white to pink or deep-purple flowers. Trilliums are also called Wake-Robin for their springtime appearance, which coincides with the territorial singing of robins.

CALIFORNIA CORN LILY
Veratrum californicum
Trillium/Death-Camas Family (Melanthiaceae)

Description: Perennial, grows 3'–8' tall from thick rhizomes. Large, oval- to egg-shaped leaves are 8"–15" long and up to 8" wide. Small flowers are arranged in elongated clusters, up to 2' long, that branch upward from the main stalk. The elongated clusters may contain hundreds of flowers. Individual flowers are 1" wide and have 6 whitish to greenish tepals, with a Y-shaped gland located at the base of each tepal. The mature capsule contains numerous winged, papery seeds.

Bloom Season: Summer

Habitat/Range: Moist and wet meadows or riparian areas from mid elevations to subalpine forests from Alaska to eastern Canada and south to Oregon and Idaho.

Comments: *Veratrum* is from the Latin words *vere* ("true") and *ater* ("black"), after the black roots of another species. *Californicum* ("of California") is in reference to where the first specimen was collected for science. Toxic to livestock and humans; at one time an insecticide was made from the plant's powdered roots.

BEARGRASS
Xerophyllum tenax
Trillium/Death-Camas Family (Melanthiaceae)

Description: Perennial, growing 2'–5' tall. Evergreen basal leaves, up to 3' long, grow in clumps and are grasslike with fine-toothed edges. The stem leaves are similar but get smaller as they progress up the stem. Cream-colored flowers are borne in dense clusters called racemes at the end of the flowering stalk. The individual flowers are borne on long stems, have 6 tepals, and are fragrant. The fruit is a capsule.

Bloom Season: Summer

Habitat/Range: From sea level to subalpine elevations and found in meadows, clearings, or the undergrowth of open dense forests from British Columbia to California and east to Wyoming.

Comments: *Xerophyllum* is from the Greek *xeros* ("dry"), *phylum* ("leaf"), and *tenax* ("tough"). Native peoples wove the tough leaves into durable capes, baskets, or hats; even Lewis and Clark had Beargrass rain hats made for their crew. In spring, bears consume the softer, fleshy leaf bases; hence, the common name.

PUSSYPAWS
Calyptridium umbellatum
Claytonia/Lewisia Family (Montiaceae)

Description: Perennial (at higher elevations and sometimes annual at lower), with 2"–10" flowering stems radiating outward and sprawling over the ground. Club- to spatula-shaped leaves, ½"–2" long, are arranged in a basal pattern and are smooth and shiny. Reddish flowering stalks extend from the leaves and bear a round cluster of fuzzy white to pink flowers. Each ¼"-wide flower has 2 round and papery sepals that surround the 4 smaller petals and stamens. The petals wither before the sepals. Fruit is a seed.

Bloom Season: Late spring into summer

Habitat/Range: Dry, sandy, pumice, or gravelly sites at mid to alpine elevations across the region and into Utah.

Comments: *Calyptridium* ("having a calyptra") for the caplike covering of the flowers. *Umbellatum* ("flowers in an umbel") describes the arrangement of the flowers in an umbrellalike pattern. During the day, the stems may elevate the flowers protecting the leaves from overheating and perhaps making the flowers more attractive to pollinators. The common name is after the clusters of flowers resembling a cat's upturned paw.

LANCELEAF SPRINGBEAUTY
Claytonia lanceolata
Claytonia/Lewisia Family (Montiaceae)

Description: Perennial, often forming a thick carpet with plants up to 8" tall. Basal leaves may or may not be absent, but lance- to wedge-shaped stem leaves clasp the upper stem. Leaves are somewhat fleshy. Flower stalks bear 3–20 star-shaped flowers that have white or pinkish petals striped with pink veins and yellow spots near the base. Fruit is a capsule with 2 seeds.

Bloom Season: Mid spring to midsummer

Habitat/Range: Seasonally moist grasslands, shrub steppe, and forests on both sides of the Cascades from low to high elevations from British Columbia to southern California and east to New Mexico.

Comments: *Claytonia* is for John Clayton (1685-1773), a Colonial botanist that collected plants mostly in Virginia and who served at one time as the Attorney General for Virginia. *Lanceolata* ("lance-shaped") pertains to the shape of the leaves. Plants arise from corms that are edible and said to taste like potato.

WESTERN SPRING BEAUTY
Claytonia sibirica
Claytonia/Lewisia Family (Montiaceae)

Description: Annual, plants 2"–16" tall. Basal leaves are fleshy and have long stems and elliptical to strap-shaped blades that are pointed. The small ¼"–¾" flowers are white to pink and have a notch at the tip. Fruit is a capsule.

Bloom Season: Early spring to fall

Habitat/Range: Widespread at sea level to mid elevations along the coast and in wet meadows and forests from Siberia and Alaska south to California.

Comments: *Claytonia* is for John Clayton (1685–1773), an American botanist who collected plants in Virginia. *Sibirica* ("of Siberia") represents a portion of its distribution. The leaves are edible.

BITTERROOT
Lewisia rediviva
Claytonia/Lewisia Family (Montiaceae)

Description: Low-growing perennial arising from a fleshy, carrot-shaped root. Basal leaves are fleshy and rounded and often wither before the flowers mature. Upper stem leaves are very small and bract-like. White- to rose-colored flowers are showy, 1"–3" wide, and made up of 12–18 petals. The fruit is a capsule.

Bloom Season: Mid spring to midsummer

Habitat/Range: Gravelly, rocky, or sandy soils from sagebrush steppe to low elevation woodlands from British Columbia to California and east to Montana and Colorado.

Comments: Named for Meriwether Lewis (1774–1809), expedition co-leader of the Corps of Discovery. *Rediviva* ("brought back to life") refers to the dried root's ability to sprout, as one of Lewis's collected specimens was able to sprout in President Jefferson's garden. Northwest tribes collected the prized roots in spring and boiled them before eating. Bitterroot is the state flower of Montana. The flowers open up by midday and attract a variety of pollinators.

AMERICAN WATERLILY
Nymphaea odorata
Water Lily Family (Nymphaeaceae)

Description: Aquatic perennial. Large, pad-like leaves are up to 13" wide and have a cleft near their stem that keeps them from being round. The showy flowers are 1½"–4" wide and have many white (sometimes pinkish) petals and numerous stamens and pistils. Fruit is a leathery capsule.

Bloom Season: Midsummer to fall

Habitat/Range: Lowland lakes on both sides of the Cascades; introduced from eastern North America.

Comments: *Nymphaea* ("water nymph") refers to the plant's aquatic habitat and nymphlike, pure white petals. *Odorata* ("scented") refers to the sweet smell of the flowers. Eastern tribes ate the leaves, flower buds, roots, and capsules and used the plant for its medicinal qualities in treating internal disorders. The flowers open in the morning and close in the afternoon and attract beetles as their primary pollinators.

TUFTED EVENING PRIMROSE
Oenothera caespitosa
Evening-Primrose Family (Onagraceae)

Description: Low-growing perennial with long-stalked, lance- to inversely lance-shaped leaves that are up to 8" long. Leaf margins variable from entire to deeply lobed. White flowers are 2"–4" wide with a long, thin corolla tube. Fruit is a woody capsule.

Bloom Season: Spring and early summer

Habitat/Range: Dry hills and rocky slopes from low to mid elevations across much of the western and central United States.

Comments: *Oenothera* ("wine-scented") refers to the use of the powdered roots in winemaking. *Caespitosa* ("low-growing") refers to the low stature of the plant. Sphinx moths are a primary pollinator of these flowers that bloom in the evening. There are several varieties of this plant in the Northwest.

PALE EVENING PRIMROSE
Oenothera pallida
Evening-Primrose Family (Onagraceae)

Description: Perennial. Reddish stems, smooth or hairy, arise erect or low growing, 4"–28" long. Leaves are lance-shaped to linear, and are 1"–2½" long. White flowers consist of 4 petals, numerous stamens, and a 4-lobed stigma. Fruit is a long, narrow capsule.

Bloom Season: Early to midsummer

Habitat/Range: Dry sandy or gravelly areas east of the Cascades from Washington to Arizona and east to New Mexico.

Comments: *Oenothera* ("wine-scented") refers to the use of the powdered roots in winemaking. *Pallida* ("pale") refers to the petal color. Individual flowers open in the afternoon and bloom for about a day, then fade to a pinkish color. Wildlife, such as pronghorn, eat the blossoms.

WESTERN RATTLESNAKE PLANTAIN
Goodyera oblongifolia
Orchid Family (Orchidaceae)

Description: Perennial with dark green oval or narrow elliptical leaves that are mottled or have white stripes down the center. A stout flowering stalk arises from the basal leaves 10-16" high and covered with sticky hairs. Numerous small, dull white to greenish flowers, mostly arranged on one side of the stem, are borne at the tip. The petals and a sepal form a hood over the lip. Fruit is a capsule.

Bloom Season: Mid to late summer

Habitat/Range: Shady coniferous forests, from lowlands to higher elevations, and in moist or dry humus throughout much of western North America.

Comments: *Goodyera* is for John Goodyear (1592-1664) an English botanist. *Oblongifolia* ("oblong-shaped leaves") refers to the leaf shape. The common name is a reference to the snakeskin-like markings on the leaves. The plant was also used to treat snakebites.

WHITE BOG ORCHID
Platanthera dilatata
Orchid Family (Orchidaceae)

Description: Perennial, up to 30" tall and bearing leaves along the entire stem. Leaves are oblong- to lance-shaped and are smaller toward the top of the stem. The small flowers are white to pale greenish, very fragrant, and arranged in a dense, candle-like cluster. The upper sepals and 2 petals form a hood, while the lower 2 sepals spread outward. The lower petal forms a wide lower lip. Behind this lip is a slender nectar tube called the spur. Fruit is a many-seeded, egg-shaped capsule.

Bloom Season: Summer

Habitat/Range: Swamps, bogs, meadows, stream edges, and marshes at mid to subalpine elevations across much of the Pacific Northwest and into the eastern and southwestern United States.

Comments: Because the flower stem twists, the upper flower petal appears to be the lower one. *Platanthera* ("broad anther") describes the anther, and *dilatata* ("spread out") refers to the lower sepals. Native Americans in British Columbia would wash themselves with this sweet-scented flower. Moths with long proboscises reach the nectar deep in the flower's spurs.

HOODED LADIES' TRESSES
Spiranthes romanzoffiana
Orchid Family (Orchidaceae)

Description: From fleshy roots arise 2–5 basal leaves that are strap-like and up to 10" long. The flowering stalk, which averages 2"–6" tall, bears numerous creamy to greenish-white flowers arranged in distinct longitudinal rows. Individual flowers have sticky, hairy sepals and petals that form a hood, with the lower petal sharply bent downward. Fruit is a capsule.

Bloom Season: Mid to late summer

Habitat/Range: Low to mid elevations in dry to moist meadows, stream sides, bogs, and woodlands across the Pacific Northwest.

Comments: *Spiranthes* is from the Greek *speira* ("coil") and *anthos* ("flower"), in reference to the twisted or braided appearance of the flowers. *Romanzoffiana* honors Count Romanzoff (Nikolai Rumyantsev, 1754–1826), a Russian who sent Kotzebue to explore Alaska.

SICKLETOP LOUSEWORT
Pedicularis racemosa
Broomrape/Paintbrush Family (Orobanchaceae)

Description: Upright perennial that may grow to 2' tall. Upper lance-shaped leaves are larger than lower ones and have short stalks. Leaf edges are doubly saw-toothed. Flowers are whitish but mostly pink to purplish. Flower's upper lip tapers into a sickle-shaped, curved beak, while petals in the larger, lower lip spread outward. Fruit is a flat, curved capsule.

Bloom Season: Summer

Habitat/Range: Coniferous woods at mid to subalpine elevations throughout the region and across much of the West.

Comments: *Pedicularis* ("pertaining to lice") refers to the idea that grazing livestock became infected with lice when foraging in fields with members of this genus. The common name describes the sickle-shaped flowers. *Racemosa* refers to the arrangement of the stalked flowers along an unbranched stem (a raceme), where the flowers mature from the base upward.

OREGON OXALIS
Oxalis oregana
Wood Sorrel Family (Oxalidaceae)

Description: Perennial, ground cover. Flower and leaf stems arise from root nodes. Leaf stems are hairy, 2"–8" tall, bearing shamrock-like leaves made up of 3 heart-shaped leaflets. Flowering stalks generally are shorter than the leaf stalks and bear a single, white or pink, funnel-shaped flower. The 1" wide flowers have red or purple veins on the 5 petals. Fruit is a football-shaped capsule.

Bloom Season: Spring

Habitat/Range: Grows in shady wood at low to mid elevations on both sides of the Cascades from Washington to northern California.

Comments: *Oxalis* is from the Greek *oxys* ("acid"), referring to the sour flavor of the leaves that contain oxalic acid. *Oregana* ("of Oregon") refers to the type locality where the plant was first collected for science. Also called Redwood Sorrel. This plant may form a dense understory, and the leaves fold up a night or during rainstorms.

DUTCHMAN'S BREECHES
Dicentra cucullaria
Poppy/Dicentra Family (Papaveraceae)

Description: This perennial has compound, succulent leaves that are almost fern-like as the stems branch several times and the numerous leaflets also divide into many segments. Flowers are borne alongside a common stalk; the white or pale-pink flowers resemble a pair of baggy pants. The outer 2 petals have ½"-long spurs (the pant legs) and flaring tips surrounded by yellow (the waistband). Fruit is a seedpod.

Bloom Season: Spring

Habitat/Range: Moist woods, stream banks, and from low to mid elevations along the Columbia River Gorge and into the Blue Mountains area of eastern Oregon, Washington, and Idaho.

Comments: *Dicentra* ("two spurs") refers to the flower's "baggy pants," and *cucullaria* ("hoodlike") also refers to the petals. The sealed flowers are protected from the elements and small pollinators. Large female bumblebees can reach the nectar with their long tongues. Plants contain a hallucinogenic compound; hence, ranchers call these plants Staggerweed for their effect upon livestock.

LONGHORN STEER'S HEAD
Dicentra uniflora
Poppy/Dicentra Family (Papaveraceae)

Description: Perennial, very low-growing, up to 4" tall. Basal leaves are compound and highly divided. The segments have various lobed tips. The single flower is borne on a short stalk, is white to pinkish, and resembles a steer's head, since the 2 sepals curve outward like horns. Fruit is a seedpod.

Bloom Season: Early summer

Habitat/Range: Open areas, meadows, or from mid to subalpine elevations from Washington to California, mostly east of the Cascades.

Comments: *Dicentra* ("two spurs") refers to the flower's 2 spurred petals. *Uniflora* ("one flower") refers to the solitary flower. Easily overlooked due to its small size.

SCABLAND PENSTEMON
Penstemon deustus
Beardtongue Family (Plantaginaceae)

Description: Perennial to 16" tall. The woody stems branch at the base and tend to form dense clumps of flowering stalks. The variable shaped leaves are mostly toothed along the margin and lance- or inversely lance-shaped. The upper leaves lack petioles and are much smaller than the lower leaves. Long, flowering stalks bear a dense cluster of white or creamy (occasionally yellow), 2-lipped flowers. The upper lip is shorter than the lower lip and often appears shriveled. The lower petals have purplish nectar guidelines near the throat. Fruit is a small capsule.

Bloom Season: Early summer

Habitat/Range: Dry and rocky outcrops or cliffs from low to subalpine elevations from central Washington to southern California and east to northern Utah.

Comments: *Penstemon* is from *pen* ("almost") and *stemon* ("stamen"), which refers to the sterile stamen called a staminode typical of this genus. *Deustus* ("scorched or burned up") refers to the color of the upper petals. The sterile stamen is hairless or sparsely hairy at the tip.

NUTTALL'S LINANTHUS
Leptosiphon nuttallii
Phlox Family (Polemoniaceae)

Description: Perennial, often growing in a patch, with hairy stems 4"–13" tall. Leaves are divided into 5 narrow, needlelike lobes. Flowers borne in clusters, each flower is about ½"-wide with a yellowish throat. The petals form a slender throat that projects above the calyx. Fruit is a seed.

Bloom Season: Mid to late summer

Habitat/Range: Open woodlands, rocky slopes, and forest openings at mid to high elevations across much of the western United States.

Comments: *Leptosiphon* is Greek for "slender tube," a reference to the corolla tube. *Nuttallii* honors Thomas Nuttall (1786–1859), an English botanist and Harvard professor, who collected plants widely across the United States. When in bloom, the flowers cloak the plants.

TALUS COLLOMIA
Collomia larsenii
Phlox Family (Polemoniaceae)

Description: Perennial, mat-like growth up to 1' wide. Grayish leaves are highly divided and covered with fine hairs. The ¾"-wide tubular flowers are white to pink or lavender and have 5 lobes with light-purple lines. Fruit is a seed.

Bloom Season: Late summer

Habitat/Range: Scree and talus slopes at subalpine to alpine elevations from Washington to California and east to Wyoming and Utah.

Comments: *Collomia* is from the Greek *kola* ("glue"), which refers to the seeds becoming sticky when wet. The tiny stature is protection against the alpine elements for these short-lived perennials. Also called Larsen's Mountain Trumpet.

GRANITE PRICKLY-PHLOX
Linanthus pungens
Phlox Family (Polemoniaceae)

Description: Perennial, mat-like growth up to 20" long. The ¼"–½" long, needlelike leaves form dense clusters along the stems. The leaves are divided into 3–7 segments, similar to fingers on a hand. Flowers are funnel-shaped and white and have 5 flaring petals that may be tinged with pink. In bud, the 1"-long flowers are twisted shut. Fruit is a tiny seed.

Bloom Season: Spring to midsummer

Habitat/Range: Rocky or sandy sites in dry areas from low to mid elevations east of the Cascades and into Idaho.

Comments: *Linanthus* is from a Greek word meaning "Flax [*Linum*] like flower." *Pungens* ("sharp-pointed") describes the tips of the leaves. The flowers unfurl at night and attract moth pollinators with nectar. Also called Prickly Phlox or Desert Trumpet.

HOOD'S PHLOX
Phlox hoodii
Phlox Family (Polemoniaceae)

Description: Perennial, cushion-like growth. Leaves are spiny and ¼" long. White, 5-petaled flowers barely rise above the leaves. The flowers are ½" wide and have a yellow center. Fruit is a capsule.

Bloom Season: Spring

Habitat/Range: Dry areas in grasslands, sagebrush steppe, and open woodlands from low to mid elevations from British Columbia to the southwestern and midwestern United States.

Comments: *Phlox* ("flame") refers to the color of some species. *Hoodii* is for Lieutenant Robert Hood of Britain's Franklin Arctic Expedition (1819–1821). Hood was the expedition's mapmaker and artist. Sometimes known as *P. canescens*.

POKE KNOTWEED
Aconogonon phytolaccifolium
Smartweed-Buckwheat Family (Polygonaceae)

Description: Perennial, grows 2'–6' tall with reddish stems. Lance-shaped leaves are 4"–8" long, pointed at the tip, and are subtended by large stipules that turn reddish. Flowers are arranged in branching clusters of numerous small, white or greenish flowers that are less than a ¼" long and have stamens that protrude above the flowers. Fruit is a seed.

Bloom Season: Summer

Habitat/Range: Moist meadows and forest openings from Alaska to California and east to Montana and Idaho.

Comments: *Aconogonon* is from the Greek *acon* ("whetstone") and *yovn* ("seed or offspring") and refers to the rough texture of the seeds. *Phytolaccifolium* ("with leaves like *Phytolacca*") refers to the leaves of this plant resembling those of Pokeweed (*Phytolacca americana*), which grows in the eastern United States.

AMERICAN BISTORT
Bistorta bistortoides
Smartweed-Buckwheat Family (Polygonaceae)

Description: Perennial, with 1 to several unbranched stems, 10"–35" tall, arising from a central base. Stems bear a few long-stalked, lance-shaped, or elliptical leaves along the lower stem. Leaves are 7"–10" long, while the upper leaves are smaller and stalkless. Small, white to pinkish flowers are borne in dense clusters, 1"–3" long. Fruits are small, 3-angled, yellowish-brown seeds.

Bloom Season: Summer

Habitat/Range: Wet meadows or stream banks at higher elevations across the western United States and Canada.

Comments: *Bistorta* is from *bis* ("twice") and *tortus* ("twisted"), meaning twice-twisted. *Bistortoides* ("twice-twisted") refers to the plant's thick, twisted root and earns the plant the nickname Snakeroot. Native Americans roasted or boiled the roots for food. Lewis and Clark collected the first specimen of this plant for science in 1806.

NORTHERN BUCKWHEAT
Eriogonum compositum
Smartweed-Buckwheat Family (Polygonaceae)

Description: Perennial, clump forming. Large basal leaves, hairy below, are up to 10" long, but the oval- to heart-shaped leaves are borne on stems longer than the leaf blade. Flower heads arise on stems 7"–21" long and bear flat-topped clusters of white to yellow tiny flowers. Fruit is a seed.

Bloom Season: Late spring through summer

Habitat/Range: Dry slopes, rocky sites, sagebrush steppe, and juniper woodlands at low to high elevations from eastern Washington to Oregon and east to Idaho.

Comments: *Eriogonum* ("woolly knees") refers to the hairs growing at the stem and leaf joints. *Compositum* ("like another but different") may refer to the plant resembling another species of *Eriogonum*.

WYETH BUCKWHEAT
Eriogonum heracleoides
Smartweed-Buckwheat Family (Polygonaceae)

Description: Perennial, clump forming. Leaves borne in whorls along the woody stems are narrow, 1-2" long, mostly basal, and hairy on the undersides. Flat-topped clusters of tiny white or yellow flowers are borne on elongated stems with a whorl of leaflike bracts midway up the stem. The stems may reach up to 20" high. Fruit is a seed.

Bloom Season: Early to mid summer

Habitat/Range: Grows in dry locations from low to high elevations in open locations, sagebrush steppe, and ponderosa pine habitats east of the Cascades from British Columbia to Utah.

Comments: *Eriogonum* ("woolly knees") refers to the hairs growing at the stem and leaf joints. *Heracleoides* ("*Heracleum*-like") refers to the flowers resembling those of Cow Parsnip (*Heracleum maximum*). Attracts a wide variety of insect pollinators such as flies, bees, beetles, and butterflies. Also called Parsnip-flowered Buckwheat.

BARESTEM WILD BUCKWHEAT
Eriogonum nudum
Smartweed-Buckwheat Family (Polygonaceae)

Description: Annual, stems grow from 1'–5' tall from a set of basal leaves that are long-stemmed and egg-shaped with a blunt end. Undersides are white, and upper sides are grayish-green with slightly crisped margins. Floral stems smooth and lacking leaves. Small clusters of white flowers are borne in a loose branching pattern. Fruit is a seed.

Bloom Season: Summer

Habitat/Range: Open, dry or damp meadows, rocky slopes, roadsides, and open forests from mid to high elevations on both sides of the Cascades from Washington to southern California.

Comments: *Eriogonum* ("woolly knees") refers to the hairs growing at the stem and leaf joints. *Nudum* ("naked") refers to the leafless flowering stalk. Attracts numerous species of butterflies as pollinators.

CUSHION WILD BUCKWHEAT
Eriogonum ovalifolium
Smartweed-Buckwheat Family (Polygonaceae)

Description: Mound-forming perennial, 2"–16" across. Basal leaves are round or spatula-shaped and covered with woolly hairs. Leaf blades are ¾"–2½" long, and petioles are up to 2" long. Leafless flowering stalks bear a rounded cluster of small, white flowers striped with purple; 6 petal-like segments are similar.

Bloom Season: Early spring to midsummer

Habitat/Range: Shrublands to alpine communities in drier sites across much of the West.

Comments: *Eriogonum* ("woolly knees") refers to the hairs growing at the stem and leaf joints. *Ovalifolium* ("oval leaves") refers to the shape of the leaves. A highly variable species.

ALPINE WILD BUCKWHEAT
Eriogonum pyrolifolium
Smartweed-Buckwheat Family (Polygonaceae)

Description: Perennial, low-growing with reddish stems up to 7" tall. The oval-shaped basal leaves are ½"–1½" long, borne on stalks, and are smooth above and hairy below. The small flat-topped clusters of white, greenish-white, or pinkish-rose flowers arise from a 3"–4" stem with reddish hairs. Two leaflike bracts sit below the flower clusters. The turban-shaped flowers have petallike sepals that are less than ¼" long and have white- to rose-colored hairs. The flowers also have an unpleasant odor. Fruit is a 3-angled seed.

Bloom Season: Late summer

Habitat/Range: Rocky outcrops, pumice, and sandy ridges at subalpine and alpine elevations in the Cascades from Washington to California and east to the Rocky Mountains.

Comments: *Eriogonum* ("woolly knees") refers to the hairs growing at the stem and leaf joints. *Pyrolifolium* ("*Pyrola*-like leaves") refers to the leaf's similarity to those in the *Pyrola* genus. Also called Dirty Socks after the floral aroma; this odor attracts numerous pollinators including small butterflies and flies.

BEACH KNOTWEED
Polygonum paronychia
Smartweed-Buckwheat Family (Polygonaceae)

Description: Perennial, sprawling plant with upright or horizontal woody stems. The leaves have sheathing, paperlike bases where they attach to the stem. The elliptical leaves are 1" long and tough with margins that roll under the edge. The flowers are borne in clusters at the branch tips; the white to pink flowers are less than ¼" long and have 8 stamens. Fruit is a black seed.

Bloom Season: Summer

Habitat/Range: Coastal sand dunes and beaches from Vancouver Island to southern California.

Description: *Polygonum* ("many knees") refers to the many joints along the stems. *Paronychia* refers to a "whitlow" or infection near a finger or toenail, for which a poultice of Beach Knotweed was applied. This plant is also called Black Knotweed after the black seeds. This knotweed colonizes sand dunes and may grow with Beach Morning Glory (*Convolvulus soldanella*) with its pinkish-purple funnel-shaped flowers.

SHASTA KNOTWEED
Polygonum shastense
Smartweed-Buckwheat Family (Polygonaceae)

Description: Perennial, low growing to upright small shrub. Lance-shaped leaves are about 1/3" long with pointed or rounded tips and 2 parallel veins that separate raised areas on the leaf's surface. As the leaves mature, they twist. Small, white flowers are borne in leaf axils in clusters that may be several inches wide. Flowers are 1/3" wide with 5 petals and a green or pink stripe vein. Fruit is a seed.

Bloom Season: Midsummer

Habitat/Range: Rocky or gravelly sites at subalpine to alpine environments from southwest Oregon to central California.

Comments: *Polygonum* ("many knees") refers to the many joints along the stems. *Shastense* ("of Mount Shasta") refers to this plant growing in pumice-rich soils on Mount Shasta.

WESTERN STARFLOWER
Trientalis latifolia
Primrose Family (Primulaceae)

Description: Perennial, low-growing mostly 4"–8" high but may be up to 15" tall. Egg-shaped leaves, 1"–4" long, are arranged in whorls around the stem. Three to 8 leaves occur just below the flowers; lacks other stem leaves. The 1/2"-wide, white to pink flowers have 4–9 (mostly 6–7) pointed petals and are borne on slender stalks with 1–4 flowers in a cluster. Fruit is a rounded capsule.

Bloom Season: Late spring to midsummer

Habitat/Range: Meadow edges, roadsides, and shaded woods in low to mid elevations from British Columbia south to central California and also in northeastern Washington and northern Idaho.

Comments: *Trientalis* ("one-third of a foot") refers to the height of this plant. *Latifolia* ("wide leaves") refers to the plant's leaves. The common name is after the star-shaped arrangement of the petals. Northern Starflower (*T. europaea*) also grows in the Northwest, has white flowers and several stem leaves below the upper whorl of leaves, and grows in wetland habitats.

BANEBERRY
Actaea rubra
Buttercup Family (Ranunculaceae)

Description: Perennial, grows up to 3' tall. Plants bear few leaves, generally one near the base and others higher on the stem. Leaves are divided 2 or 3 times into division-bearing 3 leaflets (ternately compound). Leaflets are sharply toothed and lobed. Terminal rounded cluster of tiny, white flowers with protruding stamens resembles an elongated, white ball. Fruits are mostly reddish (white also) smooth berries.

Bloom Season: Spring to early summer

Habitat/Range: Moist, shady locations from sea level to subalpine elevations across most of the Northwest and temperate North America.

Comments: Baneberry is from the Anglo-Saxon word *bana* ("murderous") and refers to the highly toxic compounds in the berries, roots, and leaves. *Actaea* is from the Greek word *aktea* ("elder") referring to the similarity of Baneberry leaves to those of Elderberry. *Rubra* ("red") defines the primary color of the berries. Plants contain berberine and other toxic compounds.

COLUMBIA WINDFLOWER
Anemone deltoidea
Buttercup Family (Ranunculaceae)

Description: Perennial, 6"–15" tall. Basal leaves divided into 3 segments while stem leaves are a whorl of 3 broadly lance-shaped leaves with toothed margins. Leaves are 1"–2" long. White flowers are up to 1½" wide and have 5 white sepals and numerous stamens arising from a green center. The fruit is a seed with long hairs.

Bloom Season: Mid spring to midsummer

Habitat/Range: Grows in moist or shady sites from low to subalpine forests mostly west of the Cascades into northern California.

Comments: The derivation of *Anemone* is unclear. *Deltoidea* ("triangular") refers to the triangular pattern of the stem leaves. Windflowers produce greater quantities of pollen than nectar to attract pollinators.

WESTERN PASQUEFLOWER
Anemone occidentalis
Buttercup Family (Ranunculaceae)

Description: Perennial with upright stout floral stem to 20" or more. Basal leaves borne on long stalks, while upper leaves are stemless; both are divided 2–3 times into deep lobes. The single, 1"–2"-long, white- or purplish-tinged flowers have 5–8 oblong sepals and numerous stamens and pistils. The flowers lack petals. Fruit is a seed with long, silky hairs.

Bloom Season: Late spring through summer

Habitat/Range: Open, rocky slopes and moist meadows at subalpine to alpine elevations from British Columbia to California and east to Montana.

Comments: The derivation of *Anemone* is unclear. *Occidentalis* ("western") refers to the distribution of this plant. The common name refers to the Easter blooming time of another species. Locally called Hippie-on-a-Stick after the resemblance of the seed heads to an Oregon hippie.

WHITE MARSH MARIGOLD
Caltha leptosepala
Buttercup Family (Ranunculaceae)

Description: Perennial, stems smooth and fleshy, growing 4"–16". Basal leaves are oval to oblong, longer than broad, and somewhat arrowhead-shaped at the base. The white or greenish flowers, borne 1–2 per stem, are 1"–2" wide. The outside of the flower is often tinged with blue. Fruit is a dry follicle that splits open when the seeds are mature.

Bloom Season: Summer

Habitat/Range: Wet mountain meadows (meadows, seeps, and stream banks) at higher elevations in subalpine and alpine regions from Alaska to Colorado and east to central Idaho.

Comments: *Caltha* ("cup or goblet") describes the shape of the flower, and *leptosepala* ("with slender sepals") describes the sepals. Native Alaskan peoples ate the leaves and flower buds, as well as the plant's slender, white roots. Elk browse on the leaves that contain toxic alkaloids without harm; hence, Cowslip and Elk's Lip are two other common names for the plant. Beetles are a common pollinator of these Marsh Marigolds.

WESTERN CLEMATIS
Clematis ligusticifolia
Buttercup Family (Ranunculaceae)

Description: Perennial vine. Stems climb on vegetation or trail along the ground and may reach 10'–40' long. The opposite leaves are compound with 5–7 egg-shaped leaflets that are lobed and toothed along the margin. The loosely arranged flowering cluster bears numerous white flowers, ½" wide, that are composed of 4 petallike sepals and numerous stamens. Male and female flowers are borne separately on the same plant. The fruit is a seed with a long, feathery tail.

Bloom Season: Mid spring to summer

Habitat/Range: Stream banks and canyon bottoms at low to mid elevations from British Columbia to California and east to the Rocky Mountains.

Comments: *Clematis* is a Greek name for different climbing plants. *Ligusticifolia* ("with leaves like *Ligusticum*") refers to the leaves resembling those of Lovage (*L. officinale*). Chopped, dried leaves and stems are steeped as a tea to treat headaches and migraines.

CAROLINA BUGBANE
Trautvetteria carolinensis
Buttercup Family (Ranunculaceae)

Description: Perennial, up to 1'–3' tall. Large, maple-like leaves, 2"–15" wide, are lobed similar to a hand with 5–11 lobes. The lobes are toothed along the margin; upper leaves are smaller. The flattish flower heads are borne on long stalks; the 1"-wide white flowers lack petals and have numerous (50–70) white stamens. The sepals fall off as the flower matures. Fruit is a papery seed with a hooked tip.

Bloom Season: Late spring and summer

Habitat/Range: Moist, open woods and along streams and waterways from low to mid elevations throughout the western United States and British Columbia.

Comments: *Trautvetteria* is for Ernst Rudolf von Trautvetter (1809–1889), a Russian botanist associated with the St. Petersburg Botanical Garden. *Carolinensis* ("of North or South Carolina") refers to an eastern variety collected in 1788 in the Carolinas. The plants have protoanemonin, an alkaloid that causes blistering or redness to the skin. Tall Bugbane (*Cimicifuga elata*) is similar but taller and with larger leaves and flowers in a narrow, elongated cluster. The hooked seeds of False Bugbane disperse by attaching to passing mammals or hikers.

SNOWBRUSH
Ceanothus velutinus
Buckthorn Family (Rhamnaceae)

Description: Shrub, 3'–8' tall. Evergreen leaves are egg-shaped and glossy above and hairy below. A sticky varnish covers the leaves. The tiny, white flowers grow in thick clusters; individual flowers have 5 petals that narrow at the base. Fruit is a seed.

Bloom Season: Midsummer

Habitat/Range: Dry hillsides and forests at low to mid elevations from British Columbia to California.

Comments: *Ceanothus* is the Greek name for a related spiny shrub. *Velutinus* ("velvety") refers to the leaf texture. Bees pollinate the aromatic flowers; the abundant blooms seem to "hum" due to the numerous bees attracted to the flowers. Snowbrush is also an important winter browse plant for deer and elk. This is a fire-adapted species with seeds that need fire to germinate. Shrubs will regrow after a fire from underground roots.

WESTERN SERVICEBERRY
Amelanchier alnifolia
Rose Family (Rosaceae)

Description: Shrub, generally 3'–15' tall but reaches 30'. Bark is gray to reddish. The deciduous leaves are round to oval and toothed along the upper margin. Five-petaled flowers are white, ½"–1½" wide, and grow in small clusters. Narrow petals surround a dense cluster of yellow stamens. Fruit is a pome (apple-like) that changes color from red to purplish black at maturity.

Bloom Season: Spring to summer

Habitat/Range: Widespread in meadows, forest edges, rocky slopes, and dry to moist open forests from low to mid elevations throughout western North America.

Comments: *Amelanchier* is from the archaic French *amelancier* that refers to another individual of this genus. *Alnifolia* ("alder-like leaves") refers to the resemblance of these leaves to those of Alder. Native Americans collected the edible fruits and mixed them with buffalo or venison to form pemmican. Deer, elk, and rabbits browse on the twigs and leaves. The leaves turn yellow and are deciduous.

GOAT'S BEARD
Aruncus dioicus
Rose Family (Rosaceae)

Description: Perennial, with hairless stems 3'–6' tall. Lower leaves are 3 times compound, large and with pointed leaflets with a pointed tip. Upper leaves smaller and 1–2 times compound. The tiny, white flowers are borne in long plumes of male and female flowers on separate plants. Fruit is a narrow pod.

Bloom Season: Early to midsummer

Habitat/Range: Edges of forests, roadsides, or streams at low to mid elevations from Alaska to California and eastward from British Columbia to Idaho; also found in Eurasia.

Comments: *Aruncus* is from the Greek *aryngos* ("a goat's beard") and refers to the flower plumes' resemblance to the hairs on a goat's chin. *Dioicus* ("two homes") refers to the male and female flowers being borne on separate plants. Northwest bribes used the plants to cure blood diseases, as a diuretic, to treat smallpox or sore throats, and as a poultice for bruises and swelling.

FERN BUSH
Chamaebatiaria millefolium
Rose Family (Rosaceae)

Description: Shrub, 3'–6' tall with spreading stems covered with sticky and star-shaped hairs. Fernlike leaves, 1"–2½" long, are highly divided several times. Flower clusters are 2"–10" long and bear ½"-wide, white, bell-shaped flowers with numerous stamens. Fruit is a several-seeded, narrow pod.

Bloom Season: Early to midsummer

Habitat/Range: Drier sites in desert canyons or mountain slopes at mid elevations east of the Cascades from central Oregon to southern California and east to Idaho.

Comments: *Chamaebatiaria* is from the Greek *Chamaibatos* ("a dwarf bramble") and refers to the low, sprawling nature of this shrub. *Millefolium* ("with 1,000 leaves") refers to the highly dissected leaves with numerous leaflets.

BEACH STRAWBERRY
Fragaria chiloensis
Rose Family (Rosaceae)

Description: Perennial, with long runners. The stiff, leathery compound leaves are made up of 3 leaflets that are toothed along the margin. The upper sides of the leaves have prominent veins, and the lower sides have silky, white hairs. The white flowers are 1"–2" wide with 5–7 petals and numerous stamens. Fruit is a small, red berry about ¾"–1" wide.

Bloom Season: Spring through summer

Habitat/Range: Coastal sand dunes and rocky outcrops at low elevations from Alaska to central California but also found in Hawaii and the coast of South America.

Comments: *Fragaria* is the Roman name for strawberries. *Chiloensis* ("of Chile") refers to the South American distribution of this plant. Rodents, birds, and humans consume the edible fruits. Numerous species of flies and bees are attracted to the flowers. The plants can spread and root by aboveground runners.

WOODLAND STRAWBERRY
Fragaria vesca
Rose Family (Rosaceae)

Description: Perennial, 4"–13" long, trailing along the ground. Divided thin, green leaves have 3 oval leaflets that are toothed along the edges and show deep veins; leaflets are slightly hairy and bear a tiny tip at each tooth. White, saucer-shaped flowers are 1"–1¼" wide and have numerous stamens. Fruit is a berry.

Bloom Season: Late spring to early summer

Habitat/Range: In shaded forests or along forest edges at low elevations, widely distributed across the western United States and into Canada.

Comments: *Fragaria* is the Roman name for strawberries. *Vesca* ("little") refers to the small, edible fruits. Sometimes grows with Broadpetal Strawberry (*F. virginia*), but Woodland Strawberry has darker, glossier leaves with deep venation.

VIRGINIA STRAWBERRY
Fragaria virginiana
Rose Family (Rosaceae)

Description: Perennial, low-growing with runners. Bluish-green leaves are elliptical to oblong and toothed along the margins. The terminal tooth is smaller than the ones to its side. The white flowers are 1" wide and have 5 petals and numerous stamens. Fruit is a red berry.

Bloom Season: Mid spring to midsummer

Habitat/Range: Open wood, meadows, stream banks, and grasslands from low to mid elevations mostly on the east side of the Cascades from Alaska to California and east to the Atlantic coast.

Comments: *Fragaria* is the Roman name for strawberries. *Virginiana* ("of Virginia") refers to the location of the first collected specimen for science. The small, edible berries are very sweet. Woodland Strawberry (*F. vesca*) also occurs in Oregon but has prominent veins on the leaves and the leaflets' terminal tooth is longer than the side ones.

OCEAN SPRAY
Holodiscus discolor
Rose Family (Rosaceae)

Description: Shrub, up to 15' tall. Stems are reddish brown with prominent ribs. The oval leaves are 1"–3" long, have shallow lobes, and are hairy below and toothed along the margins. White flowers are borne in dense, lacy clusters. Fruit is a flat seed.

Bloom Season: Summer

Habitat/Range: Open areas in woodlands or rocky slopes from coastal to subalpine elevations from British Columbia to California and east to Montana.

Comments: *Holodiscus* is from the Greek *holos* ("entire") and *diskos* ("a disc"), which is in reference to the unlobed, saucer-shaped, floral disk. *Discolor* ("of 2 different colors") refers to the white flowers that fade to tan when mature.

ROCK SPIREA
Holodiscus microphyllus
Rose Family (Rosaceae)

Description: Shrub, 1'–5' tall. New stems reddish, and older stems grayish. Alternate leaves are broad and toothed along the margin. The terminal flower cluster is made up of tiny ¼"-long flowers with 5 petals and numerous stamens. Fruit is a seed.

Bloom Season: Late spring through summer

Habitat/Range: Rocky outcrops or slopes and forest openings from mid to high elevations from central Oregon to California and east to Arizona and Utah.

Comments: *Holodiscus* is from the Greek *holos* ("entire") and *diskos* ("a disc"), which is in reference to the unlobed, saucer-shaped, floral disk. *Microphyllus* ("small leaves") refers to the leaf size.

PINEWOODS HORKELIA
Horkelia fusca
Rose Family (Rosaceae)

Description: Perennial; either low-growing or with upright, reddish-brown stems that may reach 30" tall. Basal tuft of leaves compound, 5"–12" long, *Potentilla*-like, and divided into bright-green, wedge-shaped or rounded leaflets with toothed or lobed edges. Floral stems bear several clusters of flowers at the top. Flowers are ½" wide, white to pink, and have petals that are narrow at the base and wider at the top. A ring, known as the hypanthium, bears 10 stamens and 10–20 pistils. Fruit is a seed.

Bloom Season: Late spring to midsummer

Habitat/Range: Grows in wet meadows, rocky slopes, and forest openings from mid to subalpine elevations east of the Cascade Crest from Washington to California and east to Wyoming.

Comments: *Horkelia* honors German plant physiologist Johann Horkel (1769–1846). *Fusca* ("dusky" or "dark") refers to the stems. This Horkelia is a host plant for larvae of the two-banded checkered skipper. Also known as Dusky Horkelia or Pink Pinwheels, since the flowers resemble a child's pinwheel toy.

PARTRIDGEFOOT
Luetkea pectinata
Rose Family (Rosaceae)

Description: Small, mat-forming perennial; plants 2"–7" high. The densely clustered basal leaves are finely divided and fan-shaped. Stem leaves may be absent. Upright flowering stems bear dense clusters of tiny, white to cream-colored flowers. Fruit is a small capsule that splits open at maturity.

Bloom Season: Summer

Habitat/Range: Prefers moist or shady sites in meadows or rocky sites from mid to alpine elevations in the northern mountains of western North America.

Comments: *Luetkea* honors Count F. P. Luetke (1797–1882), a Russian explorer and sea captain. *Pectinata* ("like the teeth of a comb") describes the finely divided leaf. The common name refers to the outline of the leaf, which resembles the track of a partridge or ptarmigan. Also called Alaska Spirea.

INDIAN PLUM
Oemleria cerasiformis
Rose Family (Rosaceae)

Description: A small tree or large shrub with purplish bark that grows up to 15' tall. Narrow, egg-shaped leaves, 2"–6" long, have smooth or rolled under edges, and have a cucumber-like aroma when crushed. Male and female flowers bloom on separate plants as the leaves develop. Clusters of downward-hanging, greenish-white, bell-shaped flowers; male flowers with 15 stamens, and female flowers with 5 pistils. Fruit is edible but bitter and is bluish-black and plumlike.

Bloom Season: Spring

Habitat/Range: Moist to dry, open forests at low elevations mainly west of the Cascades from British Columbia to California.

Comments: *Oemleria* honors Augustus Gottlieb Oemler (1773–1852), a German-American pharmacist who collected plants in the South and supplied them to the German botanist H. G. L. Reichenbach and others in the mid-1800s. *Cerasiformis* ("cherry-shaped") refers to the fruits. Native Americans ate the fruits and made tea from the bark for medicinal purposes. Also known as Osoberry; this early season plant may bloom in late winter.

PACIFIC NINEBARK
Physocarpus capitatus
Rose Family (Rosaceae)

Description: Shrub, 3'–8' tall with flaky bark. Maplelike lobed leaves are 1"–5½" long and broad, arranged alternately along the stems, and have star-shaped hairs on the undersides. Small white flowers are borne in rounded clusters; each flower has 5 petals and roughly 30 pinkish stamens. Fruit is an inflated red pod that splits open when dry.

Bloom Season: Late spring to midsummer

Habitat/Range: Stream banks, river edges, wetlands, and moist forests from low to mid elevations across western North America.

Comments: *Physocarpus* is from the Greek *physa* ("bellows") and *karpos* ("fruit"), which refers to the inflated seedpod. *Capitatus* ("rounded") refers to the flower arrangement. The common name refers to the scaly bark, which was once believed to be in 9 layers. Mallow Ninebark (*P. malvaceus*) is similar but is found mostly in northeast and eastern Oregon.

BITTER CHERRY
Prunus emarginata
Rose Family (Rosaceae)

Description: Shrub or small tree with reddish-purple bark on young twigs that becomes grayish with age, 3'–45' tall, and often forming thickets. Leaves are 1½"–4" long, egg-shaped or broadly lance-shaped, and with a rounded tip and fine teeth along the upper margins. Flowers borne in flat-topped clusters. Individual flowers have 5 white petals that arise from a cup-shaped calyx and bear roughly 20 stamens and 1 pistil. Fruit is a bitter cherry.

Bloom Season: Mid spring to early summer

Habitat/Range: Moist sites in woodlands from sea level to mid elevations on both sides of the Cascades in the Northwest and east to the Rocky Mountains.

Comments: *Prunus* is an ancient Latin name for plum, and *emarginata* ("notched") refers to the edges of the leaves. Wildlife will consume the bitter-tasting fruits.

CHOKECHERRY
Prunus virginiana
Rose Family (Rosaceae)

Description: Shrub or small tree up to 25' tall. Leaves are 2"–4" long, egg-shaped to inversely egg-shaped, ½"–3" wide, and toothed along the margin tapering to a point. Dense clusters of ½"-long, white flowers with 5 petals and around 20 stamens arise at the ends of branches or short, lateral shoots. Fruit is a red to blackish berry.

Bloom Season: Mid spring to midsummer

Habitat/Range: Moist locations such as along stream banks, canyon bottoms, or roadsides from mid to high elevations on both sides of the Cascades and across the western United States and Canada.

Comments: *Prunus* is an ancient Latin name for plum, a related species. *Virginiana* ("of Virginia") refers to the type locality for this wide-ranging species. Birds glean the fruit from the plants, and people harvest the berries to make jams, jellies, cordials, and other products. Crushed leaves have an almond scent.

HIMALAYAN BLACKBERRY
Rubus bifrons
Rose Family (Rosaceae)

Description: Thick, thorny stems, which may reach up to 30' in length, form massive brambles. Leaves are palmately compound with 3–5 egg-shaped leaflets that are toothed along the margin. Clusters of white to pinkish, 5-petaled flowers with numerous stamens are borne along elongated stalks. Fruit is a blackberry.

Bloom Season: Summer

Habitat/Range: Disturbed sites along roads, forest clearings, fallow fields, and other moist sites from low to mid elevations mainly west of the Cascades in the Pacific Northwest but in other states as well. Introduced from Europe, this plant has naturalized in the United States.

Comments: *Rubus* is the Latin name for blackberries, raspberries, and brambles. *Bifrons* ("two-fronded") refers to the two different sized leaflets of the compound leaf.

CUTLEAF BLACKBERRY
Rubus laciniatus
Rose Family (Rosaceae)

Description: Sprawling stems that may trail 30' or more and bear recurved thorns. Evergreen leaves are palmately divided into 3–5 deeply lobed leaflets; each leaflet is toothed along the margin and pointed at the tip. White to pink, 5-petaled flowers are borne in loose clusters along the stems, and are 1" wide. Fruit is an edible blackberry.

Bloom Season: Summer

Habitat/Range: Cutleaf Blackberry does well in disturbed ground such as a forest after a fire or cutting at low to mid elevations mainly west of the Cascades throughout the Northwest. Native to Europe but now naturalized in the West.

Comments: *Rubus* is the Latin name for blackberries, raspberries, or brambles. *Laciniatus* ("with milky flowers") refers to the flower color. The delicious berries are harvested carefully due to the thorns.

BLACKCAP RASPBERRY
Rubus leucodermis
Rose Family (Rosaceae)

Description: Shrub or vine that has prickly shoots. Pinnately compound leaves have 5 leaflets on growing stems and 3 leaves on stems that bear flowers (leaves may be palmately compound, also). Leaflets toothed and hairy below. Five-petaled flowers are white to pink, ½"–1" wide; the sepals are longer than the petals. Fruit is a black berry when mature.

Bloom Season: Spring and summer

Habitat/Range: Forests, logged or burned areas, and mountain slopes at mid elevations from Alaska to Mexico and east to Utah and Montana.

Comments: *Rubus* is the Latin name for blackberries, raspberries, or brambles. *Leucodermis* ("white skin") refers to the color of the bark. The fruits are edible.

THIMBLEBERRY
Rubus parviflorus
Rose Family (Rosaceae)

Description: Shrub, generally 2'–6' tall. Stems lack spines. Leaves 3"–8" long and broad. They are covered with soft hairs, lobed like a maple leaf, and finely toothed along the margin. White flowers are 1"–2" wide, with 5 wrinkled, papery petals and numerous yellow stamens. Fruit is a thimble-shaped red berry, resembling a raspberry.

Bloom Season: Mid spring to early summer

Habitat/Range: Widespread. Forest from low to high elevations from Alaska to Mexico and east to the Great Lakes region. Thimbleberries may colonize disturbed sites along roads, clearcuts, or burned areas.

Comments: *Rubus* is the Latin name for blackberries, raspberries, or brambles. *Parviflorus* ("with small flowers") refers to the size of the flowers. The thimble shape of the edible fruits gives the common name to this plant, which Lewis and Clark collected along the Columbia River on April 15, 1806. A notation on their herbarium specimen written by Frederick Pursh read: "A Shrub of which the natives eat the young Sprout without kooking." Black-tailed deer browse on the young leaves and stems, while birds and bears consume the fruits.

TRAILING BLACKBERRY
Rubus ursinus
Rose Family (Rosaceae)

Description: Perennial with sprawling, prickle-bearing stems that may reach 15' long or upright stems to 50" tall. The deciduous leaves are compound with 3 deeply lobed leaflets that are toothed along the margin. The tip leaflet is dark green and 3 lobed. The white to pink, 5-petaled flowers have numerous stamens and may be up to 2" wide. Male and female flowers are borne on separate plants. Fruit is an edible berry.

Bloom Season: Late spring and midsummer

Habitat/Range: Widespread throughout the region west of the Cascades and into California in disturbed areas, open woodlands, thickets, and urban areas from low to mid elevations. This is the only native blackberry in the Northwest.

Comments: *Rubus* is the Latin name for blackberries, raspberries, and brambles. *Ursinus* ("like a bear") may refer to the color of the berry or the shape of the prickle resembling a bear's claw. The fragrant flowers attract bees, flies, wasps, and butterflies as pollinators.

MOUNTAIN ASH
Sorbus sitchensis
Rose Family (Rosaceae)

Description: Shrub, up to 12' tall with multiple stems or a small tree with a single trunk. Compound leaves are 6"–10" long and comprised of 7–11 leaflets that are lance- to oval-shaped, rounded at the tip, and toothed along the margins from the middle to the end. Small, white flowers are borne in dense, flat-topped clusters that are 3"–5" wide. Fruit is a reddish or orange berry.

Bloom Season: Summer

Habitat/Range: Found in second-growth forests, forest edges, and thickets from mid to high elevations on both sides of the Cascades from Alaska to northern California and east to Montana.

Comments: *Sorbus* is from the Latin *sorbum*, which refers to the fruit of a tree similar to those of Mountain Ash. *Sitchensis* ("of Sitka") refers to the northern distribution of this plant. The fruits are not very edible, although birds such as robins, thrushes, or waxwings will eat them in winter.

BASTARD TOADFLAX
Comandra umbellata
Mistletoe/Toadflax Family (Santalaceae)

Description: Perennial, often spreading by lateral roots. Plants are up to 13" tall. Erect stems bear linear, lance-shaped or narrowly elliptical leaves that are ⅛"–1¼" long. Flowers are arranged in a flat-topped cluster. They lack petals but have 5 whitish-green sepals. Fruit is a 1-seeded nut covered with a fleshy coating that is purplish or brown.

Bloom Season: Spring

Habitat/Range: Sandy soils in grasslands or sagebrush steppe habitats across much of the semi-arid western United States.

Comments: *Comandra* is from the Greek *kome* ("hair") and *andros* ("man"); the stamens are hairy at the base. *Umbellata* ("with an umbel") refers to the flat-topped floral clusters. Bastard Toadflax is known to be parasitic on over 200 plant species, although it can survive without a host. Rootlike connections called haustoria attach to a host's roots and pirate water and nutrients from those roots.

ROUNDLEAF ALUMROOT
Heuchera cylindrica
Saxifrage Family (Saxifragaceae)

Description: Perennial, mat-forming. Basal leaves are rounded to kidney-shaped, fleshy, and with 5–7 lobes that are toothed. Leaf blades are ½"–2½" long and are borne on smooth or hairy stems, 1"–4" long. Leafless flowering stems rise above the basal leaves ½'–2' or more depending upon the growing site, in height. Small white or pinkish cup-shaped flowers are borne in a tight cluster; each flower is made up of 5 sepals and short stamens. Fruit is a seed.

Bloom Season: Mid spring through summer

Habitat/Range: Rocky ledges, cliffs, crevices, and slopes from mid to high elevations on the east side of the Cascades from British Columbia to northeastern California and east to Wyoming and Nevada.

Comments: *Heuchera* is for Johann Heinrich von Heucher (1677–1747) of Wittenberg, Germany. He was a physician, professor, and botanist. *Cylindrica* ("roll" or "cylinder") is in reference to the flower clusters. Also called Lava Alumroot.

SMALL-FLOWERED ALUMROOT
Heuchera micrantha
Saxifrage Family (Saxifragaceae)

Description: Perennial up to 3' tall with dense, white to brownish hairs on leaf stems and lower portion of flowering stalk. Leaf blades longer than broad with rounded, shallow lobes. Flowers borne in open clusters, and the individual white flowers are very small. Fruit is a many-seeded capsule; seeds are covered with rows of tiny spines.

Bloom Season: Mid to late spring

Habitat/Range: Moist areas along stream banks, slopes, or rocky outcrops from low to subalpine elevations from British Columbia to California and east to western Idaho.

Comments: *Heuchera* honors Johann Henrich von Heucher (1677–1747), professor of medicine in Wittenberg, Germany. *Micrantha* ("small-flowered") refers to the tiny flowers. Smooth Alumroots (*H. glabra*), which has wider instead of longer leaves and hairless stems, is similar. Native coastal people made a poultice from the pounded root that was applied to cuts.

WHOLELEAF SAXIFRAGE
Micranthes integrifolia
Saxifrage Family (Saxifragaceae)

Description: Perennial, often 4" but may reach 16" tall. Reddish stems may be hairy. Basal leaves are reddish and densely hairy below, variable in shape, and fringed with fine hairs on edges. Flowers are borne in small clusters at the tip of a long stem, and the individual flowers have white or greenish petals and are ¼" up to ½" wide. Seeds have small ridges.

Bloom Season: Early spring

Habitat/Range: Moist or dry grassy areas, stream banks, and subalpine meadows from low to mid elevations in British Columbia to California and east to central Idaho.

Comments: *Micranthes* is from the Greek words *micro* ("small") and *anthos* ("flower"), which is in reference to the tiny flowers. *Integrifolia* ("entire leaves") refers to the smooth leaf edge. More than 20 species of saxifrage occur in the Pacific Northwest. Blooms early in the spring and often in profusion.

WESTERN SAXIFRAGE
Micranthes occidentalis
Saxifrage Family (Saxifragaceae)

Description: Perennial, 3"–15" tall. Basal leaves are 1"–3" long, leathery, egg-shaped, and toothed along the margin. Single, flowering stems bear clusters of small, white flowers that arise on reddish, woolly stems. Ten orangish stamens arise from the flowers. Fruit is a tiny seed.

Bloom Season: Spring

Habitat/Range: Moist meadows, grassy openings, and rocky slopes or outcrops from mid to subalpine elevations from British Columbia to Oregon and east to Idaho and northwest Wyoming but mainly east of the Cascades.

Comments: *Micranthes* is from the Greek words *micro* ("small") and *anthos* ("flower"), which is in reference to the tiny flowers. *Occidentalis* ("western") refers to the plant's Northwest distribution.

TOLMIE'S SAXIFRAGE
Micranthes tolmiei
Saxifrage Family (Saxifragaceae)

Description: Perennial, forming dense mats up to 24" wide. The basal leaves are fleshy, linear, up to ½" long, and form dense mats. The red flowering stalks are 2"–4" tall and bear ½"-wide white, star-shaped flowers. Located between the 5 white, paddle-like petals are white petallike rods that contain stamens with black anthers. The greenish center contains the stigma and ovaries. Fruit is an oval capsule that has purplish mottling.

Bloom Season: Summer

Habitat/Range: Rocky outcrops, cliff faces, or bare, moist soil mostly in subalpine or alpine areas from Alaska to central California and east into central Idaho.

Comments: *Micranthes* is from the Greek words *micro* ("small") and *anthos* ("flower"), which is in reference to the tiny flowers. *Tolmiei* is for William Fraser Tolmie (1812–1886), a Scottish physician for the Hudson Bay Company stationed at Fort Vancouver in the early 1830s who collected plants in the Northwest. Tolmie Peak near Mount Rainier is named after him.

FRAGRANT FRINGECUP
Tellima grandiflora
Saxifrage Family (Saxifragaceae)

Description: Perennial, 1'–3½' tall. Basal leaves are heart-shaped and 2"–4" wide with 5–7 shallow lobes that are toothed. The few stem leaves are similar but smaller. Tubular, bell-shaped flowers have 10 stamens and are borne along in loose clusters on a long stalk. Petals are frilled and greenish white or pink but turn dark red with age. Fruit is a capsule.

Bloom Season: Late spring to midsummer

Habitat/Range: Moist woods, stream banks, and up to lower elevation mountain slopes from southern Alaska to California on the west side of the Cascades but also in the Columbia River Gorge and into northern Idaho.

Comments: *Tellima* is an anagram of *Mitella*, another genus in the Saxifrage Family. *Grandiflora* ("large-flowered") refers to the sizeable flowers, and the common name refers to the fringe around the flower's rim.

FOAMFLOWER
Tiarella trifoliata
Saxifrage Family (Saxifragaceae)

Description: Perennial, from creeping underground stems (rhizomes). Upright stems clustered or single and 6"–20" tall. Basal leaves either 3-lobed, divided into segments, or with 3 leaflets. Leaves are coarsely hairy and up to 6" wide. Upper leaves smaller. Small, white flowers, ½" long, are borne in a loose cluster above the leaves. The narrow petals resemble the stamen stems. Fruit is a low-seeded capsule.

Bloom Season: Summer

Habitat/Range: Forms a low ground cover in moist woodland from low to subalpine elevations from Alaska to California and east to Montana.

Comments: *Tiarella* is from the Greek *tiara* ("ancient Persian headdress"), which the fruit resembles. *Trifoliata* ("3 leaves") refers to the divided leaves. The common name refers to the flower color resembling specks of foam. The large leaves collect filtered sunlight that penetrates to the forest floor in the dense woodlands. Bees and other pollinators clasp the flowers in search of nectar or pollen, often bending the entire flowering stalk under their weight.

COYOTE TOBACCO
Nicotiana attenuata
Nightshade Family (Solanaceae)

Description: Annual. Plants 1'–4' tall, with sticky hairs on stems and leaves. Leaves are elliptical to broadly lance-shaped. White flowers are trumpet- or funnel-shaped and 1"–2" long, and the lobes on the calyx are shorter than the calyx tube. The stamens are borne on either long or short stalks. Fruit is a capsule that contains numerous tiny, black seeds.

Bloom Season: Mid to late summer

Habitat/Range: Dry sandy sites at low to mid elevations east of the Cascades.

Comments: *Nicotiana* honors Jean Nicot de Villemain (1530–1600), the French ambassador to Portugal who is credited with introducing tobacco plants into France in the sixteenth century. *Attenuata* ("pointed") refers to the sepal tips. Moths pollinate the deep, night-blooming flowers.

EUROPEAN BUR-REED
Sparganium emersum
Bur-Reed/Cattail Family (Typhaceae)

Description: Aquatic perennial. Floating stems up to 6½' long. Strap-like leaves are flat with a tri-angular keel and either float or are stiff and erect. Flowers are either male or female; male flowers are spherical with stamens projecting outward, and female flowers are also spherical below the male flowers. Fruit is a bur-like cluster of seeds.

Bloom Season: Spring and summer

Habitat/Range: Aquatic, shallow ponds, marshes, and lakes at low to high elevations from British Columbia to California and east to Colorado but also circumboreal in distribution in Eurasia.

Comments: *Sparganium* ("banded") refers to the narrow leaves. *Emersum* ("emerging") refers to the plants rising above the water surface.

LONGHORN PLECTRITIS
Plectritis macrocera
Valerian Family (Valerianaceae)

Description: Annual, low-growing, and often in profusion. Stems are 2"–30" tall and bear opposite, ovalish leaves, 1"–2" long, with smooth margins. Upper leaves lack stems. A tight cluster of flowers is borne at the top of the stem. The white to pale-pink flowers are about ½" long, divided into 5 lobes, and have a short spur. Fruit is a seed.

Bloom Season: Mid spring

Habitat/Range: Wet meadows, moist slopes, and along stream banks at low to mid elevations on both sides of the Cascades from southern British Columbia to California and east to Utah.

Comments: *Plectritus* ("with a spur") refers to the flower. *Macrocera* ("with long horns") also refers to the floral spurs.

SITKA VALERIAN
Valeriana sitchensis
Valerian Family (Valerianaceae)

Description: Perennial. Square stems range from 1'–3' (up to 5') tall and are mostly smooth and somewhat succulent. Two or more pairs of leaves arise oppositely at points along the flowering stem. The compound leaves have 3–7 oval- or lance-shaped leaflets, with the end leaflet being the largest. Leaf margins are coarsely toothed. Tiny, white to pinkish flowers are arranged in 1"–3"-wide, flat-topped or hemispherical clusters at the top of the plant. The stamens arise above the 5-petaled, fragrant flowers. The fruit is a seed with feathery hairs on the top.

Bloom Season: Late spring to early summer

Habitat/Range: Widespread from mid to subalpine elevations in moist meadows, stream banks, moist forested slopes, and subalpine forests from Alaska to Montana and south to California.

Comments: *Valeriana* is probably derived from the Latin word *valere* ("to be healthy or strong") and refers to the plants' medicinal qualities. *Sitchensis* ("of Sitka") refers to the location of the first specimen collected for science. The roots have a strong aroma that is a sharp contrast to the sweet-smelling flowers. Northwest tribes used the pounded roots as a poultice for cuts and wounds.

This section includes flowers that range
from pale to bright yellow. Check the white,
green, red, or orange sections if you don't
find your plant here.

BIGSEED LOMATIUM
Lomatium macrocarpum
Carrot Family (Apiaceae)

Description: Perennial, from a thick taproot. Compound leaves are highly dissected (3 times), are covered with hairs, and have purple undersides. Flowering stalks bear flat-topped clusters of yellow or white flowers that may be tinged with purple. Fruits are large, ½"–¾"-long seeds.

Bloom Season: Spring

Habitat/Range: Dry, open plains or rocky area east of the Cascades from British Columbia to California.

Comments: *Lomatium* is from the Greek *loma* ("a border or edge") and refers to the dorsal ribs or "wings" that adorn the seeds. *Macrocarpum* ("large seeds") refers to the size of the seeds.

GRAY'S DESERT PARSLEY
Lomatium grayi
Carrot Family (Apiaceae)

Description: Perennial, clump-forming. Compound leaves divided into numerous, dark-green, narrow segments. The yellow flowers are arranged in dense, flat-topped clusters that arise on leafless stems. Fruit is a flattened seed.

Bloom Season: Spring

Habitat/Range: Rocky outcrops and talus slopes in dry grasslands or sagebrush steppe along the east side of the Cascades from central Washington to northern Idaho.

Comments: *Lomatium* is from the Greek *loma* ("a border or edge") and refers to the dorsal ribs or "wings" that adorn the seeds. *Grayi* honors the American botanist Asa Gray (1810–1888), a Harvard professor who wrote *Gray's Manual of Botany* in 1848. When crushed, the leaves have a strong odor. The flat-topped clusters attract numerous insect pollinators.

MARTINDALE'S LOMATIUM
Lomatium martindalei
Carrot Family (Apiaceae)

Description: Perennial, from a deep taproot with low-growing stems 2"–10" tall. Basal blue-green leaves are highly dissected and toothed or lobed along the margin. The terminal leaf segments are deeply divided. Flat-topped clusters of tiny, yellow to yellowish-white flowers are 1"–2" wide. Fruit is a flattened seed with corky ribs and papery wings.

Bloom Season: Late spring and summer

Habitat/Range: Dry sites on rocky outcrops, talus or scree slopes, or meadows at mid to alpine elevations from southern British Columbia to southern Oregon.

Comments: *Lomatium* is from the Greek *loma* ("a border or edge") and refers to the dorsal ribs of "wings" that adorn the seeds. *Martindalei* is for Isaac Martindale (1842–1893), an American who amassed a large private herbarium in the nineteenth century. The large root system stores nutrients and moisture to enable the plant to survive through long winters or drought. Also called Few-Fruited Lomatium.

BARESTEM BISCUITROOT
Lomatium nudicaule
Carrot Family (Apiaceae)

Description: Perennial. Pinnately compound leaves are divided into egg- to lance-shaped leaflets that are blue-green and borne on a long stem. The flowering stalk rises 10"–30" above the root crown and bears small flower clusters that branch outward from the top of the flowering stalk. Individual flower stalks are unequal in length. The small, yellow flowers emit a spicy aroma. Fruit is a seed.

Bloom Season: Early to mid spring

Habitat/Range: Grows in coastal or drier meadows, grasslands, shrub steppe, and forests on the east side of the Cascades at low to high elevations from southern Washington to California and east to Wyoming and Nevada.

Comments: *Lomatium* is from the Greek *loma* ("a border or edge") and refers to the dorsal ribs of "wings" that adorn the seeds. *Nudicaule* ("naked stem") refers to the leafless flowering stalk. The flowering stalk is swollen at the tip.

NINE-LEAF BISCUITROOT
Lomatium triternatum
Carrot Family (Apiaceae)

Description: Perennial, 1'–2' tall. Compound leaves dissected into 3 segments that are further divided into narrow, linear segments that are ½"–5" long. Flowers borne in small clusters combine to form larger, flat-topped clusters. Fruit is a flattened seed with papery wings and ribs.

Bloom Season: Late spring into early summer

Habitat/Range: Moist to dry sites, meadows and open slopes to low to mid elevations from British Columbia to California and east to Utah.

Comments: *Lomatium* is from the Greek *loma* ("a border or edge") and refers to the dorsal ribs of "wings" that adorn the seeds. *Triternatum* ("triply ternate") describes the highly divided leaves. This plant has several varieties and subspecies.

WESTERN SWEET CICELY
Osmorhiza occidentalis
Carrot Family (Apiaceae)

Description: Perennial, grows 1'–4' tall on smooth or hairy stems. Leaves are divided 1–3 times, and the lance- to egg-shaped leaflets are lobed and toothed along the margins. Entire blade is 4"–8" long. Flowering stalks lack leaves and terminate in umbrellalike clusters of tiny, green flowers. Fruit is a nail-like seed.

Bloom Season: Late spring to early summer

Habitat/Range: Moist meadows, mountain slopes, and forests at mid to high elevations from British Columbia to California and east to the Rocky Mountains.

Comments: *Osmorhiza* is from *osme* ("odor") and *rhiza* ("root") after the licorice aroma of the crushed roots. *Occidentalis* ("western") describes this plant's distribution. The crushed leaves also have a sweet aroma.

SKUNK CABBAGE
Lysichiton americanus
Arum/Calla-lily Family (Araceae)

Description: Perennial, which grows 1'–2½' tall. Huge, broadly lance-shaped or elliptical leaves grow in a basal rosette around a stout stem. The leaves may be 1'–4½' long and half again as wide. A bright, yellow hood partially surrounds the greenish-yellow flowering stalk (called a spadix) that bears numerous tiny, greenish-yellow flowers. The berrylike fruits are embedded in the flowering stalk.

Bloom Season: Early to late spring

Habitat/Range: Wet areas like swamps, bogs, moist forest areas, or fens at mid to lower elevations from Alaska to central California and east to Idaho.

Comments: *Lysichiton* is from the Greek *lysis* ("releasing") and *chiton* ("a cloak") and refers to the yellow hood that falls apart with age. *Americanus* ("from America") refers to the distribution of this North American species. The plant contains oxalate crystals that cause irritation and burning to the mouth and throat. Pacific Northwest natives ate the leaves, roasted or steamed, but only during desperate times. Bears eat the roots and deer may forage on the leaves. Pollinators include beetles, bees, and flies, and slugs will "pirate" the pollen.

HEARTLEAF ARNICA
Arnica cordifolia
Aster Family (Asteraceae)

Description: Perennial. The basal, heart-shaped leaves with toothed margins arise from the stem in an opposite arrangement. The upper leaves are broadly lance-shaped and toothed on the margins. The long flowering stalk (6"–20") arises above the leaves and bears a single yellow head. The 2"–3"-wide flower head has both ray and disk flower; the rays have shallowly notched tips. Fruit is a seed with white hairs.

Bloom Season: Early to midsummer

Habitat/Range: Widespread in moist, open woods in low to subalpine elevations across the region from Alaska to California often on the east side of the Cascades.

Comments: *Arnica* is from the Greek word *arnakis* ("lambskin") and refers to either the woolly bracts that subtend the flower heads or the leaves' hairy undersides. *Cordifolia* ("heart leaf") refers to the leaf shape. Arnicas are unique in this family due to the opposite leaves. Poultices and tinctures made from dried leaves are used as a disinfectant and to treat muscle strains and bruises.

RAYLESS ARNICA
Arnica discoidea
Aster Family (Asteraceae)

Description: Perennial. Plants arise from lateral roots just below the ground surface. Lower leaves are opposite, egg- to nearly heart-shaped, and arising on long stalks. The margins are irregularly toothed, and the blades are 2"–4" long. Upper leaves are smaller and lack a stalk. The flower heads are ½"–¾" wide, have numerous yellow disk flowers, and lack ray flowers. Fruit is a seed with white hairs.

Bloom Season: Summer

Habitat/Range: Open woods at mid elevations along the Cascades from Washington to California.

Comments: *Arnica* is from the Greek word *arnakis* ("lambskin") and refers to either the woolly bracts that subtend the flower heads or the leaves' hairy undersides. *Discoidea* ("without rays") refers to the rayless flower heads. Nodding Arnica (*A. parryi*) is similar but with drooping flower heads.

BROADLEAVED ARNICA
Arnica latifolia
Aster Family (Asteraceae)

Description: Perennial, up to 2½' long. Basal leaves on long stems, round to lance-shaped, and toothed along the margin. Few pairs of stem leaves are arranged oppositely and clasp the stem; the middle pair is often the largest. Flower heads borne in small clusters with 8–11 yellow ray flowers surrounding a center of brownish disk flowers. Fruit is a seed with light hairs.

Bloom Season: Summer

Habitat/Range: Forests, meadows, lakeshores, and stream banks at low to high elevations on both sides of the Cascades from Alaska to California and east to Montana.

Comments: *Arnica* is from the Greek word *arnakis* ("lambskin") and refers to either the woolly bracts that subtend the flower heads or the leaves' hairy undersides. *Latifolia* ("wide leaves") refers to the shape of the leaves.

SILVER WORMWOOD
Artemisia ludoviciana
Aster Family (Asteraceae)

Description: Perennial with upright stems, 12"–40" tall. Stem leaves are 1"–3" long, linear to lance-shaped, and grayish woolly on the upper surface and with white hairs on the underside. The lower leaves are variable and may be entire or lobed. The flowering heads are borne in a loose cluster; the small heads bear yellow disk flowers. Fruit is a smooth seed that lacks hairs.

Bloom Season: Late summer and fall

Habitat/Range: Dry and open sites from low to subalpine elevations throughout North America and into Mexico.

Comments: *Artemisia* commemorates Artemis, the Greek goddess of chastity. *Ludoviciana* ("of Louisiana") refers to the Louisiana Territory where Meriwether Lewis collected this plant in 1806 on his return journey to St. Louis. The crushed leaves are very fragrant.

BIG SAGEBRUSH
Artemisia tridentata
Aster Family (Asteraceae)

Description: Shrub, averaging 2'–7' tall, with stout trunk and shaggy bark. Leaves are silver-gray, hairy, wedge-shaped, ¼"–2" long, and 3- to 5-toothed at tips. Non-lobed leaves may appear in early winter. Flowering stems generally surpass vegetative branches and contain numerous side branches that bear dense clusters of tiny flower heads. Flowers have yellow to cream corollas. Seeds are tiny, black, and smooth.

Bloom Season: Summer to early fall

Habitat/Range: Sandy soils in the arid West from mid to high elevations. Often covers vast acreages with a mix of bunchgrasses, forbs, and other shrubs to form the sagebrush steppe.

Comments: *Artemisia* commemorates Artemis, the Greek goddess of chastity. *Tridentata* ("with 3 teeth") refers to the leaf tip. Big Sagebrush is a key species of the sagebrush steppe that covers vast acreage in the West of which many wildlife species are reliant upon for food or shelter. The state flower of Nevada.

DELTOID BALSAMROOT
Balsamorhiza deltoidea
Aster Family (Asteraceae)

Description: Perennial, clump-forming, up to 3' tall. Leaves are 8"–25" long and triangular or spear-shaped. Leaves and stems generally hairy and rough to the touch. Leaf margins are toothed. Flowering stalks, 6"–20" long, bear 1–3 flower heads comprised of 13–21 yellow ray flowers surrounding a center of disk flowers. Flowers 1"–2" wide. Fruit is a seed.

Bloom Season: Mid to late spring

Habitat/Range: Grassy slopes, open oak woodlands, and other dry, open areas from low to high elevations mainly west of the Cascades from central British Columbia to California.

Comments: *Balsamorhiza* ("balsam root") refers to the balsam-like aroma of the roots. *Deltoidea* ("deltoid") refers to the shape of the leaves. Carey's Balsamroot (*B. careyanna*) is similar but has thicker and veinier leaves.

ARROWLEAF BALSAMROOT
Balsamorhiza sagittata
Aster Family (Asteraceae)

Description: Perennials that grow ½'–2' tall and as wide or wider. Arrow-shaped leaves may be 10" long, 6" wide, and are smooth along the margin. The stout flowering stalk bears a 2"–4"-wide flower head with large, yellow ray and disk flowers. Fruit is a seed.

Bloom Season: Late spring to early summer

Habitat/Range: Drier areas in grasslands, sagebrush steppe, and woodlands from low to mid elevations from southern British Columbia to California and northern Arizona.

Comments: *Balsamorhiza* ("balsam root") refers to the balsam-like aroma of the roots. *Sagittata* ("arrow-shaped") refers to the leaf shape. Native Americans harvested the young shoots and roots of the plant in spring as food or medicine and collected the oily seeds in summer. Deer and elk browse on the leaves, and the flowers attract numerous types of pollinators.

SERRATE BALSAMROOT
Balsamorhiza serrata
Aster Family (Asteraceae)

Description: Perennial, 4"–12" tall. Basal leaves 3"–8" long, widely lance-shaped to oval, with soft hairs, and with wide lobes that have sawlike teeth; the lobes may be deep. Flower head is 1"–1½" wide, with yellow ray flowers surrounding a center of yellow disk flowers. Fruit is a seed with hairs.

Bloom Season: Mid to late spring

Habitat/Range: Shrub steppe, dry washes, and open forests at mid to high elevations east of the Cascades from northeast Washington to northern California and east to Nevada.

Comments: *Balsamorhiza* ("balsam root") refers to the balsam-like aroma of the roots. *Serrata* ("saw-toothed") refers to the shape of the leaves. Often hybridizes with Hooker's Balsamroot (*B. hookeri*).

SILVERCROWN
Cacaliopsis nardosmia
Aster Family (Asteraceae)

Description: Perennial, with stout stems 2'–4' tall. Roundish basal leaves have long stems, are 8"–10" wide, and resemble a deeply lobed maple leaf. Upper leaves fewer and smaller. Yellow flowers are borne in a dense cluster; the flower heads are ½"–1½" wide. Individual tubular disk flowers have paired stigmas that protrude above the flowers. Fruit is a seed with numerous white bristles.

Bloom Season: Early to midsummer

Habitat/Range: Open woods and meadows at mid to high elevations along the east side of the Cascades from Washington to Oregon.

Comments: *Cacaliopsis* ("*Cacalia*-like") is a reference to the similarity of this genus to *Cacalia*. *Nardosmia* ("spikenard smell") refers to the flowers having a fragrant aroma. Tongue-leaf Luina (*C. stricta*) has pale, yellow flowers, and the plants occur in subalpine meadows in the Cascades.

GOLDEN TICKSEED
Coreopsis tinctoria
Aster Family (Asteraceae)

Description: Annual or biennial with stems 1'–4' tall. The compound leaves have many linear leaflets. The flowering heads, 1"–2" wide, have yellowish ray flowers with a reddish-brown base surrounding a center of brownish disk flowers. Fruit is a black, winged seed, often with 2 dark projections.

Bloom Season: Midsummer to fall

Habitat/Range: Moist sites along streams at low elevations from Washington to Oregon and east to Idaho.

Comments: *Coreopsis* is from the Greek *koris* ("a bug") and *opsis,* indicating a resemblance to the tick-like seed. *Tinctoria* ("used in dyeing") refers to the yellowish-orange dye made from the flowers.

JOHN DAY PINCUSHION
Chaenactis nevii
Aster Family (Asteraceae)

Description: Annual, erect stems up to 12" tall. Compound leaves divided several times. Tight cluster of small, yellow disk flowers is arranged like a pincushion. Fruit is a seed.

Bloom Season: Spring

Habitat/Range: Dry grasslands, barren soil, and sagebrush steppe at mid elevations in north-central Oregon, particularly the John Day Valley.

Comments: *Chaenactis* is from *chaino* ("gape") and *actis* ("ray"). This name refers to the opening mouth of the tiny, disk flowers. *Nevii* is for Reuben Denton Nevius (1827–1913), an American missionary and botanist. During wet springs, this plant grows in abundance at the Painted Hills Unit of the John Day Fossil Beds National Monument.

GOLD STARS
Crocidium multicaule
Aster Family (Asteraceae)

Description: Annual, 3"–6" tall, and often multi-stemmed. The basal leaves are slightly fleshy and inversely lance-shaped, while the stem leaves are smaller. Woolly hairs grow between the leaf and the stem, and they often persist as the plant matures. Flower heads bear both yellow ray and disk flowers and are about ½" wide. Seed has thick hairs that become sticky when wet.

Bloom Season: Early spring

Habitat/Range: Dry, open fields, cliff edges, and sandy plains at low elevations from Vancouver Island to California.

Comments: *Crocidium* is derived from the Greek word *krose* or *krokys* ("wool or loose thread") and refers to the hairs growing in the leaf axils. *Multicaule* ("many stems") refers to the growth habit. Also called Spring Gold.

RUBBER RABBITBRUSH
Ericameria nauseosa
Aster Family (Asteraceae)

Description: Shrub, 2'–6' tall, with stems covered with dense hairs. Leaves are alternate and linear. Yellow flowers are borne in dense clusters of 5–20 disk flowers, the clusters often cloaking the plant. Fruit is a seed with fine hairs.

Bloom Season: Late summer to fall

Habitat/Range: Dry sites in sagebrush or open woodlands from low to mid elevations from southern British Columbia to California and east through Idaho.

Comments: *Ericameria* is from the Greek *Erica* ("heath") and *meris* ("division or part") in reference to the heath-like leaves. *Nauseosa* ("nauseating") refers to the plant's strong scent. Native Americans harvested the flowers in the late summer or fall for use as a yellow dye.

DESERT YELLOW FLEABANE
Erigeron linearis
Aster Family (Asteraceae)

Description: Perennial, 2"–12" tall with a cushion-like growth. The basal leaves are linear and 1"–4" long. Flower heads are borne singularly and bear 20 or more yellow ray flowers that surround a center of yellowish-orange disk flowers. The flower-head bracts have short hairs. Fruit is a seed with a tuft of white hairs.

Bloom Season: Late spring and early summer

Habitat/Range: Dry or rocky sites in sagebrush steppe or forests up to mid elevations east of the Cascades from British Columbia to northern Nevada.

Comments: *Erigeron* is from the Greek *eri* ("early") and *geron* ("old man"), referring to the white hairs on the seeds. *Linearis* ("linear") refers to the narrow, pencil-thin leaves. Also called Desert Yellow Fleabane.

OREGON SUNSHINE
Eriophyllum lanatum
Aster Family (Asteraceae)

Description: Perennial, 4"–24" tall, arises from multiple stems. Stems, leaves, and flower-head bracts are covered with dense, white hairs. Leaves are variable in shape, opposite or alternately arranged, and have 3–7 lobes at the tip. A single flower head (1"–2" wide) is borne on a long stalk and bears 7–15 yellow ray flowers that are about ¾" long. The ray flowers surround a cluster of darker-yellow disk flowers. Fruit is a smooth seed.

Bloom Season: Late spring to fall

Habitat/Range: Dry sites, meadows, and rocky slopes from sea level to subalpine areas mostly east of the Cascades from British Columbia to California and east to Montana.

Comments: *Eriophyllum* ("woolly leaf") and *lanatum* ("woolly") refer to the hairy nature of the plant. Another common name is Woolly Sunflower. Plants attract a wide variety of pollinators over the long blooming season.

BLANKET FLOWER
Gaillardia aristata
Aster Family (Asteraceae)

Description: Perennial, up to 3' tall. Leaves long-stemmed, up to 5" long, inversely lance-shaped, and lobed or toothed along the margin. Flower heads are 1"–3" wide, borne on long stalks, and bear up to a dozen deeply notched ray flowers surrounding a center of reddish-brown disk flowers. Wedge-shaped ray flowers are 1" long and 3-lobed at the tip. Fruit is a seed topped with stiff bristles.

Bloom Season: Summer

Habitat/Range: Dry or moist meadows, plains, and disturbed areas from mid elevations in southern British Columbia to northern Oregon on the east side of the Cascades.

Comments: *Gaillardia* honors Gaillard de Charentonneau, an eighteenth-century French magistrate and botanical patron. *Aristata* ("bearded") refers to the hairs that cover the receptacle.

PUGET SOUND GUMWEED
Grindelia integrifolia
Aster Family (Asteraceae)

Description: Many branched perennial that grows from 7"–40". Long, lance-shaped basal leaves and shorter, stalkless stem leaves have sticky glands. Flower heads are ½"–2" wide and bear yellow ray flowers surrounding a center of yellow disk flowers. Sticky, resin-coated, green bracts subtend the flowers. Seeds have multiple awns that fall off.

Bloom Season: Summer

Habitat/Range: Mostly coastal, found at beaches, rocky shorelines, salt marshes, and in low elevation noncoastal moist locations from Washington to Oregon.

Comments: Named after David Grindel (1776–1836), a Russian botanist. *Integrifolia* ("entire-leaved") refers to the smooth margins of the upper leaves, not the lower toothed ones.

COMMON SNEEZEWEED

Helenium autumnale
Aster Family (Asteraceae)

Description: Perennial, with angled stems, 7"–28"– tall. The numerous lance-shaped leaves are alternate and lack a stem. The flowering heads are somewhat spherical with yellow disk flowers surrounded by 10–20 yellow, 3-lobed ray flowers that project downward. The heads are ½"–1½" wide. Fruit is a seed with pointed scales.

Bloom Season: Late summer to fall

Habitat/Range: Widespread in moist locations at low elevations throughout the region.

Comments: *Helenium* is from *helinion*, a different plant named for Helen of Troy. *Autumnale* ("pertaining to autumn") refers to the blooming period of the flowers—late summer to fall. The flowers and green buds make a yellow dye. The flowers attract a variety of pollinators, including butterflies.

CURLYCUP GUMWEED

Grindelia squarrosa
Aster Family (Asteraceae)

Description: Perennial; grows up to 40" tall. The gray-green, inversely lance-shaped leaves are 1"–3" long, resinous, and sharply toothed or entire along the margin; when toothed, there is a yellow bump near the tip. Flower heads are 1"–2" wide and bear 12–40 ray flowers (occasionally fewer) that surround a center of tiny disk flowers. The bracts beneath the flower head are very resinous. Fruit is a seed.

Bloom Season: Summer

Habitat/Range: Often in disturbed sites along roads or streams from mid to high elevations east of the Cascades and into Idaho and Utah.

Comments: Named after David Grindel (1776–1836), a Russian botanist. *Squarrosa* ("having tips projecting at right angles") refers to the flower head's outward-curling bracts. The plant's resin has been used as a topical treatment for Poison Ivy.

CUSICK'S SUNFLOWER
Helianthus cusickii
Aster Family (Asteraceae)

Description: Perennial, with upright stems 1'–3' tall. Lance-shaped leaves are alternate, 2"–4" long, with short stems, and hairless; edges may be wavy. The flower heads bear mostly 8–13 (up to 21) yellow ray flowers surrounding a 1"-wide center of yellow disk flowers.

Bloom Season: Late spring to early summer

Habitat/Range: Open areas, foothills, shrub steppe at mid elevations on the east side of the Cascades from Washington to northern California.

Comments: *Helianthus* is from the Greek *helios* ("sun") and *anthos* ("flower"). *Cusickii* is for William C. Cusick (1842–1922), a self-taught, American botanist who collected plants in the Pacific Northwest. Living in eastern Oregon, Cusick learned from the minister-botanist Dr. Reuben Nevius how to document and collect plants for scientists such as Asa Gray at Harvard University.

HAIRY FALSE GOLDENASTER
Heterotheca villosa
Aster Family (Asteraceae)

Description: Perennial, generally sprawling but may grow erect to 20". Lower leaves wither before the flowers open, but the upper strap-shaped leaves do not. The yellow flower heads are about 1" wide and have 10–25 ray flowers that encircle numerous yellow disk flowers. The hairy bracts that subtend the flowering head are overlapping. Fruit is a seed.

Bloom Season: Summer

Habitat/Range: Dry, sandy ground or rocky sites from southern British Columbia throughout the Pacific Northwest.

Comments: *Heterotheca* is from *heteros* ("different") and *theke* ("ovary") for the different seeds that form from the ray and disk flowers. *Villosa* ("soft-haired") describes the fine hairs on the leaves and stems; hence, the common name reference.

DWARF ALPINEGOLD
Hulsea nana
Aster Family (Asteraceae)

Description: Low-growing perennial. Leaves mostly basal, hairy, and inversely lance-shaped with shallow lobes. Flower stalks bear a single, bell-shaped flower head with numerous yellow ray and disk flowers. The bracts that subtend the flower heads are numerous and in 2 or 3 rows. Fruit is a seed with stiff hairs.

Bloom Season: Mid to late summer

Habitat/Range: Subalpine to alpine elevations on cinder cones, pumice soils, and meadows from southern Washington to northern California, mainly in the Cascades, but found in other mountain ranges, as well.

Comments: *Hulsea* honors Dr. Gilbert White Hulse (1807–1883), a US Army surgeon and botanist. *Nana* ("dwarf") refers to the plant's low stature. These fragrant plants may bloom in profusion and attract late-season butterflies, bees, wasps, and flies as pollinators.

TANSY RAGWORT
Jacobaea vulgaris
Aster Family (Asteraceae)

Description: Biennial, stems 1'–6' tall. The stout stems bear numerous fernlike leaves, 2"–5" long, that are highly dissected and with toothed lobes. The upper leaves are smaller. The numerous flowering heads form a dense cluster at the top of the plant. Individual heads have 10–15 ray flowers surrounding a center of disk flowers. Fruit is a seed with numerous white hairs.

Bloom Season: Summer

Habitat/Range: Introduced from Europe, now found throughout North America mostly in disturbed sites.

Comments: *Jacobaea* honors St. James (Jacobus), whose saint's day is July 25 and coincides with the late-summer blooming period of this weed. *Vulgaris* ("common") refers to the plant being found a wide area. The plant contains a toxin that discourages wild or domestic herbivores and enables the plant to spread. Also called Stinking Willie; this plant was formerly in the *Senecio* genus.

SAGEBRUSH FALSE DANDELION
Nothocalais troximoides
Aster Family (Asteraceae)

Description: Perennial, low-growing. Basal leaves are long, up to 15", narrow, and have waxy or crisped margins. A solitary yellow flower head is borne at the end of a leafless stem and bears only ray flowers. The bracts below the flower clusters are more or less lance-shaped and may have dark spots. Fruit is a club-shaped seed that is not beaked and has numerous long, white hairs at the tip.

Bloom Season: Spring and early summer

Habitat/Range: Dry, open sagebrush steppe sites in the lowlands and foothills of western North America from eastern Washington to Montana and south to Utah.

Comments: *Nothocalais* is from the Greek *nothos* ("false") and *caulis* ("stem"), referring to the leafless flowering stalk that resembles a stem. The seed's long hairs act as a parachute, helping to disperse the seeds by the wind.

WOOLLY GROUNDSEL
Packera cana
Aster Family (Asteraceae)

Description: Perennial, plants 6"–18" tall with hairy stems. Basal leaves appear silvery due to numerous white hairs, are lance- to egg-shaped, and are 1"–2" long. The stem leaves are smaller and few. Flower heads are arranged in loose, flat-topped clusters; the heads have 5–8 (up to 13) yellow ray flowers surrounding a yellowish center of disk flowers. The bracts below the flowering heads have black tips. The fruit is a ribbed seed with white hairs.

Bloom Season: Early summer

Habitat/Range: Found in a variety of sites from low to subalpine elevations in western and central North America.

Comments: *Packera* honors John G. Packer, professor emeritus at the University of Alberta, who studied the origin and evolution of Arctic flora. *Cana* ("off-white") refers to the silvery appearance of the leaves.

SILVERY RAILLARDELLA
Raillardella argentea
Aster Family (Asteraceae)

Description: Perennial, low-growing. Basal leaves are 1"–2½" long, grayish green because of the numerous fine hairs. The flowering stalks are ½"–6" long and bear a single flowering head of yellow disk flowers. The bracts below the flowering head are almost equal in length and end with a pointed tip. The fruit is a flattened seed with stiff hairs at the tip.

Bloom Season: Mid to late summer

Habitat/Range: Open woodlands or bare ground in subalpine to alpine areas from central Oregon to northern California.

Comments: *Raillardella* is similar to *Raillardia* and indicates this plant's similarity to that genus. *Argentea* ("silvery") refers to the coloration of the leaves. The plant may spread by underground roots creating dense mats. Small butterflies and other insects are attracted to the plants for their nectar or pollen.

CALIFORNIA CONEFLOWER
Rudbeckia californica
Aster Family (Asteraceae)

Description: Perennial, with stout stems growing to 6' tall. Basal leaves are lance-shaped to elliptical, up to 12" long, and smooth along the edges or possibly with lobes. Flower head is an elongated cluster with several yellow ray flowers at the base; the petals extend back and downward. The cylindrical head of greenish-yellow disk flowers may be 2½" long. Fruit is a seed topped with small scales.

Bloom Season: Mid to late summer

Habitat/Range: Moist meadows, seeps, bogs, fens, and along streams at mid elevations in southern Oregon and northern California.

Comments: *Rudbeckia* is for Olof Rudbeck the Younger (1660–1740), who appointed Carl von Linnaeus as botany lecturer and head of botany demonstrations at Uppsala University in Sweden. *Californica* ("of California") describes the type locality. Bees and butterflies are the primary pollinators of these flowers.

DWARF MOUNTAIN RAGWORT
Senecio fremontii
Aster Family (Asteraceae)

Description: Perennial, low-growing in clumps or mats from 3"–6". Highly branched stems bear succulent lance- or spoon-shaped leaves that are lobed and deeply incised. Flower heads borne on short stems with 8 ray flowers surrounding a center of disk flowers. The ray flowers often curl backward. Fruit is a seed with hairs.

Bloom Season: Late spring to midsummer

Habitat/Range: Rocky slopes and flats at high elevations from British Columbia to California and east to the Rocky Mountains.

Comments: *Senecio* is from the Latin *senex* ("old man") and refers to the white hairs atop the seeds. *Fremontii* is for John Charles Fremont (1813–1890), an explorer, US topographical engineer, one-time candidate for president, and collector who explored vast areas of the West.

LAMBSTONGUE RAGWORT
Senecio integerriums
Aster Family (Asteraceae)

Description: Biennial or perennial with a single stem that grows 6"–35" tall. Linear to lance-shaped leaves are up to 12" long and are slightly hairy. Flower heads are borne in a flat-topped cluster of several heads. Eight to 13 ray flowers, yellow to white in color, surround a small center of numerous disk flowers. Some flower heads lack ray flowers. Fruit is a seed with hairs.

Bloom Season: Late spring to midsummer

Habitat/Range: Grows in moist areas in sagebrush steppe, oak or spruce woodlands, and in montane meadows from mid to subalpine elevations throughout western Canada and the western United States.

Comments: *Senecio* is from the Latin *senex* ("old man") and refers to the white hairs atop the seeds. *Integerrimus* ("entire," "whole," or "complete") refers to either the smooth margins of the leaves or the compact flower heads. Young plants are very hairy, but the hair drops off as the plant matures.

ARROWLEAF GROUNDSEL
Senecio triangularis
Aster Family (Asteraceae)

Description: Perennial; cluster of tall stems rise up to 5'. Arrow-shaped leaves are 2"–8" long, alternately arranged along the stem, strongly toothed, and more or less hairless. Flower heads bear few to 8 ray flowers that are toothed at the tip; ray flowers surround a small but dense cluster of disk flowers. Fruit is a seed.

Bloom Season: Late spring to midsummer

Habitat/Range: Grows in moist meadows, stream banks, thickets, and open forests from mid to alpine elevations throughout western Canada and the western United States.

Comments: *Senecio* is from the Latin *senex* ("old man") and refers to the white hairs atop the seeds. *Triangularis* ("triangle-shaped") refers to the shape of the leaves.

WESTERN CANADA GOLDENROD
Solidago lepida
Aster Family (Asteraceae)

Description: Perennial, tall stems grow 1'–5' tall and are hairy above and smooth on the lower half. Basal leaves wither early, and stem leaves are linear to lance-shaped, 2"–7" long, and either sharply toothed or smooth along the edges. Flower heads are borne in a dense, branching cluster, bearing small ray flowers surrounding a center of disk flowers. Fruit is a small seed.

Bloom Season: Midsummer to fall

Habitat/Range: From British Columbia to California on both sides of the Cascades and across much of the western United States.

Comments: *Solidago* is from *solidus* ("whole") and *ago* ("to make"), which is in reference to the medicinal properties of goldenrod. Goldenrods attract a variety of pollinators such as butterflies, moths, native bees, and honey bees.

STEMLESS GOLDENWEED
Stenotus acaulis
Aster Family (Asteraceae)

Description: Perennial, mat-forming or low-growing. Lance-shaped leaves are 1"–4" long, with stiff hairs along the edge. Flower heads solitary or in a cluster of several heads and contain 6–15, ½"-long yellow ray flowers surrounding a center of yellow disk flowers. Flower heads are about 1½" wide. Fruit is a seed with hairs.

Bloom Season: Late spring through summer

Habitat/Range: Rocky soils and ledges in sage-brush steppe and mountain brush at mid to high elevations across much of the western United States.

Comments: *Stenotus* is from the Greek *stenos* ("narrow"), which refers to the leaves. *Acaulis* ("stemless") refers to the flowering heads' very short stems. Also known as Stemless Mock Goldenweed.

YELLOW SALSIFY
Tragopogon dubius
Aster Family (Asteraceae)

Description: Annual or biennial with a stout, 1'–2' stem. Leaves are long and grasslike. Flower heads are 1½"–3" wide and have numerous lemon-yellow ray flowers with long and pointed flower-head bracts extending beyond the ray flowers. The seed heads are round, and the seeds are topped with stiff hairs.

Bloom Season: Summer

Habitat/Range: Widespread in disturbed sites throughout the region but more common east of the Cascades.

Comments: *Tragopogon* ("goat's beard") may refer to the silky hairs on the seeds resembling those of a goat's beard. *Dubius* ("doubtful") has an unclear meaning. The derivation of salsify translates to "sun follower," although the flowers may close during the day or on cloudy days. The roots, eaten raw or steamed, have a flavor similar to oysters; hence, another common name is Oyster Plant.

NORTHERN MULE'S EARS
Wyethia amplexicaulis
Aster Family (Asteraceae)

Description: Often growing in profusion, the plants may be 1'–2' tall. Basal, lance-shaped leaves are 12"–15" long and very glossy. Stem leaves are smaller. Yellow flowers have both ray and disk flowers and are 2"–3" wide. Fruit is a seed.

Bloom Season: Late spring

Habitat/Range: Grows in open meadows in mid to higher elevations east of the Cascades in Washington and Oregon.

Comments: *Wyethia* is for Nathaniel Wyeth (1802–1856), the "Cambridge Iceman" who led 2 expeditions to Oregon in 1832 and 1834, during which time he collected some plants. Wyeth was the first American to travel to the Northwest along the route that would later become the Oregon Trail. *Amplexicaulis* ("stem-clasping") refers to the leaves, which lack petioles.

TALL OREGON GRAPE
Berberis aquifolium
Berberis/Vancouveria Family (Berberidaceae)

Description: Shrub, 2'–4' tall. The holly-like compound leaflets have 5–11 evergreen leaves that are saw-toothed and spiny along the margin. Yellow flowers are borne in dense clusters. The petals are 2-lobed. The grapelike fruits are bluish.

Bloom Season: Spring

Habitat/Range: Both sides of the Cascades from British Columbia to Oregon and east to Idaho in forests or sagebrush steppe.

Comments: Originally placed in the genus *Mahonia*, named after Bernard McMahon (1775–1816), a Philadelphia nurseryman who grew the plant from seeds brought back east by Meriwether Lewis, the name changed to *Berberis. Aquifolium* ("shiny leaves") describes the leaf surface. This is the state flower of Oregon. The fruits make a blue dye and the roots a yellow dye.

CASCADE OREGON GRAPE
Berberis nervosa
Berberis/Vancouveria Family (Berberidaceae)

Description: Shrub, low-growing up to 2' tall. Compound leaves have 11–19 evergreen leaflets that have spiny margins. The broadly lance-shaped leaflets are up to 3" long. Flowers borne in a dense cluster that may be 8" long. Yellow flowers have similar sepals and petals that are arranged in whorls. The stamens are attached to the inner petals. Fruit is a blue to purple berry.

Bloom Season: Late spring to midsummer

Habitat/Range: Woodlands from low to mid elevations from British Columbia to central California.

Comments: *Berberis* originates from the Arabian name for the fruit. *Nervosa* ("conspicuous nerves") refers to the prominent leaf veins. When an insect lands in the center of the flower, the stamens collapse inward and dust the insect with pollen. Native tribes (as well as wildlife) ate the fruits, and a yellow dye was made from the roots.

MENZIES' FIDDLENECK
Amsinckia menziesii
Borage Family (Boraginaceae)

Description: Annual, stems 7"–35" tall. Stems, leaves, and flowers have stiff hairs. Linear leaves are ¾"–1½" long. Small, yellow-orange flowers arranged in a coiled or scorpion tail-like pattern. The fused petals form a flaring collar and a short tube. Fruit is a small nutlet.

Bloom Season: Spring

Habitat/Range: Grasslands and dry disturbed sites mostly east of the Cascades and at low elevations.

Comments: *Amsinckia* honors Wilhelm Amsinck (1752–1831), a patron of the Botanical Garden in Hamburg, Germany. *Menziesii* honors Archibald Menzies (1754–1842), a Scottish physician and naturalist who accompanied Captain George Vancouver on his 1790–1795 Pacific exploration. The common name is after the coiled spike of flowers, which resemble a fiddle's neck.

WESTERN STONESEED
Lithospermum ruderale
Borage Family (Boraginaceae)

Description: Perennial with clustered stems that may grow up to 30" tall. Leaves and stems are covered with short, stiff hairs. The leaves seem to crowd out the flowers. The small, funnel-shaped flowers are a pale yellow, ½" wide, and flare open at the end. Fruit is a nutlet.

Bloom Season: Late spring to early summer

Habitat/Range: Dry grassland or forests from low to mid elevations from British Columbia to northern California and east to Colorado.

Comments: *Lithospermum* is from the Greek words *lithos* ("stone") and *sperma* ("seed") and refers to the smooth, stonelike seed. *Ruderale* ("growing in waste places") refers to the habitat conditions where these plants may occur. The fragrant flowers attract butterflies as pollinators. California Gromwell (*L. californicum*) occurs in extreme southwestern Oregon.

NORTHERN WALLFLOWER
Erysimum capitatum
Mustard Family (Brassicaceae)

Description: Biennial, stout stems, 6"–36" tall. Leaves linear, rough textured, up to 5" long, and covered with fine hairs. Flowers borne in dense terminal clusters are yellow and 4-petaled. Petals are ½" long and arranged in a cross pattern. Fruit is a slender pod, 1"–4" long.

Bloom Season: Late spring to midsummer

Habitat/Range: Dry, sandy areas east of the Cascades at low to mid elevations from British Columbia to California and east to Texas.

Comments: *Erysimum* is from the Greek *erysio* ("to draw") after a species that was used medicinally as a poultice to induce skin blisters and draw out pain. *Capitatum* ("dense head") refers to the flowers. Sand Dwelling Wallflower (*E. perenne*) is similar and occurs in southwestern Oregon.

PLAINS PRICKLYPEAR
Opuntia polyacantha
Cactus Family (Cactaceae)

Description: Perennial, with jointed stems. Flattened stems are fleshy, straight-spined, and variable in size. Showy flowers are 3"–6" across with numerous yellow to red petals surrounding many stamens. Fruit is a spiny, many-seeded berry.

Bloom Season: Mid spring to early summer

Habitat/Range: Dry, open ground in grasslands, plains, and sagebrush steppe from low to mid elevations throughout the drier portions of the western United States.

Comments: *Opuntia* is the Greek name for a different plant growing near the ancient Greek town of Opus. *Polyacantha* ("with many thorns") describes the stems. The green stems contain chlorophyll pigments necessary for photosynthesis. The edible fruits are sweet, and the stems were also eaten with the spines burned off.

TWINBERRY HONEYSUCKLE
Lonicera involucrata
Honeysuckle Family (Caprifoliaceae)

Description: Shrub, plants mostly 3'–7' (up to 12') tall. Opposite leaves are elliptical and pointed at the tip. Yellow flowers are borne in pairs in leaf axils. The tube-shaped flowers are ½"–1" long and have two sticky, leaflike bracts at their bases. These bracts change from green to red or purple with age. Fruit is a black, round berry.

Bloom Season: Spring

Habitat t/Range: Moist woods, stream banks, and clearings from sea level to subalpine elevations across much of western North America.

Comments: *Lonicera* honors Adam Lonitzer (1528–1586), a German herbalist. *Involucrata* ("with an involucre") refers to the conspicuous floral bracts. The bitter fruit has been reported as both edible and poisonous. The dark berries were used as a dye by some coastal tribes; hence, it is also called Ink-Berry or Bush Honeysuckle.

PACIFIC STONECROP
Sedum divergens
Stonecrop Family (Crassulaceae)

Description: Perennial, mat-forming with flowering stems 2"–6" tall. The fleshy leaves are opposite, egg-shaped, ⅛"–½" wide, and are green to red in color. The flowering stalks bear clusters of yellow flowers that have long, pointed petals. The flowers are ¼"–1" wide. Fruit is a pod.

Bloom Season: Summer

Habitat/Range: Rocky outcrops and talus slopes in coastal or subalpine to alpine elevations from southern British Columbia to Oregon.

Comments: *Sedum* is from the Lain *sedo* ("to sit"), referring to the low-growing nature of the plants on rocky outcrops. *Divergens* ("spreading") refers to the outstretched petals.

GOLDEN BEE PLANT
Peritoma platycarpa
Bee-Plant Family (Cleomaceae)

Description: Annual, grows 6"–36" tall. Green stems are tinted purple and covered with sticky hairs. Compound leaves, 2" long, are divided into 3 leaflets. Yellow flowers are borne in tight clusters, with 4 sepals, 4 petals, and 6 stamens that protrude above the petals. Fruit is a flat, hairy seedpod that hangs downward.

Bloom Season: Late spring to early summer

Habitat/Range: Grows in alkaline, volcanic soils in dry shrub steppe habitats at mid elevations from northwestern California to Idaho.

Comments: *Peritoma* is from a Greek word meaning "cut around" and refers to the circular splitting of the calyx base. *Platycarpa* is from the Greek *platy* ("broad") and *karpon* ("a nut"), referring to the fruits.

CREAM STONECROP
Sedum oregonense
Stonecrop Family (Crassulaceae)

Description: Perennial, mat-forming with succulent leaves that are inversely egg-shaped (widest above the midline) and form a basal rosette from which the flowering stalk arises. Stem is up to 8" tall, and egg- to spatula-shaped succulent leaves are up to 1½" long. Leaves have a bluish cast and a slight notch at the tip. The reddish flowering stalk bears cream to pale-yellow flowers with red-tinged or white-speckled undersides and pointed tips in dense clusters. Fruit is a many-seeded pod.

Bloom Season: Mid to late summer

Habitat/Range: Rocky ledges, talus slopes, and gravelly areas at mid elevations in the Oregon Cascades and into northern California.

Comments: *Sedum* is from the Latin *sedo* ("to sit"), referring to the low-growing nature of the plants on rocky outcrops. *Oregonense* ("of Oregon") refers to the plant growing primarily in Oregon.

PINESAP
Monotropa hypopitys
Heather Family (Ericaceae)

Description: Saprophyte. Reddish stems 8"–15" tall. The scalelike leaves lack chlorophyll. The yellowish-brown, ½"–1"-long flowers are borne in dense clusters, and the flowers hang slightly downward. Fruit is a capsule.

Bloom Season: Summer

Habitat/Range: Moist, forest humus from low to subalpine elevations throughout the region. Also occurs in Europe.

Comments: *Monotropa* ("one direction") refers to the flowers facing the same direction. *Hypopitys* is from the Greek *hypo* ("under") and *pitys* ("pine tree"), in reference to its habit of growing below pine or coniferous trees. The plant derives nutrients from soil fungi associated with their roots. Blooms turn black when mature.

SEASIDE BIRD'S-FOOT TREFOIL
Hosackia gracilis
Pea Family (Fabaceae)

Description: Perennial with upright or spreading stems. Compound leaves, about ¾" long, borne on long stems, leaflets 3–7, arranged oppositely, ¼" long, and egg-shaped. Pea-shaped flowers with a bright-yellow upper petal (banner) and pink or white flower petals (wings). Fruit is a pod.

Bloom Season: Spring to midsummer

Habitat/Range: Shoreline, meadows, disturbed areas, ditches, and sea cliffs at low elevations from British Columbia to California along the coast.

Comments: *Hosackia* honors David Hosack (1769–1835), an American botanist, physician, and educator. He may be best known for treating Alexander Hamilton after his ill-fated duel with Aaron Burr in 1804. *Gracilis* ("graceful") refers to plant's stature.

WOODLAND PINEDROPS
Pterospora andromedea
Heather Family (Ericaceae)

Description: Saprophyte. One to several reddish-brown stems arise 6"–36" tall. The scalelike leaves are reddish brown and basal. The top of the plant is a dense cluster of small, urn-shaped flowers that are yellowish brown and hang downward on short stalks. Fruit is a round capsule.

Bloom Season: Summer

Habitat/Range: Found east of the Cascades in dry pine woodlands, this plant ranges from Alaska to Mexico and east to the Rocky Mountains.

Comments: *Pterospora* ("winged seeds") describes the seeds, and *andromedea* ("Andromeda") is named after the mythical maiden chained to a rock and rescued by Perseus. Like other saprophytes, this plant derives its nutrients from fungi associated with its roots.

MEADOW BIRD'S-FOOT TREFOIL
Hosackia pinnata
Pea Family (Fabaceae)

Description: Perennial, often with sprawling stems, 8"–19" long. Compound leaves borne on short stems, with 5–7 oval to elliptical leaflets. Yellow flowers are borne in small clusters, the pealike flowers have a yellow upper petal (banner) that bends backward, and white petals that form the keel. Fruit is a small pod.

Bloom Season: Late spring to early summer

Habitat/Range: Moist areas, including wetlands that dry out seasonally, at mid elevations from British Columbia to California, mostly west of the Cascades.

Comments: *Hosackia* honors David Hosack (1769–1835), an American botanist, physician, and educator. He may be best known for treating Alexander Hamilton after his ill-fated duel with Aaron Burr in 1804. *Pinnata* ("feather-like") may refer to the pinnately compound leaves.

YELLOW BUSH LUPINE
Lupinus arboreus
Pea Family (Fabacaeae)

Description: Shrubs, green or silvery in appearance that grow up to 6' tall. Stem leaves arise on 1"–2" long stalks and are palmately divided into 5–12 leaflets. Pea-shaped flowers are borne in an elongated arrangement, 4"–12" long; each flower is about ½" long. Fruit is a pod.

Bloom Season: Spring and summer

Habitat/Range: Coastal in sandy soils or stream banks and marshes at low elevations. Native to California but introduced into the rest of the Northwest.

Comments: *Lupinus* is from lupus ("wolf"), which refers to the misconception that the plant "wolfs" nutrients from the soil. Most lupines have root nodules that fix nitrogen for uptake by plants. *Arboreus* ("treelike") refers to the plant's woody growth.

SLENDER GOLDENBANNER
Thermopsis montana
Pea Family (Fabaceae)

Description: Perennial, erect stems arise 1'–2' and bear numerous compound leaves with 3 smooth, broadly egg-shaped leaflets 2"–4" long. Yellow, pea-shaped flowers are borne in a dense, elongated spike of 5–50 flowers, with each flower about 1" long. Fruit is a straight, upright seedpod that is slightly hairy.

Bloom Season: Late spring to early summer

Habitat/Range: Meadows and moist sites from low to mid elevations from British Columbia to California and east to the Rocky Mountains.

Comments: *Thermopsis* ("resembling a lupine") and *montana* ("of mountains") refer to the habitat this plant is most likely found in. This plant is unpalatable to livestock; therefore, it may grow in dense clusters.

COMMON GORSE
Ulex europaeus
Pea Family (Fabaceae)

Description: Naturalized evergreen shrub that grows 7'–10' tall with rigid, spine-tipped branches. Leaves modified into green spines ⅓"–1½" long. Yellow, pea-shaped flowers are ⅓"–1" long. Fruit is a dark purplish-brown seedpod about ¾"–1" long.

Bloom Season: Generally winter through summer, but may be found in bloom throughout the year.

Habitat/Range: Native to Europe, Gorse grows in disturbed sites and open slopes along the coast and inland, mainly west of the Cascades from British Columbia to California.

Comments: *Ulex* is the Latin name for this plant. *Europaeus* ("of Europe") describes the distribution of this plant. A fire-adapted species that burns easily but sprouts from the roots. The seeds can remain viable in the soil for over 30 years, and they will sprout after a fire.

GOLDEN CURRANT
Ribes aureum
Currant Family (Grossulariaceae)

Description: Shrub, 2'–10' tall with smooth stems. Leaves are 3-lobed, leathery, and ¾"–1½" long. The bright-yellow flowers are borne in clusters of 5–18, are trumpet-shaped with a long tube and 5 flaring lobes. Fruit is an orange, yellow, red, or black berry.

Bloom Season: Mid spring

Habitat/Range: Moist sites along streams, washes, and rivers from low to mid elevations, in grasslands up to ponderosa pine forests, from east of the Cascades from British Columbia to California and east to the Rocky Mountains.

Comments: *Ribes* is derived from the Arabic *ribas* ("acid-tasting") after the bitterness of the edible fruits. *Aureum* ("golden") refers to the flower color. Meriwether Lewis wrote that the yellow currants are "transparent as the red currant of our gardens, not so ascid, and more agreeably favord." The Northwest natives ate the berries, which are also consumed by birds and wildlife.

COMMON ST. JOHN'S WORT
Hypericum perforatum
St. John's Wort Family (Hypericaceae)

Description: Perennial, 1'–3' tall, often growing in abundance. Round stems are light green and bear opposite leaves that are oblong and about 1" long; the leaf surface is perforated by translucent dots, and black dots may be present along the edges. Yellow flowers are ½"–¾" wide with 5 petals, 3 styles, and numerous stamens. The petals also have black dots. Fruit is a capsule.

Bloom Season: Summer

Habitat/Range: An introduced plant from Europe and Eurasia that grows in disturbed areas at low to mid elevations throughout the region.

Comments: *Hypericum* is the plant's ancient Greek name. *Perforatum* ("perforated") refers to the dots on the leaves and petals. Used medicinally by the ancient Greeks and modern herbalists to treat anxiety, depression, and abrasions.

COMMON BLADDERWORT
Utricularia vulgaris
Bladderwort Family (Lentibulariaceae)

Description: Aquatic, carnivorous perennial without roots. Stems may reach 3' or longer. Compound leaves are finely divided, ½"–3½" long, and have bladderlike sacs to capture invertebrates. Leaf margins have non-green bristles. Flowering stalk rises above the water and has several, 1"-wide flowers. The spur-shaped flowers are yellow with 5 fused petals that form an upper and lower lip and 2 stamens. Fruit is a many-seeded capsule.

Bloom Season: Summer

Habitat/Range: Ponds, marshes, and edges of lakes at mid to high elevations throughout the region and worldwide.

Comments: *Utricularia* ("little bladder") refers to the inflated sacs that trap prey. *Vulgaris* ("common") refers to the abundance of these insectivorous plants worldwide.

YELLOW AVALANCHE LILY
Erythronium grandiflorum
Lily Family (Liliaceae)

Description: Perennial that grows 6"–15" tall. The large, non-mottled basal leaves are arranged in pairs and clasp the flowering stem base. Atop the leafless, flowering stem is a single (sometimes in pairs) golden-yellow flower that hangs downward. The 6 tepals curve upward, while the large, yellow stamens protrude downward. The 1"-long, club-shaped capsules contain papery seeds.

Bloom Season: Late spring to midsummer

Habitat/Range: Moist areas such as meadows or avalanche paths at mid to alpine elevations from Washington to Oregon and east to the Rocky Mountains.

Comments: *Erythronium* is from the Greek *erythros* ("red") in reference to the pink or red flowers of some species. *Grandiflorum* ("large-flowered") refers to the flower's size. Plants may bloom near edges of snowfields or glaciers; hence, the common name. The plants are able to photosynthesize under the snow, and often, the leaves and buds push up through the snow. Also called Glacier Lily.

YELLOW BELL
Fritillaria pudica
Lily Family (Liliaceae)

Description: Perennial that grows 4"–12" high from a small, white bulb. The stem bears 2–6 narrow, strap-like leaves, ½"–6" long. Flowering stalk bears 1–3 yellow, bell-shaped flowers that hang downward. Flowers have 6 tepals. Fruit is a round or egg-shaped capsule.

Bloom Season: Early to late spring

Habitat/Range: Dry grasslands, woodlands, and open meadows at low elevations from British Columbia to California and east to Alberta.

Comments: *Fritillaria* is from the Latin *fritillus* ("a dice box"), which refers to the capsules. *Pudica* ("bashful") refers to the pendulous flowers. Lewis and Clark noted that the local Northwest tribes collected and ate the onion-like bulbs. Bees, flies, and beetles pollinate the early-season flowers.

GREAT BLAZING-STAR
Mentzelia laevicaulis
Blazing-star Family (Loasaceae)

Description: Perennial or biennial, up to 3' tall. Stems are many branched and white. The basal leaves are lance-shaped, up to 4" long, toothed along the margin, and rough-textured. Starlike, yellow flowers are 2"–3" wide, with 5 pointed petals and a short, green bract between the petals. Numerous threadlike stamens project above the flower. Fruit is a capsule with tiny, black seeds.

Bloom Season: Summer and early fall

Habitat/Range: Often in sandy or gravelly soils in dry sites at lower elevations east of the Cascades.

Comments: *Mentzelia* is for Christian Mentzel (1622–1701), a German botanist and physician. *Laevicaulis* ("smooth stem") describes the texture of the stem. The flowers open in the evening and close in the morning until the petals mature; afterward, the flowers remain open. David Douglas (1799–1834) first recorded this species along the Columbia River.

YELLOW SAND VERBENA
Abronia latifolia
Verbena/Four-O'Clock Family (Nyctaginaceae)

Description: Low-growing perennial with prostrate stems up to 3' long. Stems have sticky hairs. Leaf blades are round to kidney- or oval-shaped and are oppositely arranged along the stems. Flower heads contain several to many tubular, ½"-long yellow flowers that flare open at the mouth. Fruits are cylindrical seeds adorned with thick, keel-like projections.

Bloom Season: Mid to late summer

Habitat/Range: Coastal sand dunes and beaches from British Columbia to northern California.

Comments: *Abronia* is from the Greek *abros* ("delicate or graceful"), which describes the bracts below the fragrant, slim flowers. *Latifolia* ("broad leaves") refers to the leaf shape. Sand grains adhere to the sticky hairs on the stems and leaves; hence, the common name. Shifting sands may bury portions of the plant, sometimes giving the appearance that the flowers are sprouting from the sand. Pink Sand Verbena (*A. umbellata*) has pinkish flowers.

YELLOW POND-LILY
Nuphar polysepala
Water Lilies Family (Nymphaeaceae)

Description: An aquatic perennial, the egg- to heart-shaped leaf blades are 6"–22" long and float on the water surface. Yellow flowers are 2" across and made of inconspicuous petals and small, outer, green sepals. The larger, inner sepals are yellow but may have a purple or greenish tinge. Center of the flower is a large knob-like and long-stalked stigma. The fruit is an oval, ribbed capsule that releases seeds in a jellylike mass when mature.

Bloom Season: Late spring and summer

Habitat/Range: Ponds or standing water from low to mid elevations on both sides of the Cascades from Alaska to California and east to New Mexico.

Comments: *Nuphar* is from the Arabic word *naufar*, a name for a water lily. *Polysepala* ("many sepals") refers to the flowers. Many Northwest tribes used the root for medicinal purposes and ate the seeds. Caddis flies and beetles are attracted to the flower's nectar. Also called Wokas or Wocus.

HOOKER'S EVENING PRIMROSE
Oenothera elata
Evening-Primrose Family (Onagraceae)

Description: Tall biennial that grows 1'–5' tall. Leaves are lance-shaped and smaller toward the top of the flowering stalk. The bright-yellow flowers are 2"–4" wide, with 4 slightly notched petals and 8 protruding stamens. The fruit is a capsule that splits open longitudinally when mature.

Bloom Season: Summer

Habitat/Range: Moist areas such as stream banks, springs, open meadows, and disturbed sites throughout the region.

Comments: *Oenothera* ("wine-scented") refers to the roots being added to the process of winemaking. *Elata* ("tall") refers to the plant's stature. The flowers open in the evening to attract hawk moths or sphinx moths as pollinators. Also called Giant Evening Primrose.

TANSYLEAF EVENING-PRIMROSE
Taraxia tanacetifolia
Evening-Primrose Family (Onagraceae)

Description: Perennial, lacks a stem, and is low-growing. Long leaves are highly lobed or divided; the leaves are 4" long. Yellow flowers, 1"–2" wide, arise from a basal cluster of leaves and have 4 petals and long tubes. The 4 sepals turn backward as the flower matures. Fruit is a capsule.

Bloom Season: Early summer

Habitat/Range: Grasslands, shrublands, or meadows in pine woodlands that are seasonally moist. Generally found at lower elevations east of the Cascades from Washington to northern California and east to Idaho and Montana.

Comments: *Taraxia* is from a Greek *taraxia* ("eye disorder"). *Tanacetifolia* ("tansy-leaved") refers to the tansy-like leaves.

PALE PAINTBRUSH
Castilleja oresbia
Broomrape/Paintbrush Family (Orobanchaceae)

Description: Perennial, 6"–12" tall with upright, hairy stems. Basal leaves linear, ¼"–1¼" long, smooth along the edges, and pointed at the tip. Upper leaves divided into 2–3 lobes. Pale-yellow or purplish flower bracts are divided into narrow lobes and are shorter than the leaves. Flowers are pale yellow to pink with a short, narrow beak. Fruit is a seed.

Bloom Season: Late spring to early summer

Habitat/Range: Open ridges, sagebrush steppe, and meadows at high elevations in northeastern Oregon and western Idaho.

Comments: *Castilleja* is for Domingo Castillejo (1744–1793), a Spanish professor of botany. *Oresbia* ("living in or on mountains") refers to the plant's growing location. Also called Pale Wallowa Paintbrush after its distribution in the Wallowa Mountains of northeast Oregon.

PARROTHEAD INDIAN PAINTBRUSH
Castilleja pilosa
Broomrape/Paintbrush Family (Orobanchaceae)

Description: Perennial, 6"–18" tall. Stems and leaves hairy. The linear or lance-shaped leaves are either lobed or entire. Flowers are borne on a stalk, 1"–8" long. Pale-yellow to pinkish flowers form a short tube and have 3-lobed greenish to purple leafy bracts with white edges. Fruit is a capsule.

Bloom Season: Summer

Habitat/Range: Dry meadows and grasslands in sagebrush steppe areas from mid to high elevations from eastern Oregon to northern California and Nevada.

Comments: *Castilleja* is for Domingo Castillejo (1744–1793), a Spanish professor of botany. *Pilosa* ("covered with downy hair") describes the hairy stems and leaves. A highly variable species, but one that grows in abundance.

BRACTED LOUSEWORT
Pedicularis bracteosa
Broomrape/Paintbrush Family (Orobanchaceae)

Description: Perennial, often 2'–3' tall. The divided, fernlike leaves are 1"–5" long and have saw-toothed edges. Flowers arise in a dense, elongated cluster at the end of the flowering stalk. Individual flowers are yellowish to brownish red or purple and have an upper lip that forms a hood and a leaflike bract at their base. The hood may or may not have a short beak. Fruit is a curved capsule.

Bloom Season: Summer

Habitat/Range: Thickets, meadows, forest edges, or open forests from mid to alpine elevations throughout western North America.

Comments: *Pedicularis* ("relating to lice") refers to the old belief that grazing livestock became plagued with lice after foraging in fields with a European species of *Pedicularis*. *Bracteosa* ("with well-developed bracts") refers to the flower's leaf-like bracts. Also called Wood Betony or Fernleaf.

GOLDEN CORYDALIS
Corydalis aurea
Poppy/Dicentra Family (Papaveraceae)

Description: Perennial but low-growing. Leaves are highly divided into narrow segments. Yellow flowers borne in small clusters; each flower is narrow but bilaterally symmetrical and is made up of 4 petals with a spur at the end. Fruit is a capsule.

Bloom Season: Summer

Habitat/Range: Grows in gravelly to sandy soils in sagebrush steppe or ponderosa pine woodlands, mainly east of the Cascades but throughout North America.

Comments: *Corydalis* ("a lark") refers to the floral spur, which resembles a lark's toe. *Aurea* ("golden") refers to the flower color. Bees visit these flowers to obtain nectar stored in the spur. Seedpods may explode when mature, sounding like snapping fingers while the seeds are flung from the parent plant. Pulverized and dried Corydalis roots and leaves have been used medicinally to treat nervousness or emotional upset.

YELLOW MONKEY-FLOWER
Erythranthe guttata
Monkey-flower Family (Phrymaceae)

Description: An annual or perennial, this plant varies in size from 2"–24" tall. The oval-shaped leaves grow in pairs, and the leaves may have hairs or smooth surfaces. Lower leaves are stalked, and upper leaves clasp the stem. Borne on long stalks, the trumpet-shaped flowers are ¼"–2" long, 2-lipped with one large or several smaller crimson spots on the lower lip. Fruit is a capsule.

Bloom Season: Late spring and summer

Habitat/Range: Moist sites from sea level to subalpine elevations throughout the region.

Comments: *Erythranthe* is from the Latin word for "foreign" or "the foreigner." *Guttata* ("spotted") refers to the spots on the flower's lower lip. When an insect such as a bee enters the flower, it contacts the stigma. The 2 lobes then fold together and press against the roof of the flower. This forces the insect to contact the anthers, which dusts the insect with pollen as it searches for nectar. The lower lip's spots act as nectar guides directing pollinators into the flower. Formerly in the *Mimulus* genus.

SULFUR-FLOWERED BUCKWHEAT
Eriogonum umbellatum
Smartweed-Buckwheat Family (Polygonaceae)

Description: The basal leaves of this perennial are egg- to spoon-shaped, arise on slim stalks, and are green above and gray and woolly below. From this basal cluster of leaves arise the flowering stems that vary from 2"–20" tall. Several leaflike, narrow bracts are arranged below the flower clusters. Numerous small, yellowish flowers that may be tinged with pink are clustered into umbrellalike forms. Individual flowers have 6 lobes and stamens that extend beyond the flower opening. Fruit is a 3-angled seed.

Bloom Season: Late spring and summer

Habitat/Range: Dry, rocky sites from mid to subalpine elevations from British Columbia to California and east to the Rocky Mountains.

Comments: *Eriogonum* ("woolly knees") refers to the swollen joints on many of the species. *Umbellatum* ("umbrellalike") refers to the inverted flower cluster, while the common name refers to the sulfur color of the flowers.

LESSER SPEARWORT
Ranunculus flammula
Buttercup Family (Ranunculaceae)

Description: Perennial, low-growing up to 3" tall. Lateral stems trailing along the ground root at the leaf nodes, thus the flowering stems appear to be connected. The small leaves are linear and non-lobed. The ½" yellow flowers are borne on short stalks and have 5 shiny petals and numerous stamens. Fruit is a seed with a hooked beak.

Bloom Season: Summer

Habitat/Range: Grows in moist sites along the Northwest coast but also found across Canada to the northeast United States.

Comments: *Ranunculus* is derived from the Latin *rana* ("frog") for the aquatic or moist habitat preference of the genus. *Flammula* ("a small flame") refers to the slightly bitter taste of the leaves. The open, dish-like flower attracts numerous small flying insects as pollinators.

ESCHSCHOLTZ'S BUTTERCUP
Ranunculus eschscholtzii
Buttercup Family (Ranunculaceae)

Description: Perennial, 4"–10" but may be almost prostrate. Basal round to heart-shaped leaves are divided into segments with round blades; the blades may have shallow lobes. Flowering stems bear several, 1½"-wide, yellow flowers with 5 petals with a gap between the petals. Fruit is a seed.

Bloom Season: Mid to late summer

Habitat/Range: Moist areas, rocky mountain meadows, and near shallow alpine streams at high elevations from Alaska to California and east to the Rocky Mountains.

Comments: *Ranunculus* is derived from the Latin *rana* ("frog") for the aquatic or moist habitat preference of the genus. *Eschscholtzii* honors Johann Friedrich Gustav von Eschscholtz (1793–1831), a German surgeon and professor who accompanied Otto von Kotzebue on his 1815–1818 and 1823–1826 expeditions to North America.

WESTERN BUTTERCUP
Ranunculus occidentalis
Buttercup Family (Ranunculaceae)

Description: Perennial, with 1 to many upright and spreading stems that are 7"–30" tall. The long-stalked basal leaves have 3 wedge-shaped lobes with toothed divisions. Upper leaves are smaller and more deeply divided. Several bright-yellow flowers are borne at the end of long stalks. Flowers are ½"–1" wide, and the hairy sepals fall off as the flower matures. Fruit is a smooth seed with a hooked tip.

Bloom Season: Spring

Habitat/Range: Moist meadows, grassy areas, openings, and woodland (open or shady) from coastal to subalpine elevations from Alaska to California.

Comments: *Ranunculus* is derived from the Latin *rana* ("frog") for the aquatic or moist habitat preference of the genus. *Occidentalis* ("western") describes the range of this plant. Flies, beetles, and other winged insects are attracted to the abundance of pollen produced by the flowers.

SAGEBRUSH BUTTERCUP
Ranunculus glaberrimus
Buttercup Family (Ranunculaceae)

Description: Perennial, low-growing (2"–6") from clustered roots. Basal leaves are fleshy and either broad with shallow lobes or divided into deeper lobes. The short flowering stalks bear 1"-wide, bright-yellow flowers that have 4–7 petals and numerous stamens and pistils. Each petal has a nectar gland at the base. Fruit is a seed.

Bloom Season: Early to mid spring

Habitat/Range: Seasonally moist sites in sagebrush steppe or pine woodlands at low to mid elevations from British Columbia to California and east to the Dakotas.

Comments: *Ranunculus* is derived from the Latin *rana* ("frog") for the aquatic or moist habitat preference of the genus. *Glaberrimus* ("without hairs") refers to the smooth leaves. Pollinators such as beetles, flies, wasps, and other insects visit the plentiful flowers for either nectar, located at the base of the petals, or pollen, which is produced in abundance by the stamens.

SHRUBBY CINQUEFOIL
Dasiphora fruticosa
Rose Family (Rosaceae)

Description: Shrub, 3'–5' tall, although may be low-growing along the ground. Older stems have shredding bark. Young stems and leaves are hairy. Compound leaves divided into 5–7 linear leaflets with entire margins and pointed at the tip. Yellow flowers are ¾"–1¼" long, shallow, cup-shaped, with 5 petals and numerous stamens. Seeds with long hairs.

Bloom Season: Summer

Habitat/Range: Moist soils in meadows or rocky areas at mid to high elevations throughout the western and midwestern United States and across Canada.

Comments: *Dasiphora* is from a Greek word meaning "hair-bearing," which is in reference to either the hairs on the seeds or the ones on the young branches. *Fruticosa* ("bushy") refers to the plant's stature. Shrubby Cinquefoil has many cultivars for use in landscaping.

LARGELEAF AVENS
Geum macrophyllum
Rose Family (Rosaceae)

Description: Perennial, with hairy stems up to 3' tall. Basal leaves with rough hairs are irregularly divided into small leaflets with a larger heart- to kidney-shaped leaflet at the top. The stem leaves have 3 deep lobes or divisions. The ½"-wide, saucer-shaped, yellow flowers have 5 rounded petals surrounding a center of numerous stamens. Fruit is a seed with hooked bristles.

Bloom Season: Late spring and midsummer

Habitat/Range: Open forests and edges from low to subalpine elevations from Alaska to Baja California and east to the Great Lakes.

Comments: *Geum* is the Latin name for the plant. *Macrophyllum* ("large-leaved") refers to the size of the basal leaves. Northwest tribes used the plant medicinally for eyewashes, stomach ailments, and childbirth. The seed's hooked bristles catch on the fur of passing animals to aid in seed dispersal.

YELLOW IVESIA

Ivesia gordonii
Rose Family (Rosaceae)

Description: Perennial. Basal leaves fernlike with highly dissected overlapping lobes. Stems have white or sticky hairs. Flower stems bear somewhat rounded flower clusters with 10–20 ½"-long, starlike, yellow flowers. Flower heads may be up to 8" wide. Flowers have 5 narrow petals and 5 stamens. Fruit is a seed.

Bloom Season: Mid to late summer.

Habitat/Range: Rocky ridges and talus slopes from at mid to high elevations from Washington to California and east to Utah.

Comments: *Ivesia* honors Dr. Eli Ives (1779–1861), an American botanist and physician. *Gordonii* is for Alexander Gordon (b. 1795), a British horticulturalist and nurseryman who traveled the Oregon Trail in the 1840s.

PACIFIC SILVERWEED

Potentilla anserina
Rose Family (Rosaceae)

Description: Perennial, with sprawling stems and reddish runners. The compound leaves are divided into 9–31 leaflets that are toothed along the margin and have white hairs below. The leaves are 3"–8" long. Bright-yellow flowers, ¾"–1½" wide are saucer-shaped and borne singly. Fruit is a flattened, oval seed.

Bloom Season: Late spring to summer

Habitat/Range: Coastal beaches, headlands, swales, and open areas from Alaska to California.

Comments: *Potentilla* is from the Latin *potens* ("powerful") after the medicinal uses of the plant. *Anserina* ("related to geese") refers to the plant growing where geese forage. Coastal tribes ate the roots.

ANTELOPE BITTERBRUSH
Purshia tridentata
Rose Family (Rosaceae)

Description: Shrub, 2'–6' tall. The wedge-shaped leaves are ½"–1" long, hairy below, and 3-lobed at the tip. The yellow flowers have 5 petals and numerous stamens and are ½"–1" wide. Fruit is a seed.

Bloom Season: Spring to early summer

Habitat/Range: Drier sites in sagebrush steppe or ponderosa pine forests at mid elevation from British Columbia to California and east to Colorado.

Comments: *Purshia* honors Frederick Traugott Pursh (1774–1820), a German botanist who worked on the Lewis and Clark expedition performing plant collection and wrote *Flora Americae Septentrionalis*, a flora of North America, in 1814. *Tridentata* ("three-toothed") refers to the leaf tips. This is an important winter forage plant for wildlife.

BAKER'S VIOLET
Viola bakeri
Violet Family (Violaceae)

Description: Perennial. The long-stemmed leaf blades are lance- to heart-shaped, toothed along the margin, and smooth or hairy. The leaves may be 1"–5" long. The yellow flowers have 5 lobes; the lower 3 have purple veins, and the upper ones have brownish or purplish backs. Fruit is a capsule.

Bloom Season: Spring

Habitat/Range: Dry meadows, grasslands, prairies, and sagebrush flats from low to mid elevations on the east side of the Cascades from British Columbia to California and east to the Rocky Mountains.

Comments: *Viola* is the Latin name for various sweet-scented flowers, including Violets. *Bakeri* honors Milo Samuel Baker (1868–1961), a botanist who listed thousands of plants throughout California's North Coast and was a professor of botany at Santa Rosa Junior College in California.

GOOSEFOOT VIOLET
Viola purpurea
Violet Family (Violaceae)

Description: Perennial, low-growing. Leaves variable, dark green, deeply veined, and egg-shaped to rounded. Margins may be smooth or toothed. Yellow flowers, ½"–1" long, have 5 petals with the 2 upper ones brown-purple on the back, and the lower middle petal has purple veins. Fruit is a seed.

Bloom Season: Mid spring to midsummer

Habitat/Range: Dry forest openings, slopes, and sagebrush steppe from mid to alpine elevations.

Comments: *Viola* is the Latin name for several scented flowers. *Purpurea* ("purple") refers to the color on the upper petals. Goosefoot is after the resemblance of the leaves to a goose's foot.

GREEN AND BROWN FLOWERS

This section includes flowers that are predominantly brown or green. Some flowers included here also tend toward yellow, lavender, or pale purple. Check those sections if you don't find what you're looking for.

POISON OAK

Toxicodendron diversilobum
Sumac Family (Anacardiaceae)

Description: Perennial shrub or vine with reddish or gray stems that grow 3'–40' long. Leaves divided into 3 egg-shaped to broadly egg-shaped leaflets, 1½"–3" long, which are deeply lobed along the edges. Clusters of flowers include small, greenish flowers borne in the leaf axils and consist of both male and female flowers. Fruit is a rounded, cream- to brown-colored berry.

Bloom Season: Mid spring to midsummer

Habitat/Range: Grassy shrublands, oak woodlands, and coniferous forests from low to mid elevations mainly west of the Cascades from British Columbia to California and east to Nevada. Also found in drier sites in the Columbia River Gorge.

Comments: *Toxicodendron* ("toxic tree") refers to the nonvolatile oil, urushiol, found on the leaves and stems that can cause skin irritation. *Diversilobum* ("diverse leaves") is for the variable lobes on the leaves. The plants regrow each season and hikers should be aware of the reddish stems in spring before the leaves emerge.

POISON IVY

Toxicodendron rydbergii
Sumac Family (Anacardiaceae)

Description: Perennial. Woody shrub to 3', or sparsely branched single stems in a loose cluster. Compound leaves are long-stemmed with 3 (rarely 4 or 5) toothed or lobed, dark, lusterless green leaves that are 1"–4½" long. Tiny, greenish-white male and female flowers are densely arranged in leaf axils on separate plants. Cream to yellow berries may remain over the winter.

Bloom Season: Spring to early summer

Habitat/Range: Riparian and moist locations across the West.

Comments: *Toxicodendron* ("toxic tree") refers to the nonvolatile oil, urushiol, on the leaves and stems, which may cause uncomfortable skin irritation. *Rydbergii* is for the botanist Per Axel Rydberg (1860–1931). Leaves drop off in winter, but the fruits help to identify the plant.

PALLID MILKWEED
Asclepias cryptoceras
Milkweed Family (Apocynaceae)

Description: Perennial, stems trail along the ground 4"–12". The broad leaves are opposite, smooth, and oval. The flowers are borne in loose clusters; the greenish-white petals bend backward exposing a pale-rose center. The 5 pouch-shaped hoods protect the stamens. Fruits are 2"–3"-long, slender seedpods.

Bloom Season: Late spring

Habitat/Range: Dry, gravelly, or sandy sites in southern Washington south to California and east to western Idaho.

Comments: *Asclepias* refers to Asklepios, a mortal physician who was an authority on plants and their healing properties. According to Greek mythology, Asklepios was killed by a thunderbolt from Zeus after he boasted about reviving the dead. *Cryptoceras* is from *krypto* ("hide") and *keras* ("horn"), which is in reference to the flower. The legs of small pollinators become stuck in the hood slits, and they cannot break free. Larger pollinators, such as butterflies or moths, can withdraw their legs, which have sacs of pollen wrapped around them.

WILD GINGER
Asarum caudatum
Birthwort Family (Aristolochiaceae)

Description: Perennial, creeping ground cover. Heart-shaped leaves borne on slender, hairy stalks velvety to the touch are 2"–5" long. The leaves often cover the flowers and trailing stems. The cup-shaped flower, borne at ground level, has 3 brownish-red, sometimes greenish-yellow, sepals that are broadly lance-shaped and taper to long points. The sepals are 1"–3" long and are fused together at the base. The fruit is an egg-shaped capsule.

Bloom Season: Early to midsummer.

Habitat/Range: Moist, shady woods from British Columbia to central California and east to western Montana.

Comments: *Asarum* is from the Greek name for the plant, and *caudatum* ("with a tail") refers to the slender tips of the sepals. Though the roots are edible, this plant is not related to the commercially harvested ginger species. Native Americans used the leaves and roots for various ailments, including putting the plant into the bedding of infants to quiet them. Ants or flies pollinate the ground-level flowers. Fungus gnats lay their eggs in the flowers to hatch.

SILVER BEACHWEED
Ambrosia chamissonis
Aster Family (Asteraceae)

Description: Perennial, mat-forming with stems 1'–4' long. The spatula-shaped leaves are either deeply dissected or entire with toothed margins. The leaves may be up to 3" long and are covered with dense, white hairs. The male flowering stalk resembles a tassel and bears numerous tiny pollen-producing flowers, while the female flowers are usually borne in the leaf axils or found at the base of the tassel. The fruit is a spine-covered seed.

Bloom Season: Summer

Habitat/Range: Beaches and sand dunes along the coast from British Columbia to southern California.

Comments: *Ambrosia* was the food of the gods, making all who ate it immortal. *Chamissonis* is for Adelbert von Chamisso (1781–1838), a French-born German botanist who collected plants in California in 1816. Shifting sands may cover the lower stems.

WESTERN CONEFLOWER
Rudbeckia occidentalis
Aster Family (Asteraceae)

Description: Perennial with upright stems that are 2'–6' tall. Oval-shaped leaves are 4"–12" long, with rough hairs on both sides or just below. Flower stalks are leafless and bear 1 or more dark purple-brown, cone-shaped flower heads of disk flowers. Fruit is a seed.

Bloom Season: Mid to late summer

Habitat/Range: Seasonally moist bogs, fens, wetlands, or meadows at mid elevations from Washington to California and east to Montana.

Comments: *Rudbeckia* is for Olof Rudbeck the Younger (1660–1740), who appointed Carl von Linnaeus as botany lecturer and head of botany demonstrations at Uppsala University in Sweden. *Occidentalis* ("western") refers to the plant's distribution.

FOOL'S HUCKLEBERRY
Menziesii ferruginea
Heather Family (Ericaceae)

Description: Shrub, up to 6' tall. Young stems have rust-colored, sticky hairs that have a foul odor when crushed. The elliptical to ovate leaves are light green, are 1"–2" long, have a pointed white leaf tip, and are crowded toward the branch end. The greenish-salmon, pink, or yellow urn-shaped flowers hang downward off short stems and are ¼" long. Fruit is a capsule.

Bloom Season: Late spring and summer

Habitat/Range: Shady, moist sites in coniferous forests and forest edges at low to mid elevations from British Columbia to California and east to Wyoming.

Comments: *Menziesii* honors Archibald Menzies (1754–1842), a Scottish physician and naturalist who sailed with Captain George Vancouver on his 1790–1795 Pacific exploration. *Ferruginea* ("rusty") refers to the color of the hairs on the leaves and stems. Leaves turn yellow or red in the fall.

ONE-SIDED PYROLA
Orthilia secunda
Heather Family (Ericaceae)

Description: Perennial, 2"–10" tall. Evergreen basal leaves are ovalish, toothed along the margin and 1"–2½" long. The pale-green flowers are borne on one side of a leafless flowering stalk. The bell-shaped flowers are about ¼" long with a style that projects straight beyond the flower. Fruit is a rounded capsule.

Bloom Season: Mid to late summer

Habitat/Range: Dry sites in coniferous woods from low to subalpine elevations throughout the Northwest.

Comments: *Orthilia* ("straight-spiral") and *secunda* ("side-flowering") refer to the one-sided arrangement of the flowers. Crushed leaves were used as a poultice and the pulverized roots were soaked to make an eyewash by Native Americans.

ELKWEED
Frasera speciosa
Gentian Family (Gentianaceae)

Description: Monocarpic (blooms once then dies), often 4'–6' tall. Basal leaves are spatula-shaped or elliptical, 8"–20" long, and smooth or slightly hairy. Stem leaves are smaller and lance-shaped or inversely lance-shaped. Flowers are borne in whorled clusters; each flower is ⅜"–¾" wide and has purplish dots on greenish petals and 2 glands on each petal's lobe. Fruit is a capsule.

Bloom Season: Late spring through summer

Habitat/Range: Sagebrush steppe, mountain meadows, and mountain brush at high elevations from Washington to Mexico and east to the Dakotas.

Comments: *Frasera* honors John Fraser (1750–1811), a Scottish botanist and plant collector who collected for the Kew Gardens and sold plants privately to collectors such as the Empress of Russia. *Speciosa* ("showy") refers to the flowers. Recent research has determined that these plants bloom once during their 20–80-year lifespan and then die. Also called Monument Plant due to the tall stature.

CHECKER LILY
Fritillaria affinis
Lily Family (Liliaceae)

Description: Perennial from a small fleshy-scaled bulb covered with rice-sized bulblets. The unbranched stems attain 4"–40" tall. Lance-shaped linear leaves are borne in whorls at the base and pairs along the upper stem. The bowl-shaped mottled flowers that are 1½" wide have purple, yellow, or green mottling on the 6 tepals. Flowers hang downward, and the tepals flare open. Fruit is a many-seeded capsule.

Bloom Season: Late spring to early summer

Habitat/Range: Grassy areas and woodland meadows from low to mid elevations from British Columbia to California and east to northern Idaho.

Comments: *Fritillaria* ("dice box") refers to the capsules, and *affinis* ("similar to") refers to the similarity of the flowers to other *Fritillaria* species. Flowers have a somewhat foul aroma. Also called Mission Bells or Chocolate Lily.

GIANT HELLEBORINE
Epipactis gigantea
Orchid Family (Orchidaceae)

Description: Perennial from spreading underground roots. Upright stems 1'–2' but may reach 5'. Stems bear numerous oval- to lance-shaped leaves that are 2"–8" long. The greenish to purplish flowers have 3½"-long, greenish sepals and 3 petals with purple or dull-red lines. The upper petals are smaller and greenish purple, and the lower petal is pouch-like and pinched in the middle to form a 3-lobed tip with a curled margin. Fruit is a capsule.

Bloom Season: Mid spring to midsummer

Habitat/Range: Springs, seeps, stream banks, and moist sites from desert regions to woodlands across southern British Columbia to Baja California and east to the Rocky Mountains.

Comments: *Epipactis* is from the ancient Greek name *epipakis* ("helleborine"), and *gigantea* ("large") refers to the stature of the plant. Wasps are the primary pollinators of these orchids, which are attracted in great numbers by scent. The flowers may also self-pollinate.

HEARTLEAF TWAYBLADE
Neottia cordata
Orchid Family (Orchidaceae)

Description: Perennial, grows 2"–10" tall but may be overlooked. The 2 stem leaves are heart-shaped, 1"–2½" long, and clasp the stem at the same mid-length point. The yellowish-green or purplish-brown flowers are ¼"–½" long and 2 lipped. The slightly inflated flowers have a lower lip that is deeply divided for half its length. Fruit is a capsule.

Bloom Season: Mid spring to early summer

Habitat/Range: Moist, mossy coniferous forests at mid elevations throughout the region and into Eurasia.

Comments: *Neottia* is from the Greek *neossia* ("bird's nest"), which is named for the European-growing Bird's Nest Orchid (*Neottia nidus-avis*). *Cordata* ("heart-shaped") refers to the shape of the leaf. Various species of flies, wasps, and fungus gnats are attracted to the foul-smelling flowers. When insects land upon the center column of the flower, a sticky mass of pollen explodes from the stamens and "glues" to the pollinator's legs. The pollen either falls or is scraped off at another flower. *Twayblade* ("two-blades") refers to the 2 leaves.

SMALL GROUND-CONE
Kopsiopsis hookeri
Broomrape/Paintbrush Family (Orobanchaceae)

Description: Parasitic plant, 4"–6" tall. Resembles an upright, yellow to dark-maroon pinecone. Succulent stems covered with scalelike leaves. The 2-lipped flowers arise between bracts at the terminal end of the stem. The flowers are slender and yellow to purple and have unequal lips. Fruit is a many-seeded capsule.

Bloom Season: Late spring and early summer

Habitat/Range: Forest duff and coastal woodlands from Alaska to northern California.

Comments: *Kopsiopsis* ("like or having the form of *Kopsia*") honors Jan Kops (1765–1849), a Dutch professor of botany and agronomist. *Hookeri* is for either one or both of the British botanists: Sir William J. Hooker (1785–1865), and his son, Sir Joseph Dalton Hooker (1817–1911). The fleshy roots contact and draw nutrients from their host plants, which include Salal (*Gaultheria shallon*) and Kinnikinnick (*Arctostaphylos uva-ursi*).

BROWN'S PEONY
Paeonia brownii
Peony Family (Paeoniaceae)

Description: Perennial, 8"–24" tall. Fleshy leaves are compound once or twice, and the leaflets are deeply lobed. The heavy blossoms, 3"–4" wide, weigh the flowering stems down, often to the ground. Five to 6 oval, green or reddish sepals surround 5–10 white to maroon petals that are edged with yellow. The numerous stamens surround the styles that elongate in fruits. Fruit is a 2"–3" seedpod.

Bloom Season: Mid to late spring

Habitat/Range: Sagebrush plains, open pine woodlands, and meadow edges at mid elevations from central Washington to Idaho and south to California.

Comments: *Paeonia* is from Paeon, the Greek physician to the gods. *Brownii* honors Robert Brown (1773–1858), a British botanist that led expeditions to collect plants in Australia in the mid-1850s. These peonies produce abundant pollen but little nectar, yet they still attract bees, wasps, and ants as pollinators.

SEASIDE PLANTAIN
Plantago maritima
Plantain Family (Plantaginaceae)

Description: Perennial, often low-growing but may reach 1' tall. Basal cluster of linear leaves are tough, 2"–4" in length, and smooth (toothed in one variety) along the margin. The upright flowering stalk, 1"–5" long, bears numerous tiny, 4-petaled flowers with hairy corollas. Fruit is a seed.

Bloom Season: Summer

Habitat/Range: Rock outcrops, bluffs, or beach edges along the coast from Alaska to southern California.

Comments: *Plantago* is the Latin name for this genus, and *maritima* ("maritime") refers to the coastal distribution. The young leaves are edible either raw or steamed. Several other species of Plantago occur along the coast. The stamens protrude beyond the flowers and, like many plantains, may be both wind and insect pollinated.

DAVIS' KNOTWEED
Aconogonon davisiae
Smartweed-Buckwheat Family (Polygonaceae)

Description: Perennial with nonwoody, reddish stems that often spread along the ground. The fleshy, oval- to egg-shaped leaves, 1"–3" long, are borne on short stems and taper to a point. Small, greenish-white to pink flowers are borne in leaf axils in small clusters.

Bloom Season: Summer

Habitat/Range: Open, rocky slopes at subalpine elevations from Washington to central California and east to central Idaho.

Comments: *Aconogonon* is from the Greek *acon* ("whetstone") and *youn* ("seed" or "offspring") and refers to the rough texture of the seeds. *Davisiae* honors Nancy Jane Davis (1833–1921), an American plant collector. Also called Newberry's Fleeceflower after John Strong Newberry (1822–1892).

SEASIDE DOCK
Rumex maritimus
Smartweed-Buckwheat Family (Polygonaceae)

Description: Annual, the 8"–20"-long stems sprawl across the ground. The leaf blades are lance-shaped to broadly linear, 2"–7" long, and wavy along the margins. The tiny, greenish-brown flowers are borne in clusters in leaf axils; the flowers are less than ⅛" long. Fruit is a single-seeded nut with sand-like swellings on the surface.

Bloom Season: Summer and early autumn

Habitat/Range: Coastal beaches and wet saline areas throughout the region and to the northeastern United States. Also found in South America and Eurasia.

Comments: *Rumex* is the Latin name for sorrel or dock. *Maritimus* ("maritime") refers to the coastal or saline environments where these plants grow. Also called Golden Dock after the color of the stems at maturity.

WESTERN MEADOW RUE
Thalictrum occidentale
Buttercup Family (Ranunculaceae)

Description: Perennial, stems 1'–3' tall. The compound leaf divides several times, and the 1"-wide leaflets are smooth with 3-scalloped lobes. Male and female flowers borne on separate plants. Male flowers have numerous yellow stamens and brown to purple filaments that hang downward. Female flowers are tiny, green to purplish, and are arranged in clusters. Fruit is a seed.

Bloom Season: Mid spring to midsummer

Habitat/Range: Moist woods and meadows at low to mid elevations from British Columbia to California and east to the Rocky Mountains.

Comments: *Thalictrum* is the Greek name for this plant, and *occidentale* ("western") refers to the plant's distribution. Often confused for a grass.

COFFEEBERRY
Rhamnus californicus
Buckthorn Family (Rhamnaceae)

Description: Evergreen shrub or small tree, 4'–8' tall but may reach 20'. Alternate leaves are elliptical to inversely egg-shaped, 1½"–2½" long and with rolled-in margins that may be finely toothed along the edges or smooth. Small, greenish-white flowers are borne in open clusters. Fruit is a rounded "berry" (drupe) that turns from green to red to purple-black when mature and contains 2 coffee bean-like seeds.

Bloom Season: Late spring to midsummer

Habitat/Range: Occurs in oak woodlands and chaparral at low to mid elevations from southern Oregon to Baja California.

Comments: *Rhamnus* ("a thorn bush") refers to some species in this genus. *Californicus* ("of California") refers to its distribution. Has been used medicinally to treat skin, respiratory, and intestinal disorders.

JUNIPER MISTLETOE
Phoradendron juniperinum
Mistletoe/Toadflax Family (Santalaceae)

Description: Hemiparasitic perennial, 8"–16" long and often as wide. Jointed stems have opposite leaves that are of various sizes. Male and female flowers, which are greenish-yellow, are borne separately. Fruit is a shiny, pink berry.

Bloom Season: Spring

Habitat/Range: Grows on junipers through the Great Basin and eastern portions of Oregon and California.

Comments: *Phoradendron* is from Greek words meaning "tree thief," in reference to the plant's parasitic nature. However, this mistletoe can photosynthesize, thus relying on their host for water and some nutrients. *Juniperinum* ("juniper") refers to the primary host. This mistletoe is a larval host plant for great purple hairstreak butterflies (*Atlides halesus*). Birds eat the berries and transfer the seeds to other plants through their droppings.

COBRA PLANT
Darlingtonia californica
Pitcher Plant Family (Sarraceniaceae)

Description: Perennial, insectivorous plant. Large leaves, 5"–20", are hood-shaped and greenish yellow with purple spots on the hood. At the base of the hood is an opening that has 2 moustache-like bracts. A single, 2"-long flower is borne on a leafless stalk that is 1'–3' tall. The flowers have cream-colored sepals and purplish petals, and the flowers hang downward. Fruit is a turban-shaped capsule.

Bloom Season: Mid spring through summer

Habitat/Range: Often in nitrogen-poor locations such as bogs and springs and along small streams from sea level to mid elevations in southwest Oregon to northern California.

Comments: *Darlingtonia* is for Dr. William Darlington (1782–1863), a Philadelphia botanist. *Californica* ("of California") refers to its type location. Flies, wasps, bees, ants, and beetles are attracted to the nectar source within the flower opening. However, as they try to leave, the opaque spots on the hood "confuse" the insect, which spends a lot of time and energy trying to leave. As the insect tires, it falls into the digestive fluid at the leaf base and is digested by enzymes. Best viewed at the Darlingtonia Botanical Wayside just north of Florence, Oregon, or Eight Dollar Mountain Botanical Wayside near Selma, Oregon.

LEAFY MITREWORT
Mitellastra caulescens
Saxifrage Family (Saxifragaceae)

Description: Perennials that grow up to 25" tall. The basal leaves are broad and 5-lobed; the lobes are finely toothed along the margins. Upper stem leaves are smaller. Greenish flowers have 5 stamens, are ⅛"–¼" long, saucer-shaped, and have petals with fringelike feathery tips. Fruit is a capsule.

Bloom Season: Spring and early summer

Habitat/Range: Moist woods and meadows or along stream banks at mid elevations from British Columbia to northern California and east to Montana.

Comments: *Mitellastra* is from the Greek *mitra* ("a cap") and refers to the form of the developing fruit. *Caulescens* ("having a stem") may refer to the leaves along the flowering stalk. The flowers of Leafy Mitrewort mature from the top to the bottom.

YOUTH-ON-AGE
Tolmiea menziesii
Saxifrage Family (Saxifragaceae)

Description: Perennial, grows 1'–2½' tall. The basal leaves arise on long stalks covered with soft hairs. The lobes on the broad leaves arise from a common point (palmately) and are hairy. A long floral stalk bears numerous greenish-purple to brownish flowers that are ⅓"–½" long and have a narrow corolla. The thin petals curl at the tips. Fruit is a capsule.

Bloom Season: Mid spring to midsummer

Habitat/Range: Plant grows in moist, shady forests or open areas from low to mid elevations from Alaska to California west of the Cascades.

Comments: *Tolmiea* is for William Frazier Tolmie (1812–1886), a Scottish doctor who worked for the Hudson's Bay Company in the Northwest and also collected plants in the region. *Menziesii* is for Archibald Menzies (1754–1842), the English surgeon-naturalist who sailed with Captain George Vancouver in 1792 to explore the Northwest coast. The common name refers to the vegetative reproductive ability of these plants. Young plants arise from buds located at the base of the "adult" leaf.

LANCE-LEAF FIGWORT
Scrophularia lanceolata
Figwort Family (Scrophulariaceae)

Description: Perennial with 4-angled stems, 1'–3' tall. The long leaves are toothed along the margin and long stemmed with triangular, egg-shaped blades. The 2-lipped flowers are greenish yellow with maroon, about ½" long, and slightly inflated. The upper 2-lobed lip projects over the lower, 3-lobed lip. Fruit is a capsule.

Bloom Season: Early to midsummer

Habitat/Range: Moist sites along streams and clearings at low elevations from British Columbia to California.

Comments: *Scrophularia* is from the Latin *scrofula* ("scrophula"), after the plant's medicinal usage to treat swollen glands. *Lanceolata* ("lance-shaped") refers to the leaves. California Figwort (*S. californica*) has brownish to maroon-colored flowers.

STINGING NETTLE
Urtica dioica
Nettle Family (Urticaceae)

Description: Perennial from creeping roots with stems 3'–9' tall. Stems and leaves are covered with stinging hairs. Leaves are opposite, broadly lance- to egg-shaped, and with saw-toothed margins. Clusters of tiny, nondescript, greenish flowers are borne in the upper leaf axils. The flowers may be all male, all female, or have both male and female appendages. Fruit is a flat, oval seed.

Bloom Season: Summer

Habitat/Range: Moist sites along streams, rivers, thickets, and woodlands from sea level to subalpine elevations throughout the region.

Comments: *Uro* ("to burn") is the Latin name for nettle. *Dioica* ("dioecious") refers to the male and female flowers that are borne on separate plants. The stem fibers were plaited into cordage. The cooked stems and leaves were, and still are, eaten as "wild spinach." The hollow hairs contain formic acid, which, when crushed or broken, irritates the skin.

BLUE AND PURPLE FLOWERS

This section includes flowers that range in color from pale blue to deep indigo and violet. Since these colors grade into pink and lavender, and since some plants produce flowers that range across all of these colors, you should check among the pink flowers in the red and violet section if you don't find the flower you are looking for here.

COMMON CAMAS
Camassia quamash
Camas/Triteleia/Yucca Family (Asparagaceae)

Description: Bulb is egg-shaped. Grasslike basal leaves are about 1" wide and may grow 2' long. The flowering stalk may bear numerous pale to deep-blue (sometimes white) flowers that are 1½" long; 5 of the tepals curve upward with 1 downward. Fruit is an egg-shaped capsule that splits open into 3 segments.

Bloom Season: Late spring to early summer

Habitat/Range: Low to mid elevations in grassy plains or meadows from British Columbia to California and east to Wyoming and Utah.

Comments: Scientific name is from the Native American name *camas* or *quamash*. Camas bulbs were an important food source for native tribes. The bulbs were dug with digging sticks and roasted in large pits.

HARVEST BRODIAEA
Brodiaea coronaria
Camas/Triteleia/Yucca Family (Asparagaceae)

Description: Perennial. Narrow, grasslike leaves are long and often wither before flowering. The 5"–16" long stems bear 2–10 bluish-purple flowers (white rarely) with the petals curving backward. The 1'-long flowers have distinctive purple stripes down the center of the petals. Three sterile, white stamens resemble small petals.

Bloom Season: Early to midsummer

Habitat/Range: Prairies, grassy meadows, and rocky bluffs at low to mid elevations from Vancouver Island to California and into eastern Oregon and Washington.

Comments: *Brodiaea* honors James Brodie (1744–1824), a Scottish botanist. *Coronaria* ("crowned") refers to the flower arrangement. The common name refers to Native Americans and early settlers who harvested the small, tasty bulbs.

BALLHEAD CLUSTER LILY
Dichelostemma congestum
Camas/Triteleia/Yucca Family (Asparagaceae)

Description: Perennial from a corm. Leaves are 2"–4" long with a channel down the center. Flowers borne in a cluster, less than 20, at the tip of an upright stalk. Clusters subtended by 4 purple to white bracts. Tube- or bell-shaped flowers are dark blue or purple, with 6 sepals, 3 stamens, and 3 bluish, forked, toothlike projections.

Bloom Season: Early to midsummer

Habitat/Range: Grassy meadows and open forests at low to mid elevations from Washington to central California on the west side of the Cascades.

Comments: *Dichelostemma* ("toothed crown") refers to the appendages on the anthers. *Congestum* ("congested") refers to the tight cluster of flowers. Also called Ookow.

BRIDGES' BRODIAEA
Triteleia bridgesii
Camas/Triteleia/Yucca Family (Asparagaceae)

Description: Perennial from a bulb. Linear leaves wither early. Upright stems bear several branches with 6 sepaled or petaled, purple to lavender flowers. Fruit is a capsule.

Bloom Season: Mid spring to early summer

Habitat/Range: Forest edges or rocky outcrops, often on serpentine soils, from low to mid elevations from southern Oregon to California.

Comments: *Triteleia* is from the Greek *tri* ("three") and *teleios* ("perfect"), which is in reference to the floral parts in 3s. *Bridgesii* honors Thomas Bridges (1807–1865), an English botanist who collected plants in South America and California in the nineteenth century.

HOWELL'S TRITELEIA
Triteleia grandiflora
Camas/Triteleia/Yucca Family (Asparagaceae)

Description: Perennial, plants up to 2'tall. Bears 2 grasslike leaves that may reach 1' long. Stems are unbranched, and the flowers are borne in terminal clusters. Tube-shaped flowers have dark-blue tubes and lighter blue to white flaring lobes; each flower is about 1" long. Each of the 6 tepals has a dark-blue center line; inner tepals have more wavy edges than outer ones. Fruit is a capsule.

Bloom Season: Mid spring to early summer

Habitat/Range: Grasslands and sagebrush foothills from the coast of southern British Columbia to southwest Oregon on the east side of the Cascades.

Comments: *Triteleia* is from the Greek *tri* ("three") and *teleios* ("perfect"), which is in reference to the floral parts in 3s. *Grandiflora* ("large flowers") is for the sizeable flowers. The common name is for Thomas Howell (1842–1912), who collected plants in Washington and Oregon and wrote *Flora of Northwest America* (1897–1903). Bees, butterflies, small beetles, and perhaps hummingbirds pollinate the long, tubular flowers. Bulbs are edible. Also called Bicolored Cluster Lily due to color contrasts on flowers.

ELEGANT DAISY
Erigeron elegantulus
Aster Family (Asteraceae)

Description: Low-growing perennial. Basal leaves are linear with a white, wider base and are ½"–2" long. Upright flower stems with fine white hairs are 2"–8" tall, bear a single flower head that is less than ½" wide, and is made up of 20–25 bluish, purple, or white ray flowers surrounding a center of yellow disk flowers. Fruit is a seed.

Bloom Season: Mid to late summer

Habitat/Range: Volcanic soils, sagebrush steppe, or alpine environments at high to alpine elevations from southern Oregon to California.

Comments: *Erigeron* is from the Greek words *en* ("early") and *geron* ("an old man"), which refers to the early bloom period and profusion of white seed heads. *Elegantulus* ("elegant") refers to the stature of the plant. Also called Volcanic Daisy for its growth in volcanic soils.

CUSHION FLEABANE

Erigeron poliospermus
Aster Family (Asteraceae)

Description: Perennial, cushion-like, 2"–6" tall. Narrow or spatula-shaped leaves are 1"–1½" long and covered with dense hairs. Flowering stalks also bear numerous hairs and usually end with a single floral cluster, although the stalks may branch. Flower heads are 1' wide and have 25–30 pink or lavender ray flowers (sometimes white) surrounding a cluster of yellow disk flowers. Fruit is a seed with numerous white hairs.

Bloom Season: Spring

Habitat/Range: Dry, rocky sites or slopes in sagebrush habitats from southern British Columbia to central Oregon and east to western Idaho.

Comments: *Erigeron* is from the Greek words *en* ("early") and *geron* ("an old man"), which refers to the early bloom period and profusion of white seed heads. *Poliospermus* ("gray seed") refers to the long hairs on the seed.

CASCADE ASTER

Eucephalus ledophyllus
Aster Family (Asteraceae)

Description: Perennial, 10"–30" tall. Unbranched stems bear numerous 1"–4"-long, egg- to broadly lance-shaped leaves with the larger leaves along the middle portion of the stem. Each stem bears several daisylike flower heads that have 6–21 lavender to bluish-purple ray flowers surrounding a center of yellowish disk flowers. Fruit is a seed with tawny bristles.

Bloom Season: Midsummer to fall

Habitat/Range: Dry or moist meadows, forest openings, or edges at mid to subalpine elevations on the east side of the Cascades from British Columbia to California.

Comments: *Eucephalus* is Greek for "good head." *Ledophyllus* ("rockrose leaf") refers to the lower leaves resembling those of Labrador Tea.

TUNDRA ASTER
Oreostemma alpigenum
Aster Family (Asteraceae)

Description: Perennial, 4"–10" tall. Basal leaves linear and 2"–7" long. The stem leaves are smaller. The 1–3 stems bear a single floral head, and each is about 1½" wide. Heads made of bluish-purple ray and yellow disk flowers. The petals are often twisted or drooping. Fruit is a seed with hairs.

Bloom Season: Summer

Habitat/Range: Moist meadows or open forests at subalpine to alpine elevations from Washington to California and east to the northern Rocky Mountains.

Comments: *Oreostemma* is from *aros* ("mountain") and *stemma* ("a crown or garland") because the plants bloom in profusion at higher elevations. *Alpigenum* ("alpine") refers to the plant's distribution.

ALPINE LEAFYBRACT ASTER
Symphyotrichum foliaceum
Aster Family (Asteraceae)

Description: Perennial with reddish stems 5"–28" tall. Basal leaves are lance-shaped to elliptical, borne on short stems, 2"–5" long, and with smooth margins. Middle stem leaves are 7 times longer than wide and sessile; the basal leaves wither at flowering. Flower heads borne in open clusters, subtended by leafy bracts that are egg-shaped to oval, and rounded at the tip. Some of the bracts (phyllaries) are longer and leaflike. Heads have blue to lavender ray flowers surrounding a center of yellow disk flowers. Fruit is a seed with white hairs.

Bloom Season: Early to late summer

Habitat/Range: Open woodlands, sagebrush steppe, along streams, and in higher elevation meadows throughout the western United States and British Columbia.

Comments: *Symphyotrichum* ("hairs coming together") refers to the hairs on the plant growing together in lines. *Foliaceum* ("foliage-like bracts") refers to the bracts subtending the flower heads. There are several varieties for this species, which results in a wide range of characteristics.

PURPLE SALSIFY
Tragopogon porrifolius
Aster Family (Asteraceae)

Description: Biennial, 1'–4' tall. Stems with white, sticky sap when broken. Narrow leaves are 8"–15" long and bluish. Flowers with purple ray flowers subtended by 1"–2"-long, green, leaflike bracts. Fruit is a seed with long hairs.

Bloom Season: Spring and summer

Habitat/Range: An introduced species from Europe that occurs in moist areas, meadows, and coastal areas at low elevations throughout the region.

Comments: *Tragopogon* ("goat's beard") refers to the long, silky hairs on the seeds resembling the hairs on a goat's chin. *Porrifolius* ("leaves like a leek") refers to the leaves. Edible and used in herbal medicine to treat gallbladder disorders.

PACIFIC HOUND'S TONGUE
Cynoglossum grande
Borage Family (Boraginaceae)

Description: Perennial with stout stems; may be 1'–3' tall. Large, lance-shaped to oval leaf blades are 3"–8" long and are borne on long stems. The leaves have a rough texture. The dark-blue flowers arise on a stout flowering stalk and are about ½" wide. Five petals fuse together to form a short tube that flares open and surrounds a white center collar. Fruit is a nutlet with hooked prickles at the tip.

Bloom Season: Mid to late spring

Habitat Range: Woods and forest edges in low- to mid-elevation sites from southern British Columbia to central California on the west side of the Cascades but also in the Columbia River Gorge.

Comments: *Cynoglossum* is from the Greek works *kyon* ("dog") and *glossum* ("tongue"), which is in reference to the large leaves that are shaped like a dog's tongue. *Grande* ("large") refers to the leaves of this striking plant.

LEAFY BLUEBELL
Mertensia oblongifolia
Borage Family (Boraginaceae)

Description: Perennial, with clustered stems up to 16" tall. Basal leaves 2"–3" long and have long stems and an elliptical blade. Bluish flowers are borne in a tight cluster and have a tube that ends in 5 shallow lobes. Fruit is a nutlet.

Bloom Season: Late spring to early summer

Habitat/Range: Open areas or forest edges from low to subalpine elevations throughout the region east of the Cascades.

Comments: *Mertensia* honors Franz Carl Mertens (1764–1831), a botany professor in Bremen, Germany. *Oblongifolia* ("oblong leaves") refers to the shape of the leaves.

JESSICA STICKTIGHT
Hackelia micrantha
Borage Family (Boraginaceae)

Description: Perennial with erect stems 1'–3½' tall. Lance-shaped leaves are 3"–8" long, pointed at the tip, and with stems that bear wings. Upper leaves stemless and smaller. Flowering stalks bear ⅓"-long, blue flowers with white or yellow centers and 5 rounded petals. The petals are fused together and create a small tube. Fruit is a nutlet with pointed prickles.

Bloom Season: Summer

Habitat/Range: Moist meadows, shrubby slopes, open forests, and stream banks on both sides of the Cascades at mid to high elevations across much of the western United States.

Comments: *Hackelia* is for Joseph Hackel (1783–1869), a Czech botanist who collected plants in Bohemia. *Micrantha* ("small-flowered") refers to the flowers. When mature, the nutlet's prickles catch or "stick tight" on animal fur or hiker's shoes, helping the seeds disperse.

TALL BLUEBELLS
Mertensia paniculata
Borage Family (Boraginaceae)

Description: Perennial, with several stout stems 10"–60" tall. The basal leaves are egg- to heart-shaped and long-stalked while the stem leaves are lance- to egg-shaped and may be stalkless. Leaves are hairy above and sometimes hairy below. Bell-shaped flowers are borne in clusters, and each flower is ½"–1" long and tube-shaped at the base. Flowers are pinkish when first opening and change color to blue with maturity. Fruits are 4 nutlets joined together.

Bloom Season: Early summer

Habitat/Range: Wetter sites in meadows, open forest, and along stream banks from low to high elevations, mainly east of the Cascades from British Columbia to Oregon and east to Idaho.

Comments: *Mertensia* honors Franz Carl Mertens (1764–1831), a botany professor in Bremen, Germany. His son, Karl Heinrich Mertens (1796–1830), collected plants on an Alaskan expedition is 1827 and named the genus for his father. *Paniculata* ("in a panicle") refers to the floral arrangement.

TRUE FORGET-ME-NOT
Myosotis sylvatica
Borage Family (Boraginaceae)

Description: Biennial or short-lived perennial. Plants grow to 2' tall. Leaves and stems are covered with hairs; basal leaves in a rosette and have stems while the upper leaves do not. Leaves are broadly lanceolate and are 1"–3" long. Sky-blue flowers have 5 petals surrounding a prominent, yellow, circular ridge. Flowers are ¼"–½" wide. Fruit is a nutlet.

Bloom Season: Mid spring to early summer

Habitat/Range: Disturbed sites, shady locations, woodlands, and cultivated gardens at low to high elevations across the West. Native to Europe, this plant has escaped cultivation and became naturalized in certain areas.

Comments: *Myosotis* is from the Greek *mus* ("mouse") and *otus* ("ear"), which was a name given to plants with short leaves. *Sylvatica* ("growing in the woods") describes the plant's habitat preference. Marsh Forget-Me-Not (*M. scorpioides*) is similar but grows in wet locations.

SCOULER'S BLUEBELL
Campanula scouleri
Harebell Family (Campanulaceae)

Description: Perennial, with weak stems 4"–15" tall. Basal leaves rounded, toothed along the margin, and borne on long stems. Upper leaves narrower and more lance-shaped than the basal ones. The bell-shaped, pale-blue to violet-colored flowers are ¼"–½" long. The petals form a short tube that ends with the petals curving up and backward. A single stipe extends beyond the petals and ends with a thickened stigma. Fruit is a capsule.

Bloom Season: Late spring to midsummer

Habitat/Range: Moist, shady forests or open slopes from Alaska to northern California, mostly west of the Cascades.

Comments: *Campanula* is from the Latin *campana* ("a bell") and refers to the flower shape of this genus. *Scouleri* is for John Scouler (1804–1871), a Scotsman who joined the British Navy as a surgeon and who botanized with David Douglas (1799–1834) in the Northwest. The plants are either pollinated by insects or may be self-pollinated.

COMMON BLUEBELL
Campanula rotundifolia
Harebell Family (Campanulaceae)

Description: Perennial, often growing in clumps 6"–18" tall. Rounded to heart-shaped basal leaves wither before the flowers open and the few stem leaves are narrow. Blue, bell-shaped flowers are ½" long and have 5 petals. Fruit is a capsule.

Bloom Season: Summer

Habitat/Range: Open areas, meadows, and forest edges from low to subalpine elevations throughout the mountains of North America.

Comments: *Campanula* is from the Latin *campana* ("bell"), which refers to the flower's shape. *Rotundifolia* ("round-leaved") refers to the shape of the basal leaves. Insects may overnight in the closed flowers, protected from the elements. As the wind rattles the capsule, the seeds escape through small slits. Also called Scotch Bluebell or Lady's Thimble, this plant is widely cultivated in rock gardens.

BEACH PEA
Lathyrus japonicus
Pea Family (Fabaceae)

Description: Perennial, with stems reaching 4" long. Stems either on the ground or climbing. The compound leaves have 6–12 leaflets that are smooth. Two large, triangular, leaflike stipules arise at the base of the leaves, and the leaves end in a tendril. The 1"-long, purplish, pea-shaped flowers are borne in loose clusters. The upper petal is enlarged. Fruit is a pod.

Bloom Season: Summer

Habitat/Range: Coastal beaches and foredunes from Alaska to northern California, as well as coastal Japan.

Comments: *Lathyrus* is from the Greek name for peas (*lathyros*). *Japonicus* ("of Japan") refers to the plant's distribution. The seedpod is edible. Silky Beach Pea (*L. littoralis*) also grows along the coast and has edible roots and smaller leaves with dense hairs. Beach Pea is pollinated by bees.

LONGSPUR LUPINE
Lupinus arbustus
Pea Family (Fabaceae)

Description: Perennial, 20" tall. Leaves are divided into narrow segments. The bluish-violet (sometimes white, yellow, or reddish, depending upon the subspecies) flowers are borne on an elongated stalk. The ½"-long flowers have a blunt spur on the calyx and side petals that are hairy at the tip. Fruit is a pod.

Bloom Season: Mid spring to early summer

Habitat/Range: Dry, sagebrush flats, grasslands, or pine forests at low to mid elevations on the east side of the Cascades, from Washington to California and east into Idaho and Utah.

Comments: *Lupinus* is from *lupus* ("wolf") and refers to the misconception that lupines "wolf" nutrients from the soil. Many plants in the Pea Family fix nitrogen in the soil that other plants can uptake.

TAILCUP LUPINE
Lupinus caudatus
Pea Family (Fabaceae)

Description: Perennial, upright stems and flower stalks reach 8"–24" tall. Compound leaves have 5–9 oval-shaped leaflets, 1"–2" long, that are covered with silvery hairs; basal leaves wither before flowering. Pea-shaped flowers borne in open, elongated clusters that are 3"–10" long. Individual flowers ½" long with the top petal curving upward and side petals forming a keel. Fruit is a seedpod.

Bloom Season: Late spring to mid summer

Habitat/Range: Open slopes, sagebrush steppe, and forests on the east side of the Cascades at mid to high elevations from the Pacific Northwest to the Rocky Mountains.

Comments: *Lupinus* is from *lupus* ("wolf") and refers to the misconception that lupines "wolf" nutrients from the soil. *Caudatus* ("tail") refers to the lower sepal, which forms a spur-like cup underneath the flower.

BROADLEAF LUPINE
Lupinus latifolius
Pea Family (Fabaceae)

Description: Perennial, often in clumps, 1'–3' tall, and in profusion. Leaves are palmately compound with 7–9 broadly egg-shaped or elliptical leaflets that are usually hairy. Flowers borne in a dense cluster on an elongated stalk. The blue to purplish flowers arise on short stalks and have a smooth, bent-backward upper petal and broad side petals. Fruits are hairy pods.

Bloom Season: Late spring and early summer

Habitat/Range: Widespread in moist or damp meadows, roadsides, and forest edges or openings from low to subalpine elevations mainly west of the Cascades.

Comments: *Lupinus* is from *lupus* ("wolf") and refers to the misconception that lupines "wolf" nourishment from the soil. *Latifolius* ("broad leaf") describes the leaf size. Bees are the primary pollinators of many lupines, as they can force their way into the flowers.

SEASHORE LUPINE
Lupinus littoralis
Pea Family (Fabaceae)

Description: Perennial with mostly trailing stems that may reach 2' long. Compound leaves bear 5–8 lance-shaped leaflets that are 1" long. Pea-shaped flowers borne in dense clusters; the lower petals are bluish while the upper petal is whiter with small black dots at the base. Fruit is a hairy pod.

Bloom Season: Mid spring to summer

Habitat/Range: Sandy beaches and coastal bluffs from British Columbia to northern California.

Comments: *Lupinus* is from *lupus* ("wolf") and refers to the misconception that lupines "wolf" nutrients from the soil. *Littoralis* ("shore") refers to the plant's distribution. Coastal tribes ate the fleshy roots of this plant. Like many lupines, the seedpods dry and split open at maturity, hurling the seeds.

BIGLEAF LUPINE
Lupinus polyphyllus
Pea Family (Fabaceae)

Description: Perennial with stout stems that can grow 4'–5' tall. Compound leaves palmately divided and have 9–17 elliptical to lance-shaped leaflets that are smooth above and may be slightly hairy below. Pea-shaped flowers borne on elongate stalks; flowers are blue to pink or white and about ½" long. Fruit is a seedpod.

Bloom Season: Late spring to mid summer

Habitat/Range: Moist locations at low to mid elevations throughout western North America.

Comments: *Lupinus* is from *lupus* ("wolf") and refers to the misconception that lupines "wolf" nutrients from the soil. *Polyphyllus* ("many leaves") refers to the numerous leaflets. Bees pollinate the flowers. Commonly grown in backyard gardens.

ROCK LUPINE
Lupinus saxosus
Pea Family (Fabaceae)

Description: Perennial, 6"–12" tall. Basal leaves palmately divided into 6–13 lance-shaped leaflets. Leaflets are ½"–1¾" long, smooth on top, and hairy below. Flowering stalk is 2"–9" long and bears a dense cluster of blue, pea-shaped flowers with a hairy calyx and a yellow to violet patch on the upper petal. Fruit is a hairy seedpod.

Bloom Season: Early to mid spring

Habitat/Range: Rocky slopes in sagebrush steppe at mid to high elevations from Washington to California and into the Great Basin.

Comments: *Lupinus* is from *lupus* ("wolf") and refers to the misconception that lupines "wolf" nutrients from the soil. *Saxosus* ("full of rocks") refers to the habitat where these lupines grow.

HAIRY VETCH
Vicia villosa
Pea Family (Fabaceae)

Description: Annual, with sprawling or climbing stems to 3' or more. Pinnately compound leaf has 12–18 narrowly elliptical to oblong leaflets and is hairy. Purple-blue to reddish to white flowers are borne on one side of a central stalk. The tight cluster of pea-shaped flowers may be 2"–3" long. Fruit is a pod.

Bloom Season: Spring to mid summer

Habitat/Range: An introduced plant from Europe and western Asia, it now occurs throughout the lower 48 states and elsewhere.

Comments: *Vicia* is the name for Vetch. *Villosa* ("hairy") refers to the hairs on the leaves and stem. An important cover crop, livestock may graze fields where Hairy Vetch grows, but the cattle are removed once the plant pods start to mature.

WHITESTEM FRASERA
Frasera albicaulis
Gentian Family (Gentianaceae)

Description: Perennial, 10"–30" tall. Basal leaves linear, up to 6" long with white margins. Upper leaves smaller and arranged oppositely. Flower clusters borne at the end of an elongated stalk. Blue (rarely white) flowers, ½" wide, with 4 lance-shaped, mottled petals. The petals have a hair-lined gland at the base. Fruit is a small capsule.

Bloom Season: Late spring to midsummer

Habitat/Range: Meadows and open woods of the lower mountains from British Columbia to Montana and south to Northwest California on the east side of the Cascades.

Comments: *Frasera* honors John Fraser (1750–1811), a Scottish botanist and explorer who collected plants in American and Cuba in the eighteenth century. *Albicaulis* ("white-stemmed") refers to the edges of the leaves. Several varieties exist.

MENDOCINO GENTIAN
Gentiana setigera
Gentian Family (Gentianaceae)

Description: Perennial with upright stems, 8"–18" tall. Spoon-shaped basal leaves are 1"–3" long with rounded tips. Upper leaves are smaller, and the bases clasp the stem. Funnel-shaped flowers are 1½" long and dark blue with a white throat and greenish dots inside; the 5 lobes have fringed plaits between the lobes. Fruit is a capsule with winged seeds.

Bloom Season: Summer

Habitat/Range: In serpentine soils in fen, bog, wetlands, and mountain meadows at low eleva-tions in southern Oregon and northern California.

Comments: *Gentiana* is after Gentius, king of Illyria in the second century BCE, who is often cited as the discoverer of the medicinal properties of a Gentian native to that area. The dots inside the flower are to attract pollinators.

NARROW-LEAF PHACELIA

Phacelia linearis
Waterleaf Family (Hydrophyllaceae)

Description: Annual. Plants grow 5"–20"tall. Basal leaves are narrow, and the larger, upper leaves may have split into 1–4 narrow segments. Showy, light-blue flowers are ½"–1" wide and have 5 petals. The flower buds are arranged in a coiled pattern. Fruit is a rough-textured seed.

Bloom Season: Late spring and early summer

Habitat/Range: Open areas in dry areas from low to mid elevations on the east side of the Cascades.

Comments: *Phacelia* ("fascicle") refers to the tightly clustered flowers. *Linearis* ("linear") describes the leaf shape. The dish-like flowers attract bees, flies, and beetles as pollinators.

SILKY PHACELIA

Phacelia sericea
Waterleaf Family (Hydrophyllaceae)

Description: Perennial with upright stems to 2' tall. Stem and leaves covered with silvery hairs. Lance-shaped leaves are pinnately divided once or twice and the segments have rounded lobes. Silvery, blue bell-shaped flowers borne in dense clusters along an elongated stalk. Stamens protrude beyond the petals. Fruit is a 2-chambered capsule.

Bloom Season: Late spring through summer

Habitat/Range: Open areas with rocky or sandy soils at subalpine to alpine elevations from British Columbia south to Oregon and east to Utah.

Comments: *Phacelia* ("fascicle") refers to the tightly clustered flowers. *Sericea* ("silky") refers to the abundant fine hairs on the stem and leaves. Flowers attract bees as pollinators.

OREGON FLAG
Iris tenax
Iris Family (Iridaceae)

Description: Perennial to 20" tall. The basal, grasslike leaves are up to 20" long but narrow. Stem leaves are smaller. The showy flowers range from blue to purple and may be white, pink, yellow, or lavender. The sepals have yellow and white centers and dark-purple veins; the petals are narrower and solid in color. Fruit is an angled capsule that splits open into 3 chambers.

Bloom Season: Spring to early summer

Habitat/Range: Grassy meadows, open fields, roadsides, and open forests at low to mid elevations from Washington to California on the west side of the Cascades.

Comments: *Iris* honors the Greek goddess Iris, whose message-bearing appearance was heralded by a rainbow. *Tenax* ("tough") refers to the durability of the leaves. The Scottish botanist David Douglas (1799–1834) collected and named this plant after observing native tribes in California making fishing nets and snares from the leaves to trap fish, deer, and bear.

WESTERN BLUE FLAG
Iris missouriensis
Iris Family (Iridaceae)

Description: Perennial, with grasslike leaves. Atop the 1'–2' stems are a pair (sometimes 4) of pale-blue flowers about 3" wide. The showy flowers have 3 wide sepals lined with purplish streaks and a yellow base, 3 upright petals, and 3 petallike styles. Fruit is a large capsule.

Bloom Season: Late spring to midsummer

Habitat/Range: Moist, marshy areas or along streams from low to mid elevations from Alaska to Baja California and east to Minnesota.

Comments: *Iris* honors the Greek goddess Iris, whose message-bearing appearance was heralded by a rainbow. *Missouriensis* ("of the Missouri River") is from Meriwether Lewis, who collected this plant along the Missouri. Native Americans used the pulverized roots of the Western Blue Flag to treat toothaches, and the stems and leaves were used in making weavings or cordage strong enough to snare an elk. Bumblebees land on the wide sepal and push their way under the petallike segment to suck nectar, pollinating the flowers in the process.

IDAHO BLUE-EYED GRASS
Sisyrinchium idahoense
Iris Family (Iridaceae)

Description: Perennial, flattened stems are up to 14" tall. The mostly basal leaves are long and linear and grasslike. The 1"-wide flowers arise individually or in small clusters and are blue to bluish purple with a yellow center. The 6 tepals are pointed at the tip. Fruit is a rounded or egg-shaped capsule.

Bloom Season: Late spring to midsummer

Habitat/Range: Grows in moist meadows and seasonally (spring) wet areas in juniper and ponderosa pine forests at low to mid elevations from Alaska south to Baja California and across Canada to the east side of the Rocky Mountains.

Comments: *Sisyrinchium* is the ancient Greek name for a different plant. *Idahoense* ("of Idaho") refers to the type locality. The common name refers to the grasslike leaves. Blue-Eyed Grass (*S. bellum*) is similar.

COMMON SELF-HEAL
Prunella vulgaris
Mint Family (Lamiaceae)

Description: Perennial, with square stems 6"–36" tall. The opposite leaves are broadly lance-shaped to elliptical. The flowers are borne in dense clusters of purple to blue, 2-lipped flowers. The lower lip has 3 lobes and fringe on the middle lobe. The upper lobe forms a flat hood. Fruit is a nutlet.

Blooms Season: Summer

Habitat/Range: Disturbed sites such as roadsides, fields, ditches, old clearcuts, and other open areas from low to mid elevations throughout the region.

Comments: The origin of *Prunella* is unclear because German herbalists in the fifteenth and sixteenth centuries interchanged the names *Prunella* and *Brunella. Vulgaris* ("common") refers to the widespread abundance of this plant. Self-Heal, as the name implies, was used medicinally. Aboriginal people around the world ate the leaves or used them to treat eye irritations, fevers, cuts, burns, and more. Modern herbalists also use Common Self-Heal to treat various ailments.

PURPLE SAGE
Salvia dorrii
Mint Family (Lamiaceae)

Description: Shrub, 12"–36" tall with a strong mint scent. Stems square, hairy, and upright. Lance-shaped leaves are narrow at the base and wider at the tip, about 1" long. Bluish-purple flowers are tubular, 2-lipped with the upper lip 2-lobed and the lower lip with 3 petals, and have 2 stamens that protrude above the petals.

Bloom Season: Mid spring to midsummer

Habitat/Range: Dry desert shrub and sagebrush steppe at low to high elevations from Washington to California and east to Arizona.

Comments: *Salvia* is from the Latin *salvus* ("safe"), which refers to the safe medicinal properties of the genus. *Dorrii* honors Clarendon Herbert Dorr (1816–1887), a plant collector in what was the Nevada Territory. Purple Sage was made famous in Zane Gray's Western novel *Riders of the Purple Sage* (1912). This shrub is grown commercially for landscaping.

NARROW-LEAVED SKULLCAP
Scutellaria angustifolia
Mint Family (Lamiaceae)

Description: Perennial with square stems, up to 20". Leaves are opposite and oval to lance-shaped with smooth edges. The 1"-long, bluish-purple flowers arise singularly or in pairs from the upper leaf axils and are tube-shaped. The lower petal is broad and hairy, while the upper petal forms a hood or hump. Two smaller side petals border the outside of the tube. Calyx is 2-lipped and forms a crest on the upper portion. Fruit is a hard nutlet.

Bloom Season: Late spring to midsummer

Habitat/Range: Dry plains, canyons, and foothills from low to mid elevations from southern British Columbia south to California and Idaho.

Comments: *Scutellaria* is from the Latin word *scutella* ("saucer or small disk"), which refers to the pouch on the upper side of the calyx. *Angustifolia* ("narrow-leaved") refers to the shape of the leaves, which often appear folded lengthwise. Marsh Skullcap (*S. galericulata*) grows in wet meadows or marshes and has white streaks on the blue or pinkish-purple flowers. Lewis and Clark collected this specimen on June 5, 1806, near present-day Kamiah, Idaho.

SAGEBRUSH MARIPOSA LILY
Calochortus macrocarpus
Lily Family (Liliaceae)

Description: Perennial, 8"–21" tall. The 1–3 grass-like leaves are thin but not flat. One to 3 flowers are borne on each plant, and the flowers are 2" wide. The flowers are lavender, purple, or white, with 3 narrow, pointed sepals that are longer than the 3 broad petals. A green stripe extends down the petals to the sepals. There are reddish-purple nectar lines on the lower, inner portion of the petals. Fruit is a capsule.

Bloom Season: Late spring to midsummer

Habitat/range: Dry meadows, sagebrush flats, or ponderosa pine forests from low to high elevations from southern British Columbia to California and east to Montana.

Comments: *Calochortus* ("beautiful grass") refers to the grasslike leaves. *Macrocarpus* ("large fruited") refers to the large seed capsules. The onion-like bulbs are edible.

BLUE FLAX
Linum lewisii
Flax Family (Linaceae)

Description: Perennial, sometimes with a woody base. Thin, smooth stems grow 1'–2' tall and bear linear to lance-shaped leaves that are 1"–2" long. The 1"-wide flowers have 5 blue petals that are streaked with purple and 5 styles that protrude beyond the stamens. Fruit is a rounded capsule.

Bloom Season: Mid spring to summer

Habitat/Range: Widespread in western North America in damp or dry meadow or forest openings. Cultivated, also.

Comments: *Linum* is the Latin name for flax, and *lewisii* is for Captain Meriwether Lewis (1774–1809), co-leader of the Corps of Discovery. Lewis collected and described Blue Flax on his western expedition, noting its perennial form and potential commercial properties. Some western Native tribes used flax fibers to make cordage for nets and snares, while fibers from the cultivated Common Flax (*L. usitatissimum*) have been woven into linen for over 300 years.

NAKED BROOMRAPE
Orobanche uniflora
Broomrape/Paintbrush Family (Orobanchaceae)

Description: Parasitic plant, 1"–4" tall. Leaves are basal, lance-shaped, and up to ½" long. The long, yellowish flowering stalk has sticky hairs and bears a single flower. The tubular flowers are bluish or purple, 2" long, and have 2 prominent, yellow ridges on the lower lip. Fruit is a capsule.

Bloom Season: Early spring to midsummer

Habitat/Range: Moist (at least seasonally in spring) meadows, grasslands, open areas, and open woods from low to mid elevations across much of North America.

Comments: *Orobanche* is from *orobos* ("a type of vetch or climbing plant") and *ancho* ("to strangle"), which refers to the parasitic nature. *Uniflora* ("one flower") indicates the solitary flower, which is borne on a leafless or naked flowering stalk. This species parasitizes species of Stonecrop, Saxifrage, and some Asteraceae members. A dumbbell-shaped stigma (often yellow) on the upper inside roof of the flower resembles an anther and encourages the insect pollinators to advance into the flower.

GIANT BLUE-EYED MARY
Collinsia grandiflora
Plantain Family (Plantaginaceae)

Description: Annual, often low-growing, but may reach 1½' tall. Lower leaves stalked and round, while upper leaves narrower and arranged in whorls. Flowers are ½"–¾" long and 2-lipped and multiple shades of blue, pink, lavender, or white. The 2 upper petals are generally lighter than the lower ones. Fruit is a tiny, football-shaped capsule bearing 4 smooth seeds with thick margins.

Bloom Season: Mid to late spring

Habitat/Range: Low to mid elevations in grassy fields, open areas, slopes, or rocky outcrops throughout the region. Native but considered weedy.

Comments: *Collinsia* is named for Zacchaeus Collins (1764–1831), an American botanist from Philadelphia. *Grandiflora* ("large-flowered") describes the flowers. Often associated with the Virgin Mary because of the plant's flowering around Easter. Small-flowered Blue-Eyed Mary (*C. parviflora*) has smaller flowers.

WOODLAND BEARDTONGUE

Nothochelone nemorosa
Plantain Family (Plantaginaceae)

Description: Perennial. From the woody base arise several tall stems up to 40". Leaves are arranged opposite each other along the stem, have short stalks, and are lance- to egg-shaped. The leaf margins are sharply toothed. The tubular flowers are blue purple or pink purple and 2-lipped. The upper lip is shorter than the lower lip on the 1½"-long flowers. The stamens are very hairy on the tip. Fruit is a capsule.

Bloom Season: Early to midsummer

Habitat/Range: Woods and moist, rocky slopes from low to subalpine elevations.

Comments: *Nothochelone* refers to this plant being a "false" *Chelone*, which is another genus. *Chelone* ("turtle") refers to the front of the flower resembling a turtle's head, which is another common name.

BARRETT'S PENSTEMON

Penstemon barrettiae
Plantain Family (Plantaginaceae)

Description: Perennial, spreading stems reach 6"–16" long and create a mat-like growth. The basal lance-shaped to elliptical leaves are 1½"–5" long, borne on short stems, and may have spaced teeth along the margin. The upper leaves are smaller than the lower ones, but both are bluish green and smooth. Rose-purple to lilac-colored flowers borne along one side of a flowering stalk; the 2-lipped flowers are 1"–1½" long, keeled on the top, and 2-ridged on the inner lower lip with numerous white hairs inside. Fruit is a capsule.

Bloom Season: Late spring and early summer

Habitat/Range: Basalt cliffs and rocky slopes at low elevations in the eastern end of the Columbia River Gorge.

Comments: *Penstemon* is from *pen* ("almost') and *stemon* ("stamen"), which refers to the sterile stamen, called a staminode, typical of this genus. *Barrettiae* is for Almeta Hodge Barrett, a doctor's wife living in Hood River, Oregon, who located the flower in the late 1800s. This penstemon has extensive root systems that penetrate deep within the rocky soil it inhabits. The leaves turn a striking purplish bronze in winter.

CARDWELL'S PENSTEMON
Penstemon cardwellii
Plantain Family (Plantaginaceae)

Description: Perennial, low growing and shrubby with matted stems. Leaves are evergreen, oval, ½"–1½" long, and with rounded tips. Long, tubular flowers are about 1"–2" long, blue to purplish, and the upper portion is longitudinally ridged. Fruit is a capsule.

Bloom Season: Summer

Habitat/Range: Rocky slopes and outcrops at mid to high elevations from southern Washington to southern Oregon.

Comments: *Penstemon* is from *pen* ("almost") and *stemon* ("stamen"), which refers to the sterile stamen, called a staminode, typical of this genus. *Cardwellii* honors James R. Cardwell (1830–1916), a horticulturalist who emigrated to Oregon in 1851 and who collected numerous wildlife, birds, and mineral specimens in western Oregon.

SHRUBBY PENSTEMON
Penstemon fruticosus
Plantain Family (Plantaginaceae)

Description: Perennial, may be in dense colonies. Stems are prostrate and mat-forming at the base, while the flowering stems rise 6"–16". Leaves are evergreen, linear to inversely lance-shaped, and toothed along the margin. Corolla is blue-lavender to purplish and 1"–2" long; flowers are arranged on 1 side of the flowering stem. The 2-ridged palate on the flower's lower lip has dense white or yellow hairs. Fruit is a capsule.

Bloom Season: Mid spring to midsummer

Habitat/Range: Open rocky slopes to forests, foothills to mid elevation from British Columbia to Oregon and east into Idaho.

Comments: *Penstemon* is from *pen* ("almost") and *stemon* ("stamen"), which refers to the sterile stamen, called a staminode, typical of this genus. *Fruticosus* ("shrubby or woody") refers to the stems. Separate varieties of this penstemon have slightly different leaves.

GLANDULAR PENSTEMON
Penstemon glandulosus
Plantain Family (Plantaginaceae)

Description: Tall, robust perennial with stems to 40". Basal leaves large and triangular with soft hairs and sharply toothed margins. Both the basal and smaller upper stem leaves clasp the stem, as well as end with a tapered tip. The stout flowering stalks bear numerous flowers arranged in whorls; the buds are slightly sticky. The tubular, purplish-blue flowers are 1"–2" long and have 4 fertile stamens with barely noticeable short hairs on the anthers. Fruit is a capsule.

Bloom Season: Late spring to early summer

Habitat/Range: Open areas and forest edges in mid-elevation sites from western Idaho to the foothills of the Cascades in central Washington to northern Oregon.

Comments: *Glandulosa* ("glandular") refers to the sticky hairs on the calyx. These large, showy flowers attract hummingbirds, butterflies, and bees as pollinators. Also called Sticky-Stem Penstemon.

CASCADE PENSTEMON
Penstemon serrulatus
Plantain Family (Plantaginaceae)

Description: Perennial. Stems may be 1'–3' tall. Lance-shaped to oval leaves are 1"–3" long and toothed along the margins; lower leaves borne on short stalks, and upper leaves clasp the stem. Cluster of purple-blue to light-blue flowers are borne at the top of the flowering stalk. Tubular flowers are about 1" long. Fruit is a capsule.

Bloom Season: Late spring to midsummer

Habitat/Range: Seasonally wet areas, mountain slopes, meadows, rocky outcrops, and open forests at low to high elevations from Alaska to Oregon.

Comments: *Penstemon* is from *pen* ("almost") and *stemon* ("stamen"), which refers to the sterile stamen, called a staminode, typical of this genus. *Serrulatus* ("saw-toothed") refers to the serrated leaf margins. One of the few Northwest penstemons that grows at the coast, as well as in the mountains.

COLUMBIA KITTENTAILS
Synthyris missurica
Plantain Family (Plantaginaceae)

Description: Perennial, plants 6"–16" tall. The long-stemmed, basal leaves are kidney-shaped, 1"–3" wide, and have lobes or blunt teeth along the margins. Stem leaves are much smaller. The ¼"-long blue to purplish flowers are borne along an elongated stalk and have 4 petals of unequal length and 2 stamens that project beyond the flowers. Fruit is a rounded capsule.

Bloom Season: Spring to early summer

Habitat/Range: Shady woods or rocky slopes at low elevations from southeast Washington to northeast California and east to northern Idaho and Montana.

Comments: *Synthyris* ("fused doors") refers to the notched top of the capsule. *Missurica* ("of the Missouri River") describes the location where Meriwether Lewis collected a specimen in 1806. Also called Western Mountain Synthyris or Mountain Kittentails after the long spike of flowers resembling a kitten's tail.

BALLHEAD GILIA
Gilia capitata
Phlox Family (Polemoniaceae)

Description: Annual, with thin stems 1'–3' tall. Basal and stem leaves are divided into narrow linear segments. The lower, larger leaves may be 5" long. The ¼"–½"-wide blue flowers are arranged in rounded clusters. The 5 petals form a short tube that flares outward. Fruit is a somewhat rounded capsule.

Bloom Season: Summer

Habitat/Range: Open fields, meadows, rocky outcrops, and disturbed areas at low to mid elevations from Washington to California and east to northern Idaho.

Comments: *Gilia* honors Filippo Luigi Gilii (1756–1821), an Italian naturalist and director of the Vatican Observatory who co-authored books about South American plants. *Capitata* ("dense head") refers to the clustered arrangement of the flowers. Also called Many-Flowered or Bluefield Gila. Butterflies, bees, wasps, and flies are attracted to the abundant flowers.

WESTERN JACOB'S-LADDER
Polemonium occidentale
Phlox Family (Polemoniaceae)

Description: Perennial, 8"–40" tall. Pinnately divided leaves arise on long stems and have 9–17 lance-shaped leaflets that are green to yellow green above and waxy below. Bell- or bowl-shaped blue flowers with 5 lobes and yellow throats are borne in open clusters and are about ¾" long. Fruit is a seed.

Bloom Season: Late spring through summer

Habitat/Range: Moist locations along streams, meadows, and open forests at mid to alpine elevations across much of western North America.

Comments: *Polemonium* is probably named for Polemon, a Greek philosopher. *Occidentale* ("western") refers to the distribution of this plant. The sky-blue flowers attract bees, flies, and beetles as pollinators.

MONKSHOOD
Aconitum columbianum
Buttercup Family (Ranunculaceae)

Description: Perennial, 3'–7' tall. Maplelike leaves, 2"–7" long, are divided into 3–7 lobes that might be toothed or lobed again. Dark-blue flowers, 1"–2" long, are borne at the tips of the flowering stalk and have 5 petallike sepals and 2 petals. The upper sepal is hoodlike, and the petals form a spur. Fruit is a capsule.

Bloom Season: Mid to late summer

Habitat/Range: Moist meadows, stream banks, and woodlands at mid to high elevations throughout western North America.

Comments: *Aconitum* was an ancient Greek word used for the plant. *Columbianum* ("of western North America") refers to its wide distribution. The plant is very toxic and might have been used to treat arrows or to poison wolves, resulting in another common name: Wolf's Bane.

MENZIES' LARKSPUR
Delphinium menziesii
Buttercup Family (Ranunculaceae)

Description: Perennial, 6"–24" tall. Basal leaves are deeply divided like the fingers on a hand and lobed on the edges of the segments. Basal leaves usually are withered prior to flowering. Flowering stalks bear deep-blue to purplish flowers comprised of 5 showy, petallike sepals and 4 petals. The upper 2 petals are small and white, while the lower 2 are darker. The upper sepal forms a ½"-long spur that projects straight back. Fruit is a pod that splits open at maturity.

Bloom Season: Late spring and midsummer

Habitat/Range: Variable, found in rocky outcrops and scree slopes, moist or dry meadows, or along stream banks from British Columbia to northern California.

Comments: *Delphinium* is from the Greek word *delphis* ("dolphin") and refers to the shape of the flower buds. *Menziesii* honors Archibald Menzies (1754–1842), a Scottish naval surgeon and botanist who sailed with Captain Vancouver on his 1790–1795 Pacific exploration. Plants contain a toxic alkaloid, delphinine, which diminishes with age.

PLAINS LARKSPUR
Delphinium nuttallium
Buttercup Family (Ranunculaceae)

Description: Perennial, stems upright to 20" from extensive fibrous roots. Leaves are variable, borne on long stems, and the blades are highly divided. Flowers have 5 blue sepals, and the upper one forms a spur. The petals are smaller and white. Fruit is a capsule.

Bloom Season: Spring

Habitat/Range: Drier sites in sagebrush flats, woodlands, and mountain slopes from British Columbia to California and east to Nebraska.

Comments: *Delphinium* is from the Greek word *delphis* ("dolphin") and refers to the shape of the flower buds. *Nuttallium* is for Thomas Nuttall (1786–1859), an English naturalist who collected plants and birds in the United States from 1811–1834. Bee-pollinated.

MAHALA MAT
Ceanothus prostratus
Buckthorn Family (Rhamnaceae)

Description: Perennial, mat-forming. Reddish-brown stems variable in length, but may reach up to 8' long. Evergreen leaves are oval, about 1" long, and bear teeth along the edges. Clusters of tiny, blue flowers are borne on short, upright stems. Fruit is a pod.

Bloom Season: Late spring to early summer

Habitat/Range: Open locations in forests at mid to high elevations from British Columbia to northern California and east to Nevada.

Comments: *Ceanothus* is the Greek name for a spiny shrub, referring to certain members of this genus. *Prostratus* ("prostrate") refers to the low-growing habit of this plant. Mahala Mat is a nitrogen-fixing plant, transferring atmospheric nitrogen into a usable form by roots. This plant colonizes burned or logged areas. Also called Pinemat, due to its growth in forests.

POISON LARKSPUR
Delphinium trolliifolium
Buttercup Family (Ranunculaceae)

Description: Perennial with upright, hollow stems that are 2'–6' tall. Large, shiny leaves are divided into many deep lobes, each toothed. Flowering stalk bears dark-blue flowers with ¾"-long spurs; the 2 upper petals have white in their centers. Fruit is a capsule.

Bloom Season: Late spring to early summer

Habitat/Range: Moist locations in meadows and shady forests at low to mid elevations from southern Washington to northern California, mainly west of the Cascades.

Comments: *Delphinium* is from the Greek word *delphis* ("dolphin") and refers to the shape of the flower buds. *Trolliifolium* refers to the leaves resembling those in the *Trollius* genus. Poison Larkspur is toxic to livestock; another common name is Cow Poison.

BLUE BLOSSOM
Ceanothus thyrsiflorus
Buckthorn Family (Rhamnaceae)

Description: Perennial shrub 3'–20' tall. Egg-shaped leaves are 1"–2" long, toothed along the margin, and evergreen and have 3 distinct veins running lengthwise. Blue flowers borne in dense clusters; each flower has 5 petals and stamens that protrude beyond the petals. Fruit is a capsule portioned into 3 single-seeded sections.

Bloom Season: Mid spring to early summer

Habitat/Range: Coast hills from western Washington to central California, and also the Columbia River Gorge.

Comments: *Ceanothus* is the Greek name for a spiny shrub, referring to certain members of this genus. *Thyrsiflorus* ("flowers in a thyrse") reflects the type of floral arrangement: an elongated, narrowly branched cluster of flowers with blooms that mature from the bottom or outside toward the top or center of the cluster. In California, this species may resemble a small tree growing to 25' in height with a 5"–12"-thick trunk. Also called California Lilac.

SAND VIOLET
Viola adunca
Violet Family (Violaceae)

Description: Perennial, but low-growing. Basal leaves are spear- to heart-shaped and have finely toothed margins. The upright stems bear long-stalked leaves, as well. From 1–5 floral stalks arise from the stems and bear a single, lavender-blue flower. The flowers are ¼"–¾" wide and have 5 petals; the bottom petal is the largest, and the spur is half the length of the lowest petal. The top of the style has hairs. Fruit is a capsule that bursts open at maturity.

Bloom Season: Spring

Habitat/Range: Moist meadows in mid to high elevations throughout North America.

Comments: *Viola* is the Latin name for various sweet-scented flowers, including violets. *Adunca* ("hooked") refers to the spur. Also called Hooked Violet or Western Dog Violet, this species is the state flower of Illinois, New Jersey, Rhode Island, and Wisconsin.

RED AND VIOLET FLOWERS

This section includes red and violet flowers, as well as multicolored flowers that are predominantly red or violet. Since red and violet flowers often become lighter with age, check both the orange and the blue and purple sections for the flower you are looking for.

HOOKER'S ONION

Allium acuminatum
Amaryllis Family (Amaryllidaceae)

Description: Perennial from a bulb, grows 6"–17" tall. The 1 or 2 grasslike leaves wither before the flower blooms. The floral stalk bears a cluster of pink or rose-purple flowers (occasionally white). The majority of the flowers are upright, not hanging downward, and the sepals have pointed tips that curl slightly backward. Two papery bracts sit below the flower cluster. Fruit is a capsule.

Bloom Season: Mid spring to early summer

Habitat/Range: Dry rocky or sandy sites, open hillsides, or low- to mid-elevation forests across the region from Vancouver Island to California and east to western Colorado.

Comments: *Allium* is from the Greek name for garlic, and *acuminatum* ("pointed") refers to the pointed sepal tips. The common name honors Sir William Jackson Hooker (1785–1865), a British botanist who named and cataloged hundreds of plant specimens collected by Northwest plant collectors in the nineteenth century. Nodding Onion (*A. cernuum*) has pinkish flowers arranged in a "nodding" cluster.

COLUMBIA DESERT PARSLEY

Lomatium columbianum
Carrot Family (Apiaceae)

Description: Perennial, mound-forming, usually less than 2' tall. The stems arise from a thick, woody root. The highly dissected leaves are bluish green and have numerous linear leaflets. The flowering stalks bear an umbrellalike cluster of reddish-purple flowers (rarely yellow). Fruit is a large seed with thick wings.

Bloom Season: Early spring

Habitat/Range: Rocky cliffs and canyon rims at low to mid elevations from the Columbia River Gorge north to central Washington.

Comments: *Lomatium* is from the Greek *loma* ("a border") and refers to the winged fruit. *Columbianum* ("of the Columbia River") refers to the location of the type specimen of these plants. The Day Valley Desert Parsley (*L. minus*) also bears purplish flowers in an umbrellalike cluster.

SHOWY MILKWEED

Asclepias speciosa
Milkweed Family (Apocynaceae)

Description: Perennial, with stout stems that may be up to 3' or taller. Opposite leaves are broad, hairy, and bleed a milky latex when broken. Spherical clusters of pinkish-white flowers often hang downward from short, stout stalks. The 1"–1½"-long flowers are star-shaped and have 5 rose-purple reflexed petals and 5 pinkish-cream, needlelike, pouch-shaped hoods. Fruit is a 3"–5"-long, spiny or smooth pod that contains seeds with long plumes.

Bloom Season: Mid spring through summer

Habitat/Range: Often in disturbed areas along roads, ditches, and moist sagebrush steppe areas from low to mid elevations

Comments: *Speciosa* ("showy") is in reference to the spectacular flowers. The silky down attached to the seeds, which is 5 or 6 times more buoyant than cork, was used to stuff pillows and World War II era life jackets and flight suits. Showy Milkweed is a host plant for monarch butterfly larvae. The plant is toxic to livestock.

PINK PUSSYTOES

Antennaria rosea
Aster Family (Asteraceae)

Description: Mat-forming perennial with horizontal runners and upright flowering stems from 2"–19" tall. Basal leaves that are very hairy and paddle- or lance-shaped. Stem leaves are smaller and narrow. Clusters of flower heads made up of only disk flowers. The involucre bracts are pinkish to white and about ¼" long. Fruit is a seed with white hairs.

Bloom Season: Late spring and summer

Habitat/Range: Widespread from grassy slopes and meadows in low to subalpine elevations throughout the region.

Comments: *Antennaria* is from the Latin *antenna* ("a ship's yard"), either a horizontal pole that supports the sail or a mast used to hold signal flags, and this is also the derivation for an insect's antennae; hence, the genus name after the seed's white hairs, which resemble butterfly antennae and describes the flower heads that remain intact long after the growing season. *Rosea* ("rose-colored") refers to flower color. The common name—Pussytoes—refers to the resemblance of the flower heads to the underside of a cat's paw.

SEASIDE DAISY
Erigeron glaucus
Aster Family (Asteraceae)

Description: Perennial, with mostly mat-forming stems and a stout taproot. Basal leaves are thick, inversely lance- to spatula-shaped, and toothed along the upper margins. Flowering heads have numerous pinkish to white ray flowers that surround a central cluster of yellow disk flowers. Heads are 1"–2" wide. Fruit is a seed.

Bloom Season: Summer

Habitat/Range: Coastal bluffs, headlands, and rocky outcrops from Oregon to California.

Comments: *Erigeron* is from the Greek *eri* ("early") and *geron* ("old man"), referring to the white hairs on the seeds. *Glaucus* ("white coating") refers to the leaves. The large flower surface attracts a variety of insects as pollinators in the summer.

STEENS MOUNTAIN THISTLE
Cirsium eatonii
Aster Family (Asteraceae)

Description: Perennial, 2'–5' tall. From a basal rosette of spiny leaves arises a stout, unbranched stem. The deeply divided leaves are lance-shaped and covered with long, white spines. Flower heads are pink to purplish. Fruit is a seed.

Bloom Season: Mid to late summer

Habitat/Range: Grassland, sagebrush steppe, disturbed areas, and rocky alpine areas in southeastern Oregon.

Comments: *Cirsium* is from the Greek name *kirsion* ("swollen vein"), which refers to one species of thistle that was used to treat swollen veins. *Eatonii* honors Daniel Cady Eaton (1834–1895), a Yale botany professor and plant collector. Also called Eaton's Thistle.

SICKLEPOD ROCKCRESS
Boechera sparsiflora
Mustard Family (Brassicaceae)

Description: Perennial, thin stems up to 2' tall. Lance-shaped to oval basal leaves are 1"–4" long, pointed at the tip, and have hairs. Upper leaves similar but clasping the stem. Pink to purple flowers have 4 spoon-shaped petals. Fruit is a 2"–5"-long, curved seedpod.

Bloom Season: Early to mid spring

Habitat/Range: Dry sites, grasslands, and open areas at mid elevations from Canada to California and east to Utah.

Comments: *Boechera* honors Danish botanist Tyge W. Böcher (1909–1983), who worked on the taxonomy of alpine plants. *Sparsiflora* ("few flowers") refers to the number of flowers. The long, curved pods split open to release the tiny seeds.

EUROPEAN SEAROCKET
Cakile maritima
Mustard Family (Brassicaceae)

Description: Perennial, with fleshy stems growing upright or sprawled across the sand. The 2"–4"-long leaves are also fleshy and deeply lobed. Pale pink flowers with 4 petals arise in sparse clusters and are about ½" wide. The fruits are an inflated silique with hornlike lobes.

Bloom Season: Summer

Habitat/Range: Coastal beaches from British Columbia to California. Introduced from Europe.

Comments: *Cakile* is from the old Arabic name for the plant. *Maritima* ("maritime") refers to the plant's distribution. American Searocket (*C. edentula*) has lobed or toothed leaves and lacks the hornlike projections on the fruit.

NUTTALL'S TOOTHWORT
Cardamine nuttallii
Mustard Family (Brassicaceae)

Description: Perennial, 3"–10" tall. The stem leaves have 3–5 lobes; plants lack basal leaves. The flowers are borne in loose clusters at the top of the flowering stalk. The ½"-wide flowers are pale pink and have 4 petals with dark nectar lines. Fruit is a slender pod.

Bloom Season: Early spring

Habitat/Range: Shady woods, often associated with oaks, at low elevations from British Columbia to California on the west side of the Cascades.

Comments: *Cardamine* is the ancient Greek name for related plants. *Nuttallii* is for Thomas Nuttall (1786–1859), a plant and wildlife collector, writer, and Harvard professor. Pennsylvania Bitter-Cress (*C. pensylvanica*) is a related species that has a peppery flavor to its edible leaves.

DAGGER-POD
Phoenicaulis cheiranthoides
Mustard Family (Brassicaceae)

Description: Perennial, often with sprawling, reddish-purple flowering stems. Basal leaves in clusters are grayish white, elliptical to inversely lance-shaped, and 1"–7" long. Flowering stalks are up to 8" long and bear reddish-purple, pink, or white flowers. Flowers have 4 petals and are borne in dense clusters. Fruit is a daggerlike pod.

Bloom Season: Mid spring to early summer

Habitat/Range: Open, dry areas such as grass-lands or sagebrush flats from low to mid eleva-tions from eastern Washington to Oregon and east to Idaho.

Comments: *Phoenicaulis* is from *phoni* ("reddish purple") and *caulis* ("stem"), which is in reference to the reddish stems. *Cheiranthoides* ("hand of flowers") refers to the different flowering stems spreading in different directions from the center. The shape of the seedpods gives the plant its common name.

OREGON BOXWOOD
Paxistima myrsinites
Bitter-Sweet Family (Celastraceae)

Description: Shrub, 10"–40" tall with reddish-brown branches. The evergreen leaves are opposite, oval to elliptical, ½"–1½" long, and sharply toothed along the margin. The tiny, reddish flowers are borne in small clusters in the leaf axils and have spreading petals. The 4 petals are borne on the outer rim of the floral disk. The fruit is a 1- or 2-seeded capsule covered with white.

Bloom Season: Early to mid spring

Habitat/Range: Coniferous forests at low to mid elevations from British Columbia to California and east to the Rocky Mountains.

Comments: *Paxistima* is from *pachys* ("thick") and *stigma* ("a stigma"), after the thickened stigma. *Myrsinites* ("*Myrsine*-like") refers to the plants' resemblance to myrtle. Oregon Boxwood is used extensively in the floral arranging industry. The genus may be spelled *Pachyistima*, and another common name is Mountain Lover.

ROCKY MOUNTAIN BEEPLANT
Peritoma serrulata
Bee-plant Family (Cleomaceae)

Description: Annual that grows 1'–6' or taller and may have numerous branches. Compound leaves are smooth to slightly hairy and have 3 lance-shaped to elliptical leaflets that are ¾"–3½" long. Flowering stalks bear ½"-long, pink to reddish-purple flowers (sometimes white) that have 4 petals and 7 stamens. Slender seedpods are about 2" long and bear rounded, rough-textured seeds.

Bloom Season: Summer

Habitat/Range: Disturbed sites at low to mid elevations across much of the western United States and into the Great Plains.

Comments: *Peritoma* is from the Greek *peri* ("cut around") and *tome* ("division"), referring to the cut around the calyx base. *Serrulata* ("finely saw-toothed") refers to the leaf edges. The flowers produce great quantities of nectar that attract bees, thus, the common name. Native Americans ate the cooked leaves and created black pottery paint from the boiled plants.

ROSEFLOWER STONECROP
Sedum laxum
Stonecrop Family (Crassulaceae)

Description: Perennial, succulent. Basal rosette of leaves is oval or oblong, sometimes bluish with a waxy coating, 1½" long, and tightly packed together. Reddish flowering stems, 3"–16" long, bear smaller, reddish, oblong leaves. The branched flowering stalks bear clusters of reddish to white flowers (12–80) with rounded petals.

Bloom Season: Summer

Habitat/Range: Rocky outcrops from low to mid elevations from southern Oregon to northern California.

Comments: *Sedum* is from the Latin *sedo* ("to sit"), in reference to the low-growing stature of the genus covering rocky outcrops or stone walls. *Laxum* ("growing loosely") refers to the shallow roots.

CANDY STICK
Allotropa virgata
Heather Family (Ericaceae)

Description: Saprophyte, grows 5"–18" tall. Stem is red with white stripes and bears whitish, scale-like leaves. Flowers, borne at the top of the stalk, are urn-shaped, reddish white, and have 5 sepals and 10 stamens. Fruit is a capsule.

Bloom Season: Summer

Habitat/Range: Moist coniferous woodlands in humus at low elevations from British Columbia to California.

Comments: *Allotropa* is from the Greek *allos* ("other") and *tropos* ("to turn"), in reference to the flowers, which are oriented around the stalk rather than on one side like the related Indian Pipe (*Monotropa uniflora*). *Virgata* ("twiggy") refers to the stature of the plant. Look for crab spiders on the flowers, which prey upon unsuspecting pollinators.

KINNIKINNICK

Arctostaphylos uva-ursi
Heather Family (Ericaceae)

Description: Perennial, low-growing (up to 10" tall) with stems that mostly trail along the ground. Evergreen leaves are oval- to spoon-shaped and have entire margins. Urn-shaped flowers are pinkish white, ¼" long, and hang downward in clusters. Fruit is a red berry.

Bloom Season: Mid spring to midsummer

Habitat/Range: Widespread from low elevations to alpine areas, often growing in sandy or rocky sites in clearings or forests.

Comments: *Arctostaphylos* is from the Greek *arktos* ("a bear") and *staphyle* ("a bunch of grapes"), which refers to the abundant fruits. *Uva-ursi* ("bear grape") also refers to these fruits. Native tribes collected and dried Kinnikinnick leaves for smoking, often adding it to tobacco. The mealy berries were collected and eaten, as well.

BOG LAUREL

Kalmia microphylla
Heather Family (Ericaceae)

Description: Shrub with multiple, low-growing stems but may reach 2'–3' tall. Alternate to whorled evergreen leaves are elliptical to inversely lance-shaped, ½"–1" long, and with edges that may or may not roll inward. Pale-pink flowers borne in terminal clusters are saucer-shaped, ½"–1" wide, and have 5 lobes. Ten stamens are evenly spaced around the lobes. Fruit is a 5-celled capsule.

Bloom Season: Summer

Habitat/Range: Wet areas in bogs, swamps, stream banks, and meadows from low to alpine elevations from Alaska to California and east to Colorado.

Comments: *Kalmia* is for Pehr (Peter) Kalm (1716–1779), a student of Carl Linnaeus. *Microphylla* ("small leaves") describes the stature of the leaves. Each stamen's anther is tucked into a pocket in the petal lobe and is held there under tension like a bent toothpick. A foraging insect trips the stamen's filament, and the anther pops up and dusts the insect's underbelly with pollen. The plant contains a toxic glycoside called grayanotoxin; if ingested, it may cause nausea, vomiting, dizziness, breathing difficulties, and decreased blood pressure. Also known as Alpine Laurel or Western Swamp Laurel.

PINK MOUNTAIN-HEATHER
Phyllodoce empetriformis
Heather Family (Ericaceae)

Description: Shrub, often mat-forming, with stems 4"–18" tall. Needlelike leaves are evergreen, numerous, and ½" long. Bell-shaped pink to red flowers are borne in small clusters, and the flowers have 5 sepals and are ½" long. Flowers may be erect or hanging down. Fruit is a round capsule.

Bloom Season: Summer

Habitat/Range: Moist meadows and open forests in subalpine to alpine areas throughout the region.

Comments: *Phyllodoce* is after the Greek sea nymph Phyllodoce, as Linnaeus started the custom of naming genera in the Heather Family after goddesses and sea nymphs. *Empetriformis* ("*Empetrium*-like") refers to the leaves resembling those of the Crowberry (*Empetrum nigrum*). White Mountain-Heather (*Cassiope mertensiana*) has white, bell-shaped flowers.

PINK WINTERGREEN
Pyrola asarifolia
Heather Family (Ericaceae)

Description: Perennial, 2"–14" tall. The basal cluster of leaves is glossy green, evergreen, long-stalked, and rounded. The upright, reddish floral stem bears numerous pink, cup-shaped flowers that have waxy petals. Fruit is a capsule.

Bloom Season: Summer

Habitat/Range: Moist sites in forests at low to subalpine elevations throughout most of North America.

Comments: *Pyrola* ("pear-like") refers to the pear-like leaves. *Asarifolia* ("*Asarum*-like leaves") refers to the similarity of the leaves to those of Wild Ginger. The undersides of the leaves may be pink and hence, the common name.

PACIFIC RHODODENDRON
Rhododendron macrophyllum
Heather Family (Ericaceae)

Description: Shrub, up to 24' tall. The alternate, leathery leaves are evergreen, elliptical, and 4"–10" long. Clusters of bell-shaped, rose-purple flowers are borne at the ends of branches. The flowers are 1"–2" long with 5 wavy lobes. Fruit is a capsule.

Bloom Season: Mid spring to early summer

Habitat/Range: Coniferous or mixed woodlands with acidic soils at sea level to mid elevations from southern British Columbia to northern California.

Comments: *Rhododendron* is from *rhodon* ("a rose") and *dendron* ("tree"), after the colorful blossoms growing on sizeable shrubs. *Macrophyllum* ("large-leaved") describes the leaf size. Rhododendrons contain a toxic glycoside, andromedotoxin, which, if concentrated in honeybee hives, can cause poisoning to those that consume the honey. This is the state flower of Washington.

EVERGREEN HUCKLEBERRY
Vaccinium ovatum
Heather Family (Ericaceae)

Description: Evergreen shrub, 1'–13' tall with leafy and hairy stems. Evergreen leaves are egg- to broadly lance-shaped, 1"–2" long, finely toothed along the margins, leathery, and dark green above and lighter below. Narrow, bell-shaped flowers with 5 lobes are arranged in dense clusters of 2–12 pinkish flowers along one side of a stem. Fruit is a bluish-black berry.

Bloom Season: Mid spring through summer.

Habitat/Range: Coastal woodlands from low to mid elevations, mainly west of the Cascades from British Columbia to California.

Comments: *Vaccinium* is a Latin name for blueberries or huckleberries. *Ovatum* ("egg-shaped") refers to the leaves. The edible fruits were harvested by coastal tribes and either eaten fresh or dried and baked into heavy breads, some weighing 10–15 pounds. Meriwether Lewis commented that the shrub retained its character even during the winter.

RED HUCKLEBERRY
Vaccinium parvifolium
Heather Family (Ericaceae)

Description: Deciduous shrub, 3'–12' tall. From bright-green branches arise oval leaves, ½"–1½" long, that may or may not be toothed along the margin. Urn-shaped flowers are pinkish white to greenish white, ¼" wide, and with 5 petals. Fruit is a red berry.

Bloom Season: Late spring to early summer

Habitat/Range: Grows more in moist locations or on nursery logs in coniferous or mixed forests from southeast Alaska to California west of the Cascade crest.

Comments: *Vaccinium* is a Latin name for blueberries or huckleberries. *Parvifolium* ("small leaved") refers to the size of the leaves. Fruits are eaten by birds, wildlife, and humans. Grouseberry (*V. scoparium*) is a low-growing relative with red, edible berries that birds, especially grouse, consume and that grows in drier forests mainly on the east side of the Cascades.

WOOLLY-POD MILKVETCH
Astragalus purshii
Pea Family (Fabaceae)

Description: Perennial, low-growing, 2"–6" tall. Compound basal leaves are woolly and bear 7–19 paired leaflets. The leaflets are elliptical and pointed at the tip. The pinkish, pea-shaped flowers may be white, yellow, or purplish. Flowers have a long tube that flares to a 2-lipped opening. Fruit is a woolly, ½"–1"-long seedpod.

Bloom Season: Spring

Habitat/Range: Dry sites in grasslands and sagebrush flats at low elevations from southern British Columbia to northern California and east to Montana and New Mexico.

Comments: *Astragalus* may be from the Greek *astragulos* ("anklebone"), referring to the shape of the pods. *Purshii* honors Frederick Traugott Pursh (1774–1820), a German botanist who worked on the Lewis and Clark plant collections and wrote *Flora Americae Septentrionalis*, a flora of North America, in 1814.

BLUE MOUNTAIN PRAIRIE CLOVER
Dalea ornata
Pea Family (Fabaceae)

Description: Perennial. Multiple stems arise from the woody base and are up to 2' long. Compound leaves bear 5–7 elliptical or egg-shaped leaflets with small glands, which are ½"–1½" long. Flowers arranged in tight, elongated clusters up to 2" long; flowers mature from the bottom up. The calyx may have long, silky hairs, and the ⅛"-long petals are rose to lavender colored. Fruit is a seedpod with 1–2 seeds.

Bloom Season: Mid spring to early summer

Habitat/Range: Dry rocky or sandy soil in sagebrush steppe at low to mid elevations east of the Cascades from Washington to California and east to Utah.

Comments: *Dalea* honors Samuel Dale (1659–1739), a British apothecary, physician, and amateur plant collector. *Ornata* ("ornate") refers to the flowers. Commercially harvested seed is used in landscape restoration projects and horticultural nurseries.

FEW-FLOWERED PEA
Lathyrus pauciflorus
Pea Family (Fabaceae)

Description: Perennial with upright stems, 2'–3' tall. Compound leaves have 8–10 egg-shaped leaflets and are in pairs. Tendrils arise at the leaf tip. The lavender to purple, pea-shaped flowers turn blue with age. The fruit is a pod.

Bloom Season: Spring

Habitat/Range: Drier sites in woodlands, meadows, and sagebrush flats at low to mid elevations from eastern Washington to California and east to Idaho and Arizona.

Comments: *Lathyrus* is from the Greek name for peas – *lathyros*. *Pauciflorus* is from the Latin *pauci* ("few") and *florus* ("flowers") in reference to the few flowers per stem. Pollinated by bumblebees.

BIG-HEAD CLOVER

Trifolium macrocephalum
Pea Family (Fabaceae)

Description: Perennial, mostly low-growing, although plants might reach 10"–12" high. Compound leaves have 5–7 (sometimes 9) hairy leaflets, which arise from a common point, with fine-toothed edges. Tiny, white, cream, pink, or rose-colored flowers are arranged in dense, 2"-wide, rounded clusters. Clusters may contain up to 60 flowers. Fruit is a 1-seeded pod.

Bloom Season: Spring

Habitat/Range: Abundant in dry, rocky sites in sagebrush plains and ponderosa pine woodlands on the east side of the Cascades from Washington to California and east into Idaho and Nevada.

Comments: *Trifolium* ("3 leaves") is a name given to species in this genus that have 3 leaflets, and *macrocephalum* ("large head") refers to the large flower clusters. This is a native clover species that attracts numerous bees, wasps, and flies as pollinators.

SAND CLOVER

Trifolium willdenovii
Pea Family (Fabaceae)

Description: Annual, with mat-like clusters. Compound leaves have 3 linear, sharp-pointed leaflets; the leaflets are about ½" long. Flower heads have a saucer-shaped bract with a spiny margin below the ½"–1½"-wide flowering heads. Heads contain up to 60 pink to purplish flowers with white tips. Fruit is a pod.

Bloom Season: Early spring

Habitat/Range: Grassy hillsides and meadows generally along the west side of the Cascades from British Columbia to California.

Comments: *Trifolium* ("3 leaves") is a name given to certain species in this genus that have 3 leaflets. *Willdenovii* is for Carl Ludwig Willdenow (1765–1812), a German botanist who was director of the Berlin Botanical Garden. The Scottish plant collector David Douglas recorded this plant in 1827 along the Columbia River. Also called Sand Clover.

SPRINGBANK CLOVER
Trifolium wormskioldii
Pea Family (Fabaceae)

Description: Perennial, low-growing, stems generally trail along the ground. The compound leaves are made up of 3 elliptical to inversely lance-shaped leaflets and may be greenish purple in color. Each leaflet is finely toothed along the margin and pointed at the tip. Clusters of bracts below the flower head are also toothed along the margin. White, pink, or reddish, pea-shaped flowers are arranged in a dense cluster that may be ½"–1" wide. Individual flowers often have white tips. Fruit is a pod with 1–4 seeds.

Bloom Season: Mid spring to fall

Habitat/Range: Moist, open ground along the coast or up into the mountains from British Columbia to Mexico and east into Idaho and New Mexico.

Comments: *Trifolium* ("3 leaves") refers to the leaflets of certain species in this genus. Also known as Cow Clover or Wormskjold's Clover. *Wormskioldii* honors Morten Wormskjold (1783–1845), a Danish botanist who led an expedition to Greenland and who whaled with Kotzebue on his Pacific expedition. Coastal tribes harvested the roots in the fall as a food source. An abundance of nectar produced by the flowers attracts bees as pollinators.

GIANT VETCH
Vicia nigricans
Pea Family (Fabaceae)

Description: Perennial, sprawling, stems to 6' long. Compound leaves have 16–30 leaflets that are broadly lance-shaped. Tendrils enable the plant to trellis up vegetation. The pea-shaped flowers are borne in dense clusters, are 1" long, and bronze to reddish purple. Fruit is a seedpod.

Bloom Season: Mid spring through summer

Habitat/Range: Beaches, stream banks, or clearings along the coast from Alaska to California and inland to the Willamette Valley.

Comments: *Vicia* is derived from the Latin *vincio* ("to bind") and refers to the twining nature of the plant. *Nigricans* ("blackish") refers to the roots. Bee-pollinated.

RICHARDSON'S GERANIUM
Geranium richardsonii
Geranium Family (Geraniaceae)

Description: Perennial, grows 1'–3½' tall. Basal leaves palmately divided, 1"–6" wide; the wedge-shaped leaves may be lobed again. Stems have stiff hairs covered with sticky glands. White, saucer-shaped flowers are about ½"–1½" wide and have 5 petals with red or purple veins. Fruit is a beaked pod.

Bloom Season: Mid spring through summer

Habitat/Range: Moist locations in woodland forests, open meadows, and sagebrush steppe from mid to high elevations from Alaska to Mexico and east to the Rocky Mountains.

Comments: *Geranium* is from the Greek *geranos* ("crane"), which refers to the beak-like fruits. *Richardsonii* honors John Richardson (1787–1865), a Scottish explorer, naturalist, and naval surgeon who explored the Arctic with John Franklin on the Coppermine Expedition of 1819–1822. Sticky Geranium (*G. viscosissimum*) attracts flies, butterflies, and bees to the flowers as pollinators; however, the plant produces enzymes that can digest insects trapped in the sticky glands, a feature called "protocarnivorous."

GUMMY GOOSEBERRY
Ribes lobbii
Currant Family (Grossulariaceae)

Description: Deciduous shrub, grows 2'–3½' tall. Stems with fine hairs, 3 slender spines arising at nodes, and bark that turns grayish red with age. Egg-shaped leaves are heart-shaped at the base, sticky, ½"–1" long, and deeply toothed with 3–5 rounded lobes. Fruit is a reddish-brown berry covered with bristles.

Bloom Season: Mid spring to midsummer

Habitat/Range: Moist forests and foothills at mid elevations from British Columbia to California.

Comments: *Ribes* is from the Arabic or Persian *ribas* ("acid-tasting"), which refers to the fruits of some species. *Lobbii* honors William Lobb (1809–1864), an English plant collector who introduced, among other tree species, the Monkey-Puzzle Tree (*Araucaria araucana*) from Chile to Europe.

RED CURRANT
Ribes sanguineum
Currant Family (Grossulariaceae)

Description: Shrub, with woody, spineless stems that are 3'–15' tall. The rough leaves have 3–5 shallow lobes, are 1"–4" long, and have minute teeth along the edges. Tubular flowers are borne in clusters of 10–30 pale to deep-pink flowers that hang down. The 5 sepals flare outward, forming a star-shaped pattern about ½" wide. The smaller white to red petals form a short tube that projects beyond this star-pattern. Fruit is a black berry.

Bloom Season: Early summer

Habitat/Range: Variable, moist, or dry woodlands or valleys from sea level to mid elevations from British Columbia to California and on the east slope of the Cascades in Washington and Oregon.

Comments: *Ribes* is from the Arabic or Persian *ribas* ("acid-tasting"), which refers to the fruits of some species. *Sanguineum* ("blood red") refers to the color of the flowers. Hummingbirds, bees, and butterflies pollinate the flowers. The flowers may appear before the leaves in the early spring. Red Currant is a host to White Pine Blister Rust (*Cronartium ribicola*), a fungus with a life cycle that includes this currant and Western White Pine (*Pinus monticola*). This species also does well in a cultivated garden.

GRASS WIDOWS
Olsynium douglasii
Iris Family (Iridaceae)

Description: Perennial, plants 6"–10" tall. Two grasslike leaves arise from the base. The reddish to lavender flowers are about 1" wide and have 6 tepals with white bases. Fruit is a capsule.

Bloom Season: Early spring

Habitat/Range: Meadows, grasslands, and open forests from low to mid elevations from British Columbia to California, mainly west of the Cascades, but occurs on the east side, as well.

Comments: The derivation of *Olsynium* is unclear. *Douglasii* is for the Scotsman David Douglas (1799–1834), who collected plants in the Northwest for the Horticultural Society of London before meeting his untimely death in Hawaii. Another Grass Widow, *O. inflatum*, is similar but occurs farther east into Idaho and Utah, and the pistil is more inflated.

NETTLE-LEAF GIANT HYSSOP

Agastache urticifolia
Mint Family (Lamiaceae)

Description: Perennial, plant may be 3'–6' tall with multiple stems. Square stems and leaves have a strong odor when crushed. Leaves broadly lance-shaped to triangular, opposite, 1"–3" long, light green below, and with toothed edges. Flower head, 1"–7" long, is a dense cluster of small, violet to white flowers with 2 upper lobes and 3 lower ones. Fruit is a brown nutlet.

Bloom Season: Summer

Habitat/Range: Dry slopes, meadows, and brushy areas from low to high elevations from British Columbia to California and east to Montana.

Comments: *Agastache* ("many spikes") refers to the numerous flowering stems. *Urticifolia* ("nettle leaved") refers to the leaves resembling those of Stinging Nettle (*Urtica dioica*). Dried leaves and flowers are brewed as an herbal tea, and the plant is used medicinally to treat rheumatism, stomach upsets, and colds.

MOUNTAIN BEEBALM

Monardella odoratissima
Mint Family (Lamiaceae)

Description: Perennial, with square stems 8"–24" tall. Lance- to egg-shaped leaves are opposite, hairy, and have entire margins. Pinkish-lavender flowers are borne in 1"–2"-wide clusters. Purplish bracts that arch backward subtend the flower clusters. Fruits are 4 nutlets.

Bloom Season: Mid to late summer

Habitat/Range: Rocky outcrops and dry slopes at mid to high elevations from British Columbia to California and east to Idaho and Nevada.

Comments: *Monardella* is a diminutive of *Monarda*, another genus in the Mint family. *Odoratissima* ("odorous") refers to the minty smell of the crushed leaves and stems. Mountain Beebalm attracts butterflies and bees as pollinators.

COOLEY'S HEDGE-NETTLE
Stachys chamissonis
Mint Family (Lamiaceae)

Description: Perennial, 3'–6' tall with square, unbranched stems with bristlelike hairs. The leaves are 3"–7" long, opposite, triangular to heart-shaped in outline, and toothed along the margin. Flowers are borne in clusters along the upper portion of the stem. Green sepals are fused into a short tube with 5 spine-tipped lobes. The reddish-purple petals are fused into an upper and lower, 3-lobed lip. Fruits are 4 small nutlets.

Bloom Season: Summer

Habitat/Range: Moist sites in clearings, wetlands, swamps, and forest edges or openings at low elevations from southern British Columbia to Oregon.

Comments: *Stachys* is Greek for "spike," in reference to the flower arrangement, and *chamissonis* is after the French-born German botanist Adelbert von Chamisso (1781–1838), who collected plants in California in 1816. The common name is for Grace Cooley, a New Jersey professor of botany who first identified this plant in 1891. The growth form of this plant resembles Stinging Nettle (*Urtica dioica*); hence, the common name. The crushed stems have an unpleasant, versus minty, odor.

STREAMBANK GLOBE MALLOW
Iliamna rivularis
Mallow Family (Malvaceae)

Description: Perennial, grows 3'–6' tall. Maplelike leaves, 4"–8" long, are palmately lobed into 3–7 rounded segments that are coarsely toothed and are sparsely coated with starlike hairs. Rose to white, disk-shaped flowers borne in loose clusters; each flower has 5 egg-shaped petals that overlap. Fruit is a capsule.

Bloom Season: Summer

Habitat/Range: Stream banks and moist meadows or slopes in riparian areas, sagebrush steppe, or aspen forests at mid to high elevations. Occurs mainly east of the Cascades from British Columbia to Oregon and east to Colorado.

Comments: *Iliamna* derivation uncertain, although might be named for Alaska's Iliamna volcano. *Rivularis* ("growing by streams") refers to the plant's habitat.

OREGON CHECKER-MALLOW
Sidalcea oregana
Mallow Family (Malvaceae)

Description: Perennial, flowering stems 1'–5' tall. Upright stems bear star-shaped hairs on the lower half and are smooth above. Leaves lobed to palmately compound. Bowl-shaped flowers are pinkish to rose-colored, made of 5 petals, borne along an elongated stalk, and bear white stamens surrounding a reddish style. Fruit is a capsule.

Bloom Season: Summer

Habitat/Range: Moist meadows, bogs, seeps, and other moist locations in sagebrush steppe or ponderosa pine woodlands from mid to high elevations on both sides of the Cascades from Washington to California.

Comments: *Sidalcea* is a combination of two other genera, *Sida* and *Alcea*. *Oregana* ("of Oregon") refers to the plant's distribution. This Checker-mallow may have plants that bear bisexual flowers (both male and female parts) or just female flowers without anthers.

FIREWEED
Chaermion angustifolium
Evening-Primrose Family (Onagraceae)

Description: Perennial. Stems may grow 2'–9' tall and are often unbranched. The stalkless leaves are lance-shaped and 2"–10" long. Clusters of flowers arise at the ends of the stems. The rose to reddish-purple flowers are 1"–2" wide with 4 petals and a 4-lobed stigma. The long, podlike capsule splits open to release numerous white-haired seeds.

Bloom Season: Midsummer to fall

Habitat/Range: Disturbed sites such as clearings, burns, meadows, avalanche paths, and roadsides from low to high elevations throughout the region.

Comments: *Chamerion* is from the Greek *chamae* ("lowly") and *nerion* ("Oleander"), referring to the plant's resemblance to a low-growing Oleander. *Augustifolium* ("having narrow leaves") indicates the lance-shaped leaves. The common name describes the habit of this plant colonizing recently burned areas. After the 1980 Mount St. Helens eruption, Fireweed was one of the first plants to sprout in the area. The upright spikes of flowers attract bees that visit the older, lower flowers first before moving up to higher flowers.

RAGGED ROBINS
Clarkia pulchella
Evening-Primrose Family (Onagraceae)

Descriptions: Annual, 4"–20" tall, but some are up to 3'. Linear leaves arranged alternately along the stem. Lavender to rose-purple flowers have 4 petals that are more or less 3-lobed at the tip and narrow (clawed) at the base. Two sets of stamens may be present, with one set being fertile and the other infertile and smaller. Fruit is a slender capsule.

Bloom Season: Late spring to early summer

Habitat/Range: Grows in dry grasslands, meadows, or open woods from British Columbia to Oregon and Idaho and east of the Cascades.

Comments: Frederick Pursh (1774–1820), the botanist charged with identifying specimens from the Lewis and Clark Expedition, named the genus after William Clark (1770–1838). *Pulchella* ("pretty") refers to the lovely flowers. Meriwether Lewis first recorded this plant on June 1, 1806: "I met with a singular plant today in blume of which I preserved a specemine…" is how Lewis began his description of this plant. Also known as Elkhorns, Deer Horn, or Beautiful Clarkia.

DIAMOND CLARKIA
Clarkia rhomboidea
Evening-Primrose Family (Onagraceae)

Description: Annual, thin stems, bent at the tip, 8"–34" tall. Lance- to egg-shaped leaves borne on long stems. Pink to lavender flowers have 4 diamond-shaped to spoon-shaped petals that are speckled with darker pink colors; the petals join together at their narrow bases. Flowers are ½"–1" wide. Fruit is an elongated capsule.

Bloom Season: Late spring to early summer

Habitat/Range: Grows in pine forests and shrub steppe habitats on both sides of the Cascades from British Columbia to California.

Comments: *Clarkia* is for William Clark (1770–1838), one of the co-leaders of the Lewis and Clark Expedition. *Rhomboidea* ("rhomboid-like") refers to the shape of the petals.

CALIFORNIA FUCHSIA
Epilobium canum
Evening-Primrose Family (Onagraceae)

Description: Perennial with upright or mat-forming stems. Stems hairy and may have sticky glands. Leaves mostly opposite, lance-shaped to oval, about 2" long, and either entire or toothed along the margin. Reddish-orange flowers are 1"–1½" long and tube-shaped with tips that flare open. The 4 petals are 2-lobed at the tip, with stamens and a pistil extending beyond the mouth of the flower. Fruit is a capsule.

Bloom Season: Midsummer to fall

Habitat/Range: Forests, rocky drainages, and talus slopes from mid to high elevations in southern Oregon south to California.

Comments: *Epilobium* ("upon the pod") refers to the placement of the flower's ovary beneath the attachment of the petals. *Canum* ("gray" or "ashy") refers to the color of the leaves. The flowers attract butterflies and hummingbirds as pollinators. Also called Hummingbird Trumpet.

ROCKFRINGE WILLOWHERB
Epilobium obcordatum
Evening-Primrose Family (Onagraceae)

Description: Mat-forming perennial. Leaves alternate, oval to rounded, ¼"–¾" long, and covered with light hairs. The tubular flowers are pinkish to rose purple, and the 4 petals flare open at the mouth and are deeply lobed—almost heart-shaped. Fruit is a club-shaped capsule.

Bloom Season: Midsummer

Habitat/Range: Rocky ledges, alpine areas, and mountain slopes at high elevations from California to Oregon and Idaho.

Comments: *Epilobium* is from the Greek *epi* ("upon") and *lobos* ("a pod"), referring to the placement of the corolla above the ovary. *Obcordatum* ("inversely heart-shaped") refers to the shape of the petal lobes.

FAIRY SLIPPER
Calypso bulbosa
Orchid Family (Orchidaceae)

Description: Perennial, growing from a marble-sized bulb. A single flowering stem arises 4"–8" from the bulb. The single oval-shaped leaf often fades during the summer. The 1"-long flower varies from pink to rose purple in color (sometimes white or cream). A single inflated petal forms the "slipper" portion of the flower and bears 2 hornlike projections at the base. This petal has purplish spots and streaks. Above this petal is the hood, which cloaks the stamens and styles. Above the hood are 2 more petals and 3 sepals that are lance-shaped and project up and outward. Fruit is a capsule.

Bloom Season: Late spring and early summer

Habitat/Range: Found throughout the Northwest in coniferous forests from sea level to high elevations, and it occurs from Alaska throughout Canada and south to California, Colorado, and Arizona.

Comments: *Calypso* is named after the sea nymph Kalypso, which is from a Greek word meaning "covered or hidden." *Bulbosa* ("bulbous") refers to the swollen underground stem. These orchids are pollinated by inexperienced bees, which seek nectar rewards that the plants advertise through their fragrance and coloration. However, the flowers produce no nectar for these pollinators. Mature bees leave the flowers alone, and the plants depend upon successive generations of immature bees to continue the pollination process. Also called Deer Orchid.

SPOTTED CORALROOT
Corallorhiza maculata
Orchid Family (Orchidaceae)

Description: Saprophyte, often with numerous upright, yellowish-red or brown stems, 8"–18" tall. Plants lack green leaves but have small translucent scales along the stem. The pink or reddish (reddish-orange) flowers are borne in a loose cluster at the top of the stem. There are 3 reddish sepals and 3 petals; the lower petal forms a white, 3-lobed lip with several reddish spots. The other 2 petals are reddish and arch around and over the third petal. Fruit is a capsule with numerous seeds.

Bloom Season: Late spring and summer

Habitat/Range: Grows in humus or forest duff at low to mid elevations across the region and North America.

Comments: *Corallorhiza* is from the Greek *korallion* ("coral") and *rhiza* ("root") and refers to the knobby, coral-like roots. *Maculata* ("spotted") refers to the crimson spots on the flower. As saprophytes, these plants do not photosynthesize but obtain nutrients from soil fungi. The spotted lip offers a wide landing platform for insect pollinators such as flies or bees. As the insects search for nectar, they are dusted with pollen from stamens located in the upper hood of the flowers. Striped Coralroot (*C. striata*) has pinkish flowers with reddish-brown or purple stripes.

WESTERN CORALROOT

Corallorhiza mertensiana
Orchid Family (Orchidaceae)

Description: Saprophyte, often with numerous upright, reddish stems, 8"–20" tall. The plants lack green leaves but have semitranslucent, leaflike sheaths. The pink to reddish-brown flowers are borne in a loose cluster at the top of the stem and have 3 slender sepals and 3 petals. The lower, pink to red lip lacks spots or stripes but may have a white tip. Two narrow sepals project outward from the sides, while the third sepal is fused to the 2 upper petals, forming a hood. Fruit is a capsule with numerous seeds.

Bloom Season: Summer

Habitat/Range: Grows in humus or duff at low to mid elevations from Alaska to California and east to Montana and Wyoming. Sometimes found in close proximity to Spotted Coralroot (*C. maculata*).

Comments: *Corallorhiza* is from the Greek *korallion* ("coral") and *rhiza* ("root") and refers to the knobby, coral-like roots. *Mertensiana* is for Franz Carl Mertens (1764–1831), a professor of botany at Bremen, Germany. The knobby roots resemble coral; hence, the common name. As saprophytes, these plants do not photosynthesize but instead obtain nutrients from soil fungi. Similar to Spotted Coralroot, the wide lower lip provides a landing platform for insects that proceed into the flower in search of nectar.

APPLEGATE'S PAINTBRUSH

Castilleja applegatei
Broomrape/Paintbrush Family (Orobanchaceae)

Description: Perennial, with sticky-haired stems, 4"–24" tall. The variable leaves are linear (lower) and 3-lobed (upper) with wavy margins. The reddish bracts have 3–5 lobes and surround a spout-like, tubular, green corolla. Fruit is a capsule.

Bloom Season: Summer

Habitat/Range: Rocky outcrops or open woods at mid elevations from Oregon to California and east to Idaho.

Comments: *Castilleja* is for Domingo Castillejo (1744–1793), a Spanish professor of botany. *Applegatei* honors Elmer Applegate (1867–1949), a student of Oregon flora. Hummingbirds pollinate this species.

COTTONY PAINTBRUSH
Castilleja arachnoidea
Broomrape/Paintbrush Family (Orobanchaceae)

Description: Perennial, often with multiple stems 4"–10" tall. The leaves are hairy. Small, greenish flowers are hairy and enclosed by reddish-orange to greenish-yellow bracts. Fruit is a capsule.

Bloom Season: Midsummer to fall

Habitat/Range: Dry, sandy, gravelly, or pumice soils at mid to alpine elevations in Oregon, California, and Nevada.

Comments: *Castilleja* is for Domingo Castillejo (1744–1793), a Spanish professor of botany. *Arachnoidea* ("resembling spider hairs") refers to the hairy leaves and bracts. Many Indian paintbrush species are difficult to distinguish from each other. Hummingbirds or butterflies pollinate most species of paintbrush.

COMMON RED PAINTBRUSH
Castilleja miniata
Broomrape/Paintbrush Family (Orobanchaceae)

Description: Perennial, with stems 10"–36" tall. The entire leaves are smooth and lance-shaped with entire margins. The hairy, reddish bracts are 3-lobed and surround a greenish corolla. Fruit is a capsule.

Bloom Season: Late spring to early fall

Habitat/Range: Moist open meadows or along streams from sea level to subalpine elevations throughout the region.

Comments: *Castilleja* is for Domingo Castillejo (1744–1793), a Spanish professor of botany. *Miniata* ("Saturn-red") is for the scarlet-red bracts. Elmer's Paintbrush (*C. elmeri*) also has entire leaves, but the flowers are purplish red with sticky hairs. Hummingbird-pollinated.

ANNUAL INDIAN PAINTBRUSH
Castilleja minor
Broomrape/Paintbrush Family (Orobanchaceae)

Description: Annual, with stems 4–32" tall. The stems have sticky hairs. The leaves are narrowly lance-shaped. The upper floral bracts are tipped with red, while the corollas are yellow. Fruit is a capsule.

Bloom Season: Summer and early fall

Habitat/Range: Moist sites in meadows, marshes, or alkaline flats at low elevations throughout the western United States.

Comments: *Castilleja* is for Domingo Castillejo (1744–1793), a Spanish professor of botany. *Minor* ("smaller") refers to the small galea or upper helmetlike portion of the flower. Hummingbird-pollinated.

MOUNTAIN OWL CLOVER
Orthocarpus imbricatus
Broomrape/Paintbrush Family (Orobanchaceae)

Description: Annual, 4"–15" tall. Linear or narrowly lance-shaped leaves are 2" long with smooth margins. Showy, pink-purple bracts subtend the ½"-long, purplish-red flowers that barely show above the bracts. Fruit is a capsule.

Bloom Season: Mid to late summer

Habitat/Range: Dry meadows and mountain ridges at mid to high elevations from British Columbia to California.

Comments: *Orthocarpus* is from the Latin *orth* ("straight") and *karpos* ("fruit"), which is in reference to the symmetrical capsules. *Imbricatus* ("overlapping") refers to the overlapping, showy bracts. The common name may be from the spots resembling owl's eyes on some of the related species.

DWARF LOUSEWORT
Pedicularis centranthera
Broomrape/Paintbrush Family (Orobanchaceae)

Description: Perennial, with stems 1½"–2½" tall. Leaves are divided to midrib, 2"–6" long, linear to lance-shaped, and with "ruffled," toothed edges with white tips. Flowers grow in tight clusters; 5 lobes of the calyx are of unequal length and slightly hairy. Corolla is purple or yellowish, ¾" long, with the 2-lipped upper lip being hooded and the lower lip being 3-lobed.

Bloom Season: Late spring through summer

Habitat/Range: Juniper woodlands and mountain brush at mid elevations from southeast Oregon through the Great Basin.

Comments: *Pedicularis* ("of lice") refers to the ancient use of the seeds to destroy lice. This lousewort is partially parasitic on other plants. *Centranthera* is from the Greek *centrum* ("pointed") and *anther* ("anthers"), referring to the shape of the anthers.

ELEPHANTHEAD
Pedicularis groenlandica
Broomrape/Paintbrush Family (Orobanchaceae)

Description: Perennial, may be 6"–20" tall. Leaves are fernlike, 2"–6" long, and toothed along the margins. Reddish-purple, unbranched stems bear dense clusters of flowers at the terminal end. Each small, pinkish flower resembles an elephant's head. The upper petal is round, resembling the head, and then tapers to the long trunk. Three lower petals resemble the 2 large ears and the lower mouth. Fruit is a capsule.

Bloom Season: Late spring and early summer

Habitat/Range: Wet meadows and stream banks at mid to high elevations across Canada and south throughout the Cascade Range and east to the Rocky Mountains.

Comments: *Pedicularis* ("of lice") refers to the belief that livestock grazing in fields of these plants would become infested with lice. *Groenlandica* ("of Greenland") refers to the type locality. Bumblebees pollinate these flowers by perching on the trunk and forcing their way into the flower. Little Elephant's Head (*P. attollens*) is a similar species that occurs at subalpine elevations, but the trunk barely extends beyond the flower's throat.

WESTERN CORYDALIS
Corydalis scouleri
Poppy/Dicentra Family (Papaveraceae)

Description: Perennial, often in dense clusters with stems 2'–4' tall. The compound leaves divide 2–4 times, and the leaflets are oval- or lance-shaped and 1"–2½" long. The pinkish (white to rose to purplish) flowers are borne in a tight cluster along an elongated stalk and face one direction. The 4-petaled flowers are borne on short stems attached to their middle. The upper petal forms a hood and long spur, while the lower petal flares at the mouth. The side petals have crests. Fruit is a capsule.

Bloom Season: Mid spring to midsummer

Habitat/Range: Moist, shady woods from low to high elevations on the west side of the Cascades from southern British Columbia to northern Oregon.

Comments: *Corydalis* ("a lark") refers to the resemblance of the floral spur to that of the lark. *Scouleri* is for John Scouler (1804–1871), a Scotsman who joined the British Navy as a surgeon and who botanized with David Douglas in the Northwest. The flower's spur contains nectar that bumblebees seek, landing on the lateral petals joined together at their tips. This forces the upper petal apart and dusts the bees with pollen.

WILD BLEEDING HEART
Dicentra formosa
Poppy/Dicentra Family (Papaveraceae)

Description: Perennial, spreading by underground roots. The stout stems are 8"–20" tall and bear basal compound leaves on long stems that are fernlike—highly dissected and lobed. The flowering stalk bears 4–15 pinkish (sometimes white), heart-shaped flowers that hang downward. Of the 4 petals, the outer 2 have short spurs that spread outward. Fruit is a podlike capsule with black seeds.

Bloom Season: Late spring and summer

Habitat/Range: Moist sites in woodlands and along streams from low to mid elevations from British Columbia to central California.

Comments: *Dicentra* is from the Greek *dis* ("twice") and *kentron* ("a spur") after the 2 spurs formed by the petals. *Formosa* ("beautiful") describes the flower. The seed tips have a tiny, white appendage that is rich in oil and is coveted by ants. The ants carry the seeds to their nest, acting as dispersal agents for the seeds. Hummingbirds pollinate the flowers.

RED MONKEY-FLOWER
Erythranthe cardinalis
Monkey-flower Family (Phrymaceae)

Description: Perennial with upright or spreading stems, 1'–3' tall. Leaves are downy, opposite, palmately veined, and toothed along the margin. Reddish-orange flowers are about 1½" long, sub-tended by a green, hairy calyx, and the upper lip arches forward, and the lower lip curves backward. Fruit is a capsule.

Bloom Season: Late spring through summer

Habitat/Range: Moist sites, seeps, and wetland from low to mid elevations from Washington to Baja California and east to Utah.

Comments: *Frythranthe* is from the Greek *erythros* ("red") and *anthos* ("flowers"), which is in refer-ence to the flower color of some species in this genus. *Cardinalis* ("red") refers to the flower color. Hummingbird- and butterfly-pollinated, this plant sometimes escapes cultivation.

LEWIS' MONKEY-FLOWER
Erythranthe lewisii
Monkey-flower Family (Phrymaceae)

Description: Perennial, often growing in thick clusters. Stems are 15"–45" tall and covered with soft, sticky hairs. The oval-shaped leaves clasp the stem and are arranged oppositely. The leaves are toothed along the margin. Trumpet-shaped, rose-red, or pinkish flowers are 1½"–2" long and 2-lipped. The lower lip has 2 yellowish, hairy ridges. Fruit is a capsule.

Bloom Season: Summer

Habitat/Range: Moist clearings, stream banks, and rocky seeps from mid to high elevations from British Columbia to California and east to Colorado.

Comments: *Erythranthe* is from the Greek *erythros* ("red") and *anthos* ("flowers"), which is in reference to the flower color of some species in this genus. *Lewisii* honors Meriwether Lewis (1774–1809), co-leader of the Corps of Discovery Exploration with William Clark and who was a statesman, soldier, and explorer. The insides of the flowers have flypaper-like glands that trap insects.

FOXGLOVE

Digitalis purpurea
Plantain Family (Plantaginaceae)

Description: Perennial, stout stems reach 1'–7' tall. Basal leaves borne on long stems are 7"–20" long, egg- to lance-shaped, and finely toothed along the margins. Upper leaves smaller. The flowering stalk bears numerous tube-shaped flowers that flare open at the mouth, droop slightly downward, and are 2"–3" long. The flowers are white, pink, red, or purple (or intergrades of these colors) and have spots inside the lower lip. Fruit is an egg-shaped capsule.

Bloom Season: Late spring and summer

Habitat/Range: Widespread in disturbed areas such as roadways, fields, fallow meadows, and forest edges from low elevation. Introduced from Europe, this plant occurs throughout the Northwest.

Comments: *Digitalis* is from the Latin *digitus* ("finger") and refers to the flower's resemblance to a glove's finger. *Purpurea* ("purple") describes the flower color. Flowering stalks mature from the bottom up. Plants produce the compound digitalin, which is made into digitalis, a potent heart medicine that is used in modern cardiac treatment.

PALMER'S PENSTEMON

Penstemon palmeri
Plantain Family (Plantaginaceae)

Description: Perennial, stout stems 20"–56" tall. Basal and lower stem leaves are egg-shaped and up to 4" long with a short stalk. Upper leaves are triangular or heart-shaped and clasp the stem. Leaf edges are smooth or toothed. Floral stalk bears large, tubular flowers that are 1"–1½" long and have wide openings. The pink, lavender, or whitish 2-lipped flowers have prominent, purplish nectar lines on the lower lips and throat and have a bearded sterile stamen that protrudes beyond the flower opening. Fruit is a capsule.

Bloom Season: Summer

Habitat/Range: Roadsides and cultivated areas, sagebrush flats, and pine woodlands from low to mid elevation in Idaho and eastern Oregon.

Comments: *Palmeri* honors Edward Palmer (1829–1911), an avid plant collector in North and South America, with over 200 species named for him. Though mainly a Southwestern species, this penstemon has been seeded for highway beautification projects and cultivated gardens and is now naturalized in Idaho. Bumblebees muscle into the flowers to seek nectar and pollen using the nectar lines as guides.

ROCK PENSTEMON
Penstemon rupicola
Plantain Family (Plantaginaceae)

Description: Perennial, growing in dense mats. Evergreen leaves are opposite, short-stemmed, and egg-shaped with finely toothed margins. Tubular flowers are 1"–1½" long, pink to reddish purple, and 2-lipped. The upper lip has a keel on the outside, while the lower lip has 2 white, hairy ridges. The anthers have long, white hairs. Fruit is a capsule.

Bloom Season: Late spring to midsummer

Habitat/Range: Rocky outcrops and basalt cliffs from low to high elevations in the Cascades from southern Washington to northern California.

Comments: *Rupicola* ("rocky") refers to the habitat preference of this penstemon. Also known as Cliff Penstemon, this species has woolly anther sacs. Davidson's Penstemon (*P. davidsonii*) is another low-growing, mat-forming penstemon with purple to lavender flowers that grows on rocky outcrops.

SEA THRIFT
Armeria maritima
Plumbago Family (Plumbaginaceae)

Description: Perennial, flowering stems up to 10". The linear basal leaves are stiff and spiny and form dense, mat-like clusters. Flowering stalks bear rounded clusters, ½"–1½" wide, of tiny, pink or lavender flowers. Papery bracts arise below the flower clusters, and the petals are also papery and may last on the plant long after the blooming season. Fruit is a single seed enclosed within a bladder that is often enclosed by the sepals.

Bloom Season: Mid spring to summer

Habitat/Range: Coastal bluffs and beaches, although may grow inland in grassy meadows. Sea Thrift has a circumboreal distribution.

Comments: *Armeria* is from the French name *armoires* ("cluster-headed *Dianthus*"), which refers to a different, although similar looking, plant. *Maritima* ("coastal") refers to the plant's distribution. This species occurs in both coastal and inland horticultural gardens.

SPREADING PHLOX
Phlox diffusa
Phlox Family (Polemoniaceae)

Description: Perennial with low, matted growth. Numerous needlelike, yellowish-green leaves are opposite, ½"–¾" long, and sharply pointed. The flowers are ½"–¾" wide, trumpet-shaped, and vary in color from pink to white to bluish. The 5 petals are fused together for most of their length. Fruit is a small capsule.

Bloom Season: Spring to late summer

Habitat/Range: Dry, open sites that are rocky or in woodlands from mid to higher elevations from British Columbia to California and east to western Montana.

Comments: *Phlox* ("flame") refers to the flower color, and *diffusa* ("spreading") describes the plants' spreading nature. These plants often form a quilt-like pattern of flowers against a spring hillside, attracting a number of early season pollinators.

SCARLET GILIA
Ipomopsis aggregata
Phlox Family (Polemoniaceae)

Description: Biennial or short-lived perennial. One to several flowering stalks arise 1'–3' from a basal rosette of highly dissected leaves. Stem leaves are smaller. Flowers are borne in loose clusters and are mostly red, although orange or yellow forms exist. Flowers have white to yellowish speckles, and the corolla tube flares open to form a 5-pointed star. Fruit is a capsule.

Blooms Season: Summer

Habitat/Range: Widespread in dry meadows, roadsides, rocky outcrops, or lightly wooded areas from low to high elevations east of the Cascades to Idaho and the Rocky Mountains.

Comments: *Ipomopsis* is from the Greek *ipo* ("to strike") and *opsis* ("resembling"), which is in reference to the striking flowers. *Gilia* honors Filippo Luigi Gilli (1756–1821), an Italian astronomer and co-author of *Osservazioni Fitologiche* (1789–1792). *Aggregata* ("aggregated") refers to the cluster of basal leaves. Hummingbirds, butterflies, and certain moths are the primary pollinators that can reach the flower's nectar. Also called Skyrocket Gilia.

SHOWY PHLOX
Phlox speciosa
Phlox Family (Polemoniaceae)

Description: Perennial, low growing, 6"–16" tall. Linear-shaped leaves are arranged oppositely along the stem, are linear to lance-shaped, ½"–2" long, and pointed at the tip. There may be some hairs and glands on the leaf's upper surface. Pink or white 5-petaled flowers are ¾"–1" wide, with a long tube, and the petals are notched or 2-lobed at the tip. Fruit is a capsule.

Bloom Season: Grasslands, shrub steppe, and open woodlands from low to mid elevations from British Columbia throughout much of the west.

Habitat/Range: Widely grows in serpentine and sandy soils in sagebrush steppe, pine forests, and mountain woodlands throughout western North America at mid elevations.

Comments: *Phlox* ("flame") refers to the flower color, and *speciosa* ("beautiful") defines the flowers.

MOUNTAIN SORREL
Oxyria digyna
Smartweed-Buckwheat Family (Polygonaceae)

Description: Perennial, generally less than 20" tall. Clustered basal leaves are round to heart-shaped, fleshy, and borne on long stems. Flowering stems rise above the leaves and bear numerous, tiny, reddish and green flowers that lack petals. Fruit is a nut surrounded by a reddish wing.

Bloom Season: Mid to late summer

Habitat/Range: Rocky soils, talus slopes, and rock crevices at higher elevation or alpine areas in the Pacific Northwest and has a circumpolar distribution occurring in other mountainous regions in the northern hemisphere.

Comments: *Oxyria* ("sour") refers to the taste of the edible leaves due to the presence of oxalic acid. *Digyna* ("with 2 pistils") refers to the flower structure.

SHEEP SORREL
Rumex acetosella
Smartweed-Buckwheat Family (Polygonaceae)

Description: Perennial, up to 12" tall. The arrowhead-shaped leaves have flaring lobes near the base. The tiny, reddish-brown flowers are borne along an elongated stalk. Male and female flowers are on different plants. Fruit is a reddish-brown, winged seed.

Bloom Season: Spring to summer

Habitat/Range: Widespread weedy species from low to subalpine elevations throughout the region.

Comments: *Rumex* is the Latin name for sorrel or dock. *Acetosella* is from the Latin *acetum* ("vinegar") in reference to the slightly bitter taste of the edible leaves, which is due to oxalic acid.

SAND DOCK
Rumex venosus
Smartweed-Buckwheat Family (Polygonaceae)

Description: Perennial that propagates from horizontally spreading roots. Stems are 4"–20" tall, stem leaves are egg-shaped to elliptical, ¾"–5½" long, and ½"–2" wide. Numerous flowers have greenish floral segments that are ⅛" long. The 3 segments become enlarged when mature and red in fruit.

Bloom Season: Mid spring to midsummer

Habitat/Range: Sandy flats and dunes at mid elevations across much of western North America.

Comments: *Rumex* is the Latin name for sorrel or dock. *Venosus* ("veined") refers to the prominent leaf veins. The common name refers to this plant's habitat preference. Boiling the roots produces red, yellow, or black dyes. A poultice from the mashed roots has been used to treat burns.

JEFFREY'S SHOOTING STAR

Primula jeffreyi
Primrose Family (Primulaceae)

Description: Perennial, up to 20" tall, with a stem that is up to ¼" thick. Leaves variable inversely lance- or spatula-shaped, 4"–7" long, and smooth or with glandular hairs. Flowering stalks may bear numerous flowers. The flowers are ½"–1" long and have 4 or 5 pink to purple petals ringed with white and a red or purple base. Stamen filaments are dark. Fruit is a capsule.

Bloom Season: Late spring to early summer

Habitat/Range: Moist meadows and marshes in the mountains from Alaska to California and east to Idaho.

Comments: *Primula* ("first") refers to this plant as an early season flowering plant. *Jeffreyi* honors John Jeffrey (1826–1854), a gardener at the Edinburgh Botanical Garden in England. Bees pollinate the flowers. Also called Tall Mountain Shooting Star.

POET'S SHOOTING STAR

Dodecatheon poeticum
Primrose Family (Primulaceae)

Description: Perennial, up to 1' tall. Leaves are variable, mostly spatula-shaped, from 1½"–6" long, and covered with fine, glandular hairs. Margins of leaves may be toothed or smooth. Star-shaped flowers have pink-purple to rose-colored petals that bend backward and are ringed with yellow and a red base. The stamen filaments are purple and short. Fruit is a capsule.

Bloom Season: Late spring to early summer

Habitat/Range: Grassy slopes and woodlands that are moist in spring but become drier in summer. Occurs from central Washington to the Columbia River Gorge.

Comments: *Dodecatheon* is from the Greek *dodeka* ("12") and *theos* ("god"), meaning that the 12 Olympian gods protected the plants. Bumblebees pollinate these flowers by hanging upside down from the yellow ring and "buzzing" their wings. Pollen shakes loose and lands on the bee's belly from which the bee gleans the pollen into leg sacs. When the bee visits another flower, leftover pollen comes in contact with that flower's stigma to complete the pollen transfer. Also called Narcissus Shooting Star.

RED COLUMBINE
Aquilegia formosa
Buttercup Family (Ranunculaceae)

Description: A striking plant growing 3' tall, bearing leaves that are twice divided into 3s. The majority of leaves are basal. The red and yellow, drooping flowers have 5 long spurs and a central cluster of yellowish stamens and styles that project beyond the flower's mouth. Seeds are tiny, numerous, and black.

Bloom Season: Summer

Habitat/Range: A variety of moist sites that may be open or partially shaded throughout the region.

Comments: *Aquilegia* ("eagle") refers to the talon-like spurs on the flowers, and *formosa* ("beautiful") refers to the flowers. The red flowers attract hummingbirds and butterflies, which use their long tongues or proboscises to reach the nectar at the bulbous base of the spurs. Does well in ornamental gardens.

DARK-THROATED SHOOTING STAR
Primula pauciflora
Primrose Family (Primulaceae)

Description: Perennial, 2"–16" tall. Basal leaves are ¾"–7" long, the blades are lance- to oblong lance-shaped, sometimes with slight serrations along the margins, and borne on a long stem. Flower stalks bear 1–25 5-petaled flowers that are about ½" long, purple to lavender with a white spot and dark ring at the base. The petals flare backward. Yellow stamen filaments are fused together and have a purple-black tip. Fruit is a capsule.

Bloom Season: Mid spring to midsummer

Habitat/Range: Moist meadows, bogs, fens, and wetlands from mid to alpine elevations from British Columbia to Oregon and east to Montana.

Comments: *Primula* ("first") refers to this genus as an early season flowering plant. *Pauciflora* ("few-flowers") refers to the plant bearing a limited number of flowers. Flowers are pollinated by bees through "buzz pollination"—bees grab the petals and vibrate their wings, which drop the pollen down onto the insect.

OLD MAN'S WHISKERS
Geum triflorum
Rose Family (Rosaceae)

Description: Perennial, 4"–20" tall. The basal leaves are fernlike and hairy. The 1'-long, vase-shaped flowers are arranged in groups of 3 and hang downward. The pink to yellowish petals are hidden beneath 5 red sepals and curved bracts. Seeds have a long, hairy plume.

Bloom Season: Late spring to midsummer

Habitat/Range: Rocky outcrops, grassy slopes, and seasonally moist meadows at low to mid elevations east of the Cascades throughout the region.

Comments: *Geum* is the classical Latin name for this genus. *Triflorum* ("3 flowers") refers to the floral clusters. First collected by Meriwether Lewis in 1806. As the seeds mature, the flower stems turn upward. The 2"-long, feathery tails on the seeds, which resemble whiskers, promote wind dispersal. Also called Prairie Smoke.

NOOTKA ROSE
Rosa nutkana
Rose Family (Rosaceae)

Description: Shrub, averaging 3'–5' in height. Stems may have prickles or large, recurved thorns that form in pairs mostly near the newly developing leaves. The compound leaves have 5–9 egg-shaped to elliptical leaflets, 1"–3½" long, with saw-toothed margins. Flowers borne singularly at the end of the stem are up to 3½" wide, fragrant, and pink- to rose-colored. The sepals remain on the plant after the flower matures. Fruits (hips) are bright red and rounded.

Bloom Season: Spring to early summer

Habitat/Range: Open woodlands, woodland edges, or thickets from sea level to mid elevations from Alaska to northern California and east to the Rocky Mountains.

Comments: *Rosa* is the Latin name for a rose. *Nutkana* refers to the Nootka Sound in British Columbia where the type specimen was collected. High in vitamin C, rose hips were eaten as a last resort against starvation. Teas or poultices were also made from the branches or leaves for treating eye problems or sores. The fragrant flowers attract bees, beetles, butterflies, and other pollinators. The Peafruit Rose (*R. pisocarpa*) also has thorns that occur near the leaf buds but has smaller (up to 1½" wide), clustered flowers and pointed leaflets and occurs in wet locations.

WOODS' ROSE
Rosa woodsii
Rose Family (Rosaceae)

Description: Shrub, up to 3½" tall. Stems bear small prickles. Compound leaves have 5–9 egg-shaped to elliptical leaflets that are ½"–1½" long and toothed along the margins. The 1"–2"-wide, pinkish flowers retain their sepals in fruit. Fruit is a red rose hip.

Bloom Season: Late spring through summer

Habitat/Range: Along streams and forest edges from low to high elevations and is widely distributed in most of western North America.

Comments: *Rosa* is the Latin name for a rose. *Woodsii* is for Joseph Woods (1776–1864), an English architect who botanized and studied plants, mostly in Europe. The edible rose hips are collected for tea or medicinal properties.

SALMONBERRY
Rubus spectabilis
Rose Family (Rosaceae)

Description: Shrub, may grow in thickets and be 3'–16' tall. Thorny on the lower stems but less so above. Leaves divided into 3 or 5 sharply toothed lobes; leaves 3"–8" long. Reddish-purple flowers are 1"–1½" wide, with 5 petals and numerous stamens. Fruit is a salmon-colored berry.

Bloom Season: Early to mid spring

Habitat/Range: Moist areas along streams, coastal woods, and forests on the east side of the Cascades from low to mid elevations from Alaska to California.

Comments: *Rubus* is the Latin name for blackberries and raspberries. *Spectabilis* ("spectacular") refers to the color of the flowers. Fruits are edible. The shrubs may flower before the plant leaves emerge. Pollinated by bees and early migrating hummingbirds.

MOUNTAIN SPIRAEA
Spiraea splendens
Rose Family (Rosaceae)

Description: Shrub, spreads by underground roots, and reaches 40" tall. The numerous branches have reddish-brown bark. The egg-shaped to elliptical leaves are 1"–2" long and toothed along the margin. The dense flowering heads are flat-topped or rounded and bear numerous pinkish flowers with stamens extending past the petals. Fruit is a few-seeded pod.

Bloom Season: Summer

Habitat/Range: Open woodlands, forest edges, and disturbed areas such as avalanche chutes or clearings at mid to subalpine elevations from southern British Columbia to California and east to Idaho and parts of Montana and Wyoming.

Comments: *Spiraea* is from the Greek *speiraira* ("a plant used for garlands"). *Splendens* ("splendid") refers to the flower heads. The stamens protrude above the petals, giving the flower heads a "fuzzy" appearance. The mass of flowers provides pollinators, such as bees, opportunities to visit numerous flowers without having to search for other plants.

DOUGLAS' SPIRAEA
Spiraea douglasii
Rose Family (Rosaceae)

Description: Shrub, 2"–7" tall with numerous upright branches. The deciduous leaves are 2"–4" long and toothed along the edge (from the middle to the tip) and have dense, wool-like, gray hairs on the undersides. Tiny flowers are arranged in dense, elongated clusters (several times longer than broad) that reach 2"–6" long. The pink- to rose-colored flowers fade with age. Fruit is a long pod.

Bloom Season: Summer

Habitat/Range: Moist locations along streams, rivers, meadows, and lakes from low to mid elevations from southern Alaska to northern California and east to central Idaho.

Comments: *Spiraea* is from the Greek *speiraira* ("a plant used for garlands"), while *douglasii* honors David Douglas (1799–1834), the Scottish botanist who collected plants in the Pacific Northwest for the Royal Horticultural Society in the mid-1820s. Look for bumblebees and butterflies sipping nectar on these flowers. The protruding stamens give the flowers a "fuzzy" appearance.

SEA BLUSH
Plectritis congesta
Valerian Family (Valerianaceae)

Description: Annual, 4"–30" tall. The short-stalked basal leaves are egg- or club-shaped while the stem leaves are egg-shaped and stalkless. Leaves vary from ½"–2" long and are arranged oppositely along the stem. Floral stalks bear a rounded cluster of pink (occasionally white) flowers. The 5-lobed individual flowers are tube-shaped and about ⅛" wide and have a short spur at the base. Fruit is a winged seed.

Bloom Season: Mid spring to early summer

Habitat/Range: Moist meadows, rocky slopes, and bluffs at low elevations that dry up in summer from Vancouver Island south to California from the Cascades west to the coast.

Comments: *Plectritis* ("plaited") refers to the interwoven flower arrangement, and *congesta* ("congested") also refers to this arrangement. These plants may bloom in profusion, covering large areas.

GREAT BASIN VIOLET
Viola beckwithii
Violet Family (Violaceae)

Description: Perennial, 2"–20" tall; much of the stem may be underground. Leaves are fleshy, compound with narrow leaflets, and borne on long stems. The upper 2 petals are maroon to purple, and the lower 3 are lavender to blue-colored with yellow centers and purple veins. The lowest petal is spurred. Fruit is a seed.

Bloom Season: Early to mid spring

Habitat/Range: Sagebrush steppe and pine woodlands in moist soil at mid elevations from Oregon to California and east to Utah.

Comments: *Viola* is the Latin name for several scented flowers. *Bechwithii* is for Lt. Edward Griffin Beckwith (1818–1881), who served with the Topographical Engineers and led an expedition along the 38th and 39th parallel searching for a possible railroad route to California.

ORANGE FLOWERS

This section includes orange flowers as well as multicolored flowers that are predominantly orange. Since orange flowers often become either paler or deeper in color with age, you should check both the yellow and red sections if you do not find the flower you are looking for in this section.

ORANGE AGOSERIS
Agoseris aurantiaca
Aster Family (Asteraceae)

Description: Perennial, 4"–24" tall. Lance- to egg-shaped basal leaves are pointed at the tip and may or may not have lobes. The leafless flowering stalk bears a single flowering head with orange ray flowers that are square-tipped and lacks disk flowers. Fruit is a seed with hairs.

Bloom Season: Summer

Habitat/Range: Meadows, grasslands, forests, moist seeps, and alpine areas across much of the western United States.

Comments: *Agoseris* ("goat chicory") presumably refers to this plant being consumed as a forage plant. *Aurantiaca* ("orange-red") refers to the color of the flowers. Also called Orange Dandelion or Mountain Dandelion for its resemblance in flower structure and seed heads to those of the common Dandelion.

ORANGE SNEEZEWEED
Hymenoxys hoopesii
Aster Family (Asteraceae)

Description: Perennial, plants 1'–3' tall. Oblong basal leaves are entire and hairy or smooth. Upper leaves are lance-shaped and lack a stem. Orange-yellow flower heads are borne on woolly stalks and have 14–26 drooping ray flowers, which are 1½" long, surround a center of orangish disk flowers. Fruit is a seed with scales.

Bloom Season: Summer

Habitat/Range: Meadows and moist locations at high elevations from the Cascades to the Rocky Mountains.

Comments: *Hymenoxys* is from the Greek *hymen* ("membrane") and *oxys* ("sharp"), which is in reference to the pointed pappus scales. *Hoopesii* honors Thomas Hoopes (1834–1925) who was a farmer, civic leader, and amateur botanist who traveled west and collected plants and seeds in Colorado.

ORANGE JEWELWEED
Impatiens capensis
Jewelweeds Family (Balsaminaceae)

Description: Perennial. The alternate leaves are elliptical to oval and toothed along the margins. The flowers are 1"–2" long and orange- or brown-spotted. The horn-shaped flowers appear inflated, but there are 4 petals and 3 sepals, 1 of which forms a curved spur. Fruit is a capsule with several seeds.

Bloom Season: Summer

Habitat/Range: Moist areas along streams, rivers, and thickets at low to mid elevations from north-west Washington to the Columbia River Gorge in Oregon, but it is also found in the eastern United States and Canada.

Comments: *Impatiens* ("impatient") refers to the dispersal mechanism of the seeds. When the ripe capsule is touched, the pods explode lengthwise; they are "impatient" with being touched and hurl the seeds outward. *Capensis* ("of the Cape of Good Hope, South Africa") refers to the resemblance of the flowers to the outline of South Africa. The succulent stems were crushed and the juice was applied to poison ivy rashes by Native Americans. Also called Touch-Me-Not after the exploding capsule.

ORANGE HONEYSUCKLE
Lonicera ciliosa
Honeysuckle Family (Caprifoliaceae)

Description: Deciduous shrub or climbing vine, reaches 6' or more. Oval leaves 1½"–4" long, oppo-site, and the last pair on a branch fuse together. Trumpet-shaped, orange flowers are ¾"–1½" long and arranged in clusters at the ends of a branch. Fruit is an orange-red berry.

Bloom Season: Late spring to midsummer

Habitat/Range: Woodlands from low to mid eleva-tions from British Columbia to Oregon and east to Montana.

Comments: *Lonicera* is named after Adam Lonitzer (1528–1586), a German naturalist. *Ciliosa* ("small, fringe-like hairs") refers to the hairs on the edges of the leaves. The fruits are edible, and the plants are often used in ornamental gardens. Humming-birds, bees, and butterflies pollinate the flowers.

TIGER LILY
Lilium columbianum
Lily Family (Liliaceae)

Description: Plants may be 1'–4' tall with hairless (usually), slender stems. Lance-shaped leaves, 2"–5" long, are arranged in several whorls of 6–9 leaves. Upper stem leaves variable. Showy, orange flowers have red or purple spots near the center. The tepals curve backward to expose the orange anthers. Fruit is a barrel-shaped capsule that contains numerous seeds.

Bloom Season: Summer

Habitat/Range: Low to subalpine elevations in meadows, clearings, or open forests from British Columbia to California and east to Nevada.

Comments: *Lilium* is from the Greek *leirion* ("a lily"). *Columbianum* ("Columbia River") refers to the area where this plant was first collected for science. The edible bulbs are peppery. Hummingbirds pollinate the flowers.

MUNRO'S GLOBEMALLOW
Sphaeralcea munroana
Mallow Family (Malvaceae)

Description: Perennial, grows up to 3' tall. Palmately lobed leaves are covered with white, star-shaped hairs and have 5 lobes that are toothed along the margins. Clusters of flowers are borne on an elongated stalk, are bowl-shaped, have orange- to salmon-colored petals, and have numerous stamens. Flowers are ½"–1" wide. Fruit is a capsule.

Bloom Season: Mid to late spring

Habitat/Range: Sandy or rocky soils in dry sagebrush steppe or mountain slopes at low to mid elevations from British Columbia throughout the western United States.

Comments: *Sphaeralcea* ("globe mallow") refers to the round capsules. *Munroana* honors Dr. Donald Munro (1789–1853), curator of the gardens at the Horticultural Society in London. Sometimes when the flowers close at night, small bees curl up inside and spend the night.

CALIFORNIA POPPY
Eschscholzia californica
Poppy/Dicentra Family (Papaveraceae)

Description: Perennial, plants 6–22" tall. The highly divided basal leaves have a bluish tint and a lacy appearance. The flowering stalks bear a single, yellow to orange, bowl-shaped flower, with 4 delicate petals that are ½"–2" long. The flower sits on a distinct rim that becomes more noticeable in fruit. Fruit is a long, slender seedpod.

Bloom Season: Mid spring through fall

Habitat/Range: Grassy slopes, rock outcrops, and disturbed areas at low elevations west of the Cascades from southwest Washington to southern California.

Comments: Named after Johann Friedrich von Eschscholtz (1793–1831), an eminent German physician, botanist, and naturalist who completed 2 circumnavigations of the globe with the explorer Otto von Kotzebue in 1815–1818 and 1823–1826. *Californicus* ("of California") refers to the location of the type specimen. The flowers close at night or during cloudy days. Bees, wasps, and beetles might be observed pollinating the flowers. A widely used ornamental, this plant is the California state flower.

LARGE-FLOWERED COLLOMIA
Collomia grandiflora
Phlox Family (Polemoniaceae)

Description: Annual, stems up to 40". These plants may have 1 or many stems. The narrow leaves are up to 2" long and linear. The 1"-long, funnel-shaped flowers are arranged in sticky clusters and are salmon, light red, yellow, or white in color. The flowers flare open to reveal (barely) the 5 stamens. Fruit is a capsule.

Bloom Season: Late spring and summer

Habitat/Range: Dry, open woodlands on either side of the Cascades from British Columbia to California and east to Montana.

Comments: *Collomia* is from the Greek *colla* ("glue") and refers to the stickiness of the wet seeds. *Grandiflora* ("large flower") refers to the flower's size. The roots and leaves were brewed by some Northwest tribes as an eyewash or laxative or to treat fevers.

GREAT POLEMONIUM
Polemonium carneum
Phlox Family (Polemoniaceae)

Description: Perennial, sprawling stems up to 15"–50" long. The compound basal leaves have numerous elliptical leaflets. Salmon to whitish or blue flowers are borne in dense clusters. The funnel-shaped flowers are about 1" wide and have 5 petals. Fruit is a capsule.

Bloom Season: Early to midsummer

Habitat/Range: Moist woods, thickets, and openings at low to mid elevations on the west side of the Cascades.

Comments: *Polemonium* is from a Greek medicinal plant often associated with the philosopher Polemon (314–270 BCE). *Carneum* ("flesh-colored") refers to the flowers. Flies, bees, and beetles are common pollinators of the flowers.

GLOSSARY

Alternate—placed singly along a stem or axis, one after another, usually each successive item on a different side from the previous; often used in reference to the arrangement of leaves on a stem (*see* Opposite).

Annual—a plant completing its life cycle, from seed germination to production of new seeds, within a year, and then dying.

Axil—the area created on the upper side of the angle between a leaf and stem.

Basal—at the base or bottom of; generally used in reference to leaves arranged at the base of the plant.

Biennial—a plant completing its life cycle in two years and normally not producing flowers during the first year.

Bract—reduced or modified leaf, often associated with flowers.

Bristle—a stiff hair, usually erect or curving away from its attachment point.

Bulb—underground plant part derived from a short, usually rounded, shoot that is covered with fleshy scales.

Calyx—the outer set of flower parts, composed of the sepals, which may be separate or joined together; usually green.

Capsule—a dry fruit that releases seeds through splits or holes.

Compound Leaf—a leaf that is divided into two to many leaflets, each of which may resemble a complete leaf but which lacks buds. Compound leaves may have leaflets arranged along an axis similar to the rays of a feather or radiating from a common point like the fingers on a hand (*see* illustration p. 9).

Corolla—the set of flower parts interior to the calyx and surrounding the stamens, composed of the petals, which may be free or united; often brightly colored.

Deciduous—referring to broad-leaved trees or shrubs that drop their leaves at the end of each growing season, as contrasted with plants that retain the leaves throughout the year (*see* Evergreen).

Disk Flowers—small, tubular flowers in the central portion of the flower head of many plants in the Aster Family (Asteraceae) (*see* illustrations p. 10).

Elliptical (Leaf Shape)—*see* illustrations p. 12.

Entire (Leaf Margin)—*see* illustrations p. 9.

Evergreen—referring to plants that bear green leaves throughout the year, as contrasted with plants that lose their leaves at the end of the growing season (*see* Deciduous).

Family—a group of plants having biologically similar features, such as flower anatomy, fruit type, etc.

Flower Head—as used in this guide, a dense and continuous group of flowers, without obvious branches or space between them; used especially in reference to the Aster Family (Asteraceae).

Forb—a herbaceous flowering plant that is not a grass.

Genus—a group of closely related species, such as the genus *Penstemon* encompassing the penstemons (*see* Specific Epithet).

Herbaceous—referring to any nonwoody plant; often reserved for wildflowers or forbs.

Hood—curving or folded, petallike structure interior to the petals and exterior to the stamens in the Milkweed Family (Apocynaceae); since most milkweeds have reflexed petals, the hoods are typically the most prominent feature of the flowers.

Inflorescence—generally a cluster of flowers, although there are many terms to specifically describe the arrangement of flowers on the plant.

Involucre—a distinct series of bracts or leaves that subtend a flower or cluster of flowers. Often used in the description of the Aster Family (Asteraceae) flower heads.

Keel—a sharp lengthwise fold or ridge, referring particularly to the two fused petals forming the lower lip in many flowers of the Pea Family (Fabaceae)

Lance (Leaf Shape)—*see* illustration p. 10.

Leaflet—a distinct, leaflike segment of a compound leaf.

Linear (Leaf Shape)—*see* illustration p. 10.

Lobe—a segment of an incompletely divided plant part, typically rounded; often used in reference to the leaves.

Midrib—the central or main vein of a leaf.

Node—the region of the stem where one or more leaves are attached. Buds are commonly borne at the node, in the axils of the leaves.

Nutlet—a descriptive term for small nutlike fruits. Used to describe the separate lobes of a mature ovary in the Borage (Boraginaceae) and Mint (Lamiaceae) families.

Oblong (Leaf Shape)—*see* illustrations p. 10.

Opposite—paired directly across from one another along a stem or axis (*see* Alternate).

Ovary—the portion of the flower where the seeds develop, usually a swollen area below the style (if present) and stigma.

Pappus—in the Aster Family (Asteraceae), the modified limb of the calyx is the pappus, which consists of a crown of bristles, hairs, or scales at the top of the seed.

Parallel—side by side, approximately the same distance apart for the entire length; often used in reference to veins or edges of leaves.

Perennial—a plant that normally lives for three or more years.

Petal—component part of the corolla, often the most brightly colored and visible part of the flower.

Petiole—the stalk of a leaf. The length of the petiole may be used in leaf descriptions.

Pinnate—referring to a compound leaf, like many of the Pea Family (Fabaceae) members, where smaller leaflets are arranged along either side of a common axis.

Pistil—the seed-producing, or female, part of a flower, consisting of the ovary, style (if present), and stigma; a flower may have one to several separate pistils.

Pollen—tiny, often powdery male reproductive cells formed in the stamens and typically necessary for seed production.

Ray Flower—flower in the Aster Family (Asteraceae) with a single, strap-shaped corolla, resembling one flower petal; several to many ray flowers may surround the disk flowers in a flower head, or in some species such as dandelions, the flower heads may be composed entirely of ray flowers (*see* illustration p. 12).

Rosette—a dense cluster of basal leaves from a common underground part, often in a flattened, circular arrangement.

Scale—any thin, membranous body that somewhat resembles the scales of fish or reptiles.

Sepal—component part of the calyx; typically green but sometimes enlarged and brightly colored.

Shrub—a perennial woody plant of relatively low height, and typically with several stems arising from or near the ground.

Silique—the pod-like fruiting body of plants in the Mustard Family (Brassicaceae) that is longer than it is wide.

Simple Leaf—a leaf that has a single leaflike blade, although this may be lobed or divided.

Spatula (Leaf Shape)—*see* illustration p. 10.

Specific Epithet—the second portion of a scientific name, identifying a particular species; for instance in Tiger Lily, *Lilium columbianum*, the specific epithet is "*columbianum.*"

Spike—an elongate, unbranched cluster of stalkless or nearly stalkless flowers.

Stalk—as used here, the stem supporting the leaf, flower, or flower cluster.

Stalkless—lacking a stalk; a stalkless leaf is attached directly to the stem at the leaf base.

Stamen—the male unit of a flower, which produces the pollen: typically consisting of a long filament with a pollen-producing tip.

Standard—the usually erect, spreading upper petal in many flowers of the Pea Family (Fabaceae).

Stigma—portion of the pistil between the ovary and the stigma; typically a slender stalk.

Style—the stalk-like part of the pistil that connects the ovary to the stigma.

Subtend—to be situated below or beneath, often encasing or enclosing something.

Toothed—bearing teeth, or sharply angled projections, along the edge.

Variety—a group of plants within a species that has a distinct range, habitat, or structure.

Whorl—three or more parts attached at the same point along a stem or axis and often surrounding the stem.

Wings—the two side petals flanking the keel in many flowers of the Pea Family (Fabaceae).

SELECTED REFERENCES

Barth, Friedrich G. *Insects and Flowers: The Biology of a Partnership.* Princeton, NJ: Princeton University Press, 1985.

Blackwell, Laird. *Great Basin Wildflowers: A Guide to Common Wildflowers of the High Deserts of Nevada, Utah, and Oregon.* Guilford, CT: Morris Book Publishing, LLC, 2006.

Chipman, Art. *Wildflower Trails of the Pacific Northwest.* Medford, OR: Pine Cone Publishers, 1970.

Coombes, Allen J. *Dictionary of Plant Names.* Portland, OR: Timber Press, Inc., 1994.

Cronquist, A., A. Homgren, N. H. Holmgren, J. L. Reveal, P. K. Homgren, and R. C. Barneby. *Intermountain Flora, Vascular Plants of the Intermountain West, U.S.A.* vols. 3–6. New York: The New York Botanical Garden, 1977–1997.

Durrant, Mary. *Who Named the Daisy? Who Named the Rose?* New York: Dodd, Mead & Co., 1976.

Fagan, Damian. *Pacific Northwest Wildflowers: A Guide to Common Wildflowers of Washington, Oregon, Northern California, Western Idaho, Southeast Alaska, and British Columbia.* Guilford, CT: Morris Book Publishing, LLC, 2006.

Gilkey, Helen M. and La Rea J. Dennis. *Handbook of Northwestern Plants*, rev. ed. Corvallis, OR : Oregon State University Press, 2001.

Haskin, Leslie L. *Wild Flowers of the Pacific Coast.* Portland, OR: Binford & Mort Publishers, 1967.

Hitchcock, C. L. and A. Cronquist. *Flora of the Pacific Northwest,* 2nd ed. Seattle: University of Washington Press, 2018.

Horn, Elizabeth L. *Coastal Wildflowers of the Pacific Northwest.* Missoula, MT: Mountain Press Publishing Co., 1993.

Ireland, Orlin L. *Plants of the Three Sisters Region, Oregon Cascade Range.* Eugene, OR: University of Oregon, 1968.

Jolley, Russ. *Wildflowers of the Columbia River Gorge.* Portland, OR: Oregon Historical Society Press, 1988.

Kleinman, Kathryn and Sara Slavin. *On Flowers.* San Francisco: Chronicle Books, 1992.

Korloff, Eugene N. *Plants and Animals of the Pacific Northwest: An Illustrated Guide to the Natural History of Western Oregon, Washington, and British Columbia.* Seattle: University of Washington Press, 1976.

Larrison, E. J., G. W. Patrick, W. H. Baker, and J. A. Yaich. *Washington Wildflowers*. Seattle: The Seattle Audubon Society, 1974.

Lyons, C. P. *Wildflowers of Washington*. Vancouver, BC: Lone Pine Publishing, 1999.

Mansfield, Donald. *Flora of Steens Mountain*. Corvallis, OR: Oregon State University Press, 2000.

Mathews, Daniel A. *Cascade-Olympic Natural History*. Portland, OR: Raven Editions, 1988.

Meeuse, Bastiaan and Sean Morris. *The Sex Life of Flowers*. New York: Facts on File Publications, 1984.

Moore, Michael. *Medicinal Plants of the Mountain West*. Santa Fe, NM: Museum of New Mexico Press, 2003.

Moulton, Gary E., ed. *Journals of the Lewis and Clark Expedition*. 12 vols. Lincoln, NE: University of Nebraska Press, 1983–1999.

Nicholis, Graham. *Alpine Plants of North America: An Encyclopedia of Mountain Flowers from the Rockies to Alaska*. Portland, OR: Timber Press, Inc., 2002.

Parish, Roberta, Ray Coupé, and Dennis Lloyd, eds. *Plants of Southern Interior British Columbia and the Inland Northwest*. Vancouver, BC: Lone Pine Publishing, 1996.

Philips, H. Wayne. *Plants of the Lewis & Clark Expedition*. Missoula, MT: Mountain Press Publishing, Co., 2003.

Pojar, Jim and Andy Mackinnon. *Plants of the Pacific Northwest Coast: Washington, Oregon, British Columbia & Alaska*. Vancouver, BC: Lone Pine Publishing, 1994.

Proctor, Michael, Peter Yeo, and Andrew Lack. *The Natural History of Pollination*. Portland, OR: Timber Press, Inc., 1996.

Ross, Robert A. and Henrietta L. Chambers. *Wildflowers of the Western Cascades*. Portland, OR: Timber Press, Inc., 1988.

Saling, Ann. *The Great Northwest Nature Factbook: Remarkable Animals, Plants & Natural Features in Washington, Oregon, Idaho & Montana*. Bothell, WA: Alaska Northwest Books, 1991.

Sanders, Jack. *Hedgemaids and Fairy Candles: The Lives and Lore of North American Wildflowers*. Camden, MA: Ragged Mountain Press, 1993.

Snowdon, Lord. *Wild Flowers*. New York: Clarkson Potter Publishers, 1993.

Stearn, William T. *Stearn's Dictionary of Plant Names for Gardeners*. Portland, OR: Timber Press, Inc., 1996.

Strickler, Dr. Dee. *Wayside Wildflowers of the Pacific Northwest*. Columbia Falls, MT: The Falcon Press, 1996.

Taylor, Ronald J. *Sagebrush Country: A Wildflower Sanctuary*. Missoula, MT: Mountain Press Publishing Co., 1992.

Taylor, Ronald J. and George W. Douglas. *Mountain Plants of the Pacific Northwest*. Missoula, MT: Mountain Press Publishing Co., 1995.

———. *Mountain Wild Flowers of the Pacific Northwest*. Portland, OR: Binford & Mort, Publishers, 1975.

Terrill, Steve. *Wildflowers of Oregon*. Englewood, CO: Westcliffe Publishers, Inc., 1995.

Turner, Mark and Phyllis Gustafson. *Wildflowers of the Pacific Northwest*. Portland, OR: Timber Press, Inc., 2006.

Whitney, Stephen R. and Rob Sandelin. *Field Guide to the Cascades & Olympics*. Seattle: The Mountaineer Books, 2003.

Wuetherner, George. *Oregon's Best Wildflower Hikes: Northwest Region*. Englewood, CO: Westcliffe Publishers, Inc. 2001.

Web Sites

Burke Museum, http/:biology.burke.washington.edu/herbarium/imagecollections/list.php

California Flora, www.caflora.org

Checklist of the Vascular Flora of Oregon, www.swsbm.com

Natural History Wanderings, https://naturalhistorywanderings.com/wildflower-reports/

Northwest Native Plant Journal, www.nwplants.com

Oregon Flora Project, www.oregonflora.org

Oregon Wildflower Reports, www.oregonwildflowers.org

Pacific Northwest Wildflower Bloom Reports, http://science.halleyhosting.com/nature/bloomtime

Washington and Oregon Native Plant Society, www.wnps.org

Social Media: Facebook

https://www.facebook.com/groups/Wildflowersofcentraloregon/

https://www.facebook.com/groups/oregonwildflowers/

INDEX

ABOUT THE AUTHOR

Damian Fagan has been exploring the Pacific Northwest for over 40 years. He graduated from the University of Washington in 1982 with a B.S. in Botany and has worked for the National Park Service, The Nature Conservancy, and Central Oregon Community College's Community Learning as a park ranger, program manager, and recreation instructor. He is an avid birder and botanizer who currently lives in Bend, Oregon, with his wife, Raven, a rotating pack of dogs, and two chickens—Buff and Mia. Visit www.damianfagan.com for more information.

RAVEN TENNYSON